ABRAHAM LINCOLN,
STATESMAN HISTORIAN

ABRAHAM LINCOLN,
Statesman Historian

JESSE DERBER

UNIVERSITY OF
ILLINOIS PRESS
Urbana, Chicago, and Springfield

Library of Congress Cataloging-in-Publication Data
Names: Derber, Jesse, 1982- author.
Title: Abraham Lincoln, statesman historian / Jesse Derber.
Description: Urbana : University of Illinois Press, 2024. | Includes bibliographical
    references and index.
Identifiers: LCCN 2024007578 (print) | LCCN 2024007579 (ebook) | ISBN
    9780252046001 (hardback) | ISBN 9780252088100 (paperback) | ISBN
    9780252047183 (ebook)
Subjects: LCSH: Lincoln, Abraham, 1809–1865. | Lincoln, Abraham, 1809–1865—
    Oratory—Historiography. | Lincoln, Abraham, 1809–1865—Political and social
    views. | Speeches, addresses, etc., American—History and criticism. | Political
    oratory—United States—Historiography. | Presidents—United States—Biography.
    | Politicians—United States—Biography. | Statesmen—United States—Biography.
Classification: LCC E457.2 .D47 2024 (print) | LCC E457.2 (ebook) | DDC
    973.7092—dc23/eng/20240226
LC record available at https://lccn.loc.gov/2024007578
LC ebook record available at https://lccn.loc.gov/2024007579

To my beloved wife, Lyndsey, and to our children—
Nathan Lee, Eliana Corinne, Elijah Owen, and Sophia Suzanne—
as well as to the generations yet to come.
May you always pursue and treasure wisdom.

CONTENTS

ABRAHAM LINCOLN,
STATESMAN HISTORIAN

Introduction

I remember, when I was eight, watching with my father the debates in the lead-up to the Persian Gulf War on the *CBS Evening News* with Dan Rather and hearing opponents arguing that, should the United States intervene militarily, it would be another Vietnam. Although I was very young, I knew enough to understand that another Vietnam War would be a very bad thing. While much could be said about the Persian Gulf War, another Vietnam it was not. While adults take it for granted that people on the news are wrong about a lot of things, I, remember wondering as a child how respected and powerful members of their communities, including members of Congress, could so confidently predict something in their day would be just like something in the past and then be just plain wrong. Ever since then, I have paid special attention to the historical arguments politicians have made to justify their actions; almost always, they have been proved wanting.

This book is born from my doubts; namely, my long-held skepticism of the ability of people to understand the past to guide the present properly. It seems evident that it is too easy to misapply supposed lessons of the past to justify one's current political views and even to feed ancient hatreds, potentially leading to violence. In my experience, it's not just politicians but many respected historians who seem to fail at translating their knowledge of the history into wisdom to guide them in the present by justifying their political beliefs by flattening the differences between past and present. Conversely, today many historians take the general view that history should be understood on its own terms, and that while history can provide greater perspective on the present, it cannot be used as a clear source of wisdom to provide guidance on decisions in the present. However, in spite of all my doubts about the utility of the past, I have always felt that arguments denying the utility of history were too limiting. Is there some way the past can be used as a useful guide for the present? What is the purpose of human memory if not to allow one to use the past to make better choices? Furthermore, what is the study of history if not a memory multiplier—a discipline in which we can learn wisdom from those who have gone before us? Despite all its misuses, I have always felt that there has to be something of value in the pursuit of history.

With these doubts and questions in my mind, as I was researching Abraham Lincoln in more depth than I had ever done previously, I was struck with how much he referenced the past in his political speeches, some of which seemed to be almost entirely about history. Since he used history so much, I naturally found myself asking, "What did Abraham Lincoln think about history?" and "How did he make use of it in his political career?" By *history*, I am using the term in its broadest sense, meaning not only the *past* but also what historians term *memory* (how individuals and societies choose to remember events in the past, sometimes referred to as heritage) and *historical study* (reasoned narratives based on extensive historical research).

In this book I argue that Abraham Lincoln used history as an essential source of wisdom to guide the nation in his political career. He believed that while there were limits to human understanding, there is a certain power in discovering the truth about history. His faith in the necessity and utility of getting things right with the past led him to rely not solely on the assertions of the historians of the day but rather to develop the skills that we now recognize as the tools of the historian to uncover the lessons of the past for himself. By using these tools, he both learned lessons about the past and shaped the people's understanding of that past. He was so successful in that regard that he continues to shape our collective memory of American history. In fact, Lincoln achieved something incredibly rare, becoming a statesman historian, or someone who understands that there is wisdom to be gained from the past that can prove to useful to the present; a statesman historian thus uses the tools and methods of the historian to uncover that wisdom and apply it to effective leadership.

Historians today typically draw a firm distinction between history and collective memory, arguing that any political use of the past cannot be the former but must be the latter. However, Lincoln was working within an older tradition—namely, within a one that believed that good history made good statesmanship and that the more accurate understanding of the past one had, the better one could make decisions in the present. This is an ancient tradition embedded in the term itself—history being derived from the ancient Greek word for inquiry. Only through inquiry can one reconstruct a reasonably accurate understanding of the past, and with this understanding one can better lead their community. Lincoln was part of a tradition that saw the past as being so important that one should not merely accept a particular viewpoint (memory) but rather use inquiry and the tools of the historian to investigate the past and to uncover wisdom that could guide the present. Lincoln was never one to simply accept the collective memory that was then evident, even the memory that had been created by his political allies. He did not merely denounce the collective memory of his opponents or attack their weakest points about the past but rather he used the methods of the historian to challenge their best historical arguments. He used these tools to shape the collective memory of the nation. He was far from the only politician of the era to attempt to do this, but he did it more effectively and honestly than any of his contemporaries.

The more research I performed, the more I became convinced that Abraham Lincoln did something rare—he did history right. For one, even though I discovered a few mistakes, Lincoln's historical narratives were often more accurate not just compared to his contemporaries, but occasionally even surpassed those crafted by subsequent generations of academically trained historians (including the "Dunning School" of a century ago as well as more recent scholars). He was able to achieve this accuracy not only through extensive research but also through his keen reasoning abilities, his emotional maturity, and his intellectual humility. Second, when he made factual errors about the past (he was no doubt influenced by his various confirmation biases), Lincoln showed a commitment to searching for the truth, readily admitting to mistakes he had made once he discovered them. Third, unlike so many, both past and present, he believed the past should be studied "as philosophy to learn wisdom from, and none of them as wrongs to be revenged."[1] He understood the natural temptation to use true events in the past to fan the flames of ancient hatreds in the present rather than to use history as a window to enlighten people about human nature in order to build a better future. Fourth, Lincoln used history to guide his present but not to define the limits of his understanding. Lincoln revered many precedents of the past, but he was never imprisoned by them. History, Lincoln felt, shows that progress is real and that the best of the past is not necessarily the best that can be achieved in the present—or in the future. He understood that there were many sources of wisdom outside of history, and thus he was not strictly a conservative pursuing a lost golden age with human potential stunted by the precedents of the past.

Lincoln's understanding and use of the past did not remain static but rather it evolved throughout his lifetime. There are four distinct elements to Lincoln's use of the past in his political career. From the very beginning Lincoln made emotional appeals to the past as it was collectively understood. Lincoln's deep personal attachment to the past is evident in the earliest surviving documents that he created. Starting about the time he turned thirty, Lincoln no longer simply relied on emotional appeals to the past but rather he began to develop logical arguments derived from careful personal research using many skills that modern historians practice today. Lincoln began making these types of arguments after studying to become a lawyer, and his legal training most likely taught him skills that were transferable to the study of history. Lincoln believed that by uncovering an accurate interpretation of the past, one could better understand the present and shape the future. Beginning in 1854 when he began his fight against the Kansas-Nebraska Act, Lincoln started to inspire people by arguing that their present would one day be someone else's past and that not only could their actions provide wisdom for the future but also live on in memory. Lincoln was motivated by the idea that, just as his generation looked to the past for wisdom, so too would the future look to his for guidance. In the later years of his life, Lincoln began to exhibit a religious sense of history. In his Second Inaugural Address, Lincoln combined two things that typically do not mix well with politics: religion and history. In this speech, he described the causes of the Civil War more accurately than professional historians would do in succeeding generations and he contemplated the role of God in history. He may never have had the faith of an orthodox Christian, but he used the language of Christianity to highlight the imponderables of the past and to argue that there are greater forces at work than human intention. Even though he developed new sensibilities about history in his later political career, he never abandoned the ones he used earlier, making highly emotional arguments about the past as well as studying it to guide his present right up to his final days.

Many doubt, for good reason, that history can be used in politics without distorting the past for the needs of the present. As author Rebecca West pithily notes, "When politics enters the door, truth flies out the window."[2] Many people, both contemporary and modern, have described Lincoln's use of history as such, saying he abandoned the truth about the past in pursuit of political power. For example, shortly after delivering his

Cooper Union Address, one newspaper said that the speech was "characterized throughout with perversions of history and facts," while another
newspaper claimed that Lincoln used "special pleading and sophistical
reasoning [to] lead the mind of his hearer and reader from the true facts
in the controversy."[3] In terms of modern scholars, Pauline Maier refers
to Lincoln's historical interpretations of the Declaration of Independence
as the "wishful suppositions" of someone who had not done research,
while another scholar, Gordon S. Wood, says that Lincoln's interpretations were useful politics but still represent a "false heritage."[4] Joseph J.
Ellis portrays Lincoln as "bending the arc of American history" to better suit his political needs.[5] Eric Foner writes that Lincoln had a highly
"selective reading of history" in his 1854 Peoria Speech that effectively
"erased proslavery Americans from the nation's founding."[6] Arguing
against such an array of distinguished historians is no easy task.

However, we should not accept this proposition that politics and
history do not mix a priori, especially about Lincoln. Despite earlier
harsh criticisms of Lincon, Frederick Douglass wrote about him in 1864
that "I have not yet come to think that honesty and politics are incom-
patible," and this honesty applied to history as much as anything else.[7]
There have been those, both during Lincon's time and after, who have
acknowledged his historical skills. In 1860 Charles C. Nott and Cephas
Brainard of the Young Men's Republican Union of New York published
Lincoln's Cooper Union Address with footnotes they provided after they
had spent weeks trying to replicate Lincoln's historical research. In the
introduction Nott and Brainard write that the Cooper Union Address,
while a political act, was also "a historical work" that was "profound,
impartial, and truthful." They praise Lincoln's efforts, stating, "No one
who has not actually attempted to verify its details can understand the
patient research and historical labor which it embodies."[8]

In terms of modern scholars, Harold Holzer, author of *Lincoln at
Cooper Union: The Speech that Made Abraham Lincoln President*, writes
that Lincoln did not "merely voice his opinions" like other politicians
but "he armed himself with facts" derived from his historical study.[9]
Speaking of Lincoln's Peoria Speech, Doris Kearns Goodwin writes, "For
the first time in his public life, his remarkable array of gifts as historian,
storyteller, and teacher combined with a lucid, relentless, yet always accessible logic."[10] Even Eric Foner, who is highly critical of Lincoln's attempt at history during his Peoria Speech, writes that Lincoln's Cooper
Union Address was a "surprisingly scholarly presentation."[11]

Virtually all modern historians mention Lincoln's appreciation for
the Founding Fathers, but that could be said about just about anyone of

that era. Many do not comment on his historical scholarship, and for those who do, Lincoln's skills as a historian were at best tangential to the arguments that they were making. Besides the editors of his Cooper Union Address in 1860, there are no scholarly works whose fundamental focus was Lincoln's use of the past in general. Two relatively recent works, Richard Brookhiser's 2014 *Founders' Son: A Life of Abraham Lincoln* and Lucas Morel's 2020 *Lincoln and the American Founding*, both shed valuable light on the inspiration the Founding Fathers had on Lincoln. This book will be broader in scope, focusing on Lincoln's thoughts on history in general and, more specifically, analyzing his philosophy of history and how he came to the conclusions he did.

This book will examine Lincoln's use of the past, including his skills as a historian, and attempt to shed greater light on an important aspect of Lincoln's political career that is little understood. My goal is to spark greater interest in this aspect of his career and inspire new avenues of research, understanding that there can be no final word on any worthwhile historical topic. Finally, it is my hope that, in some small way, this book will not only celebrate but also advance the pursuit of wisdom.

Chapter 1

A Living History (1809–39)

Two Statesmen . . . Two Historians?

One February afternoon in 1860, George Bancroft, the nation's first great historian, sat in the waiting room at the Manhattan studio of Matthew Brady, the nation's first great photographer. Going to Brady's was not just about getting a picture taken. It was meant to be an experience. According to the historian Harold Holzer, Brady installed "velvet curtains, satin wallpaper, cut-glass decorations, and highly polished marble and rosewood furniture" in his Broadway studio. Displayed throughout Brady's Gallery of Photographs and Ambrotypes were the images of the most famous Americans of the era, all of whom Brady had photographed. His impressive clientele included Presidents Van Buren, Taylor, Polk, Pierce, and Buchanan and other midcentury luminaries such as Dolley Madison, Chief Justice Roger B. Taney, Commodore Matthew Perry, Henry Clay, Jenny Lind, and Senator Stephen Douglas of Illinois, the man many people believed would be the next president. By that February afternoon in 1860 George Bancroft was a man who had seen and accomplished as much in politics as many in Brady's gallery.[1]

Born in 1800 in Worcester, Massachusetts, and educated at Harvard, Bancroft had already earned success as a Jacksonian Democrat from Massachusetts, serving as secretary of the Navy during the Mexican War and then later as the U.S. Minister to the United Kingdom. Despite his political achievements, Bancroft was best known as a pioneer in the field of history. In 1834 Bancroft published his first volume of *The History of the United States of America*, a work that earned him national fame. According to his biographer Lilian Handlin, he established a "quasi-monopoly" on the historical field for decades that "was so strong that others could only chip away at the edges, without damaging the monument." For Bancroft there was no contradiction between the two careers, but rather the work of the statesman and the work of the historian were mutually reinforcing. Justifying his dual roles, Bancroft asked rhetorically, "What possible conception can a man in his study form of public popular transactions? What mere student dreams of the manner in which negotiations are conducted by the cabinet? How then can a recluse write philosophic history?" As Handlin writes, "In a sense he entered politics to become a better historian, and he wrote history to explain his political career. . . . He turned into a historian and politician, the man of letters and intellect, as well as the man of action he had always wanted to be."[2] When the slavery issue roiled the country in 1854, Bancroft became a supporter and advisor of Stephen Douglas of Illinois. He provided research for Douglas's lengthy 1859 article arguing that the Founders supported Douglas's popular sovereignty policy.[3] He began traveling throughout the country, delivering lectures to packed audiences in the North and the South. By 1860 Bancroft achieved virtually all a historian could hope for in a career: prestige, power, influence, and wealth. His name had become synonymous with history. Today he was in Brady's studio to document and preserve the memory not of others this time, but rather of himself.

While sitting in Brady's waiting room on that February afternoon in 1860, a quiet, lanky man walked in with some men wearing a new yet heavily wrinkled suit. Unknown to him, years earlier Bancroft had inspired this man so much with one of his addresses that he attempted to become a traveling lecturer himself, albeit with much less success. A virtual unknown outside of his state until 1854, he began to make a name for himself when he challenged Bancroft's would-be savior of the Union, Stephen Douglass, debating him formally and informally throughout the Prairie State for the previous six years. This new man was Abraham Lincoln.

In many ways the differences in their life experiences could not be more striking. Lincoln was born in 1809 in a cabin his father had raised on a knoll overlooking a sinking spring in the Kentucky wilderness. Unlike Bancroft's Harvard-educated father, Lincoln's was barely literate. Lincoln wrote that his father "grew up litterally without education" and "never did more in the way of writing than to bunglingly sign his own name."[4] When he was old enough, Lincoln's father sent him to a one-room-schoolhouse for brief periods of time. One local resident remembered that Caleb Hazel, one of Lincoln's teachers, "could perhaps teach spelling reading and indifferent writing and perhaps could Cipher to the rule of three," but that his strongest qualification was his "large size and bodily Strength to thrash any boy or youth that came to his School." One humble schoolhouse he attended in Indiana was a "hewed log house—had two Chimneys—one door—holes for windows—greasy paper was pasted over the holes in winter time to admit light."[5] By Lincoln's reckoning, he spent less than a year total in these rude "A.B.C. schools." Lincoln later admitted that these "so called" schools offered "absolutely nothing to excite ambition for education."[6]

Whereas Bancroft, at the age of sixteen, was a student at Harvard, propounding on the "glories and pleasures" of his intellect that soared like an eagle over the "common sphere of mankind," regarding with "calm indifference [to] the labours of ordinary men" who were nothing but "inferior beings," Lincoln was, at the age of sixteen, one of those "inferior beings," hacking out a living in the Indiana wilderness.[7] He spent most of his days felling trees, grubbing stumps, splitting rails, cutting trails, raising cabins, hunting game, plowing fields, shucking corn, and slaughtering hogs. Unlike Bancroft, he never went to college or on a grand tour in Europe. The only opportunity he had for travel were two flatboat trips to New Orleans, in which the most remarkable thing that happened, according to Lincoln, was that, one night when the boat was off the sugar coast of Louisiana, he and his companion "were attacked by seven negroes with intent to kill and rob them."[8]

Despite his limited formal schooling and life experience, Lincoln was a reasonably educated man by the time he reached adulthood. This, according to his former law partner John T. Stuart, was because "he dug it out himself." His stepmother remembered, "He read all the books he could lay his hand on" when he was a child. If he found a passage particularly striking, he would write it down on a board with charcoal or red ochre if no paper was available, and "when the board would get too black he would shave it off with a drawing knife and go on again." If it was too noisy in the cabin, he would go out to the stable or the woods and read. According to one friend, "what Lincoln read he read and re-read—read and Studied thoroughly." One Indiana acquaintance remembered that Lincoln frequently "packed books when at work" and would read them "when he rested from laber." Another recalled that "while others would romp and lafe he would be engaged in the arithmetic or asking questions about Som history heard or red of." What he learned, he sometimes would teach his friends, using analogies to make complex concepts for children easy to understand.[9]

Lincoln continued his self-education when he grew into manhood and set out on his own in New Salem, Illinois. According to one New Salem friend, "History and poetry and the newspapers constituted the most of his reading." He did this mostly in the early morning and late at night after work. Another friend wrote that Lincoln would go off by himself down to the river or take "a strole to the Cuntry as he said for Refreshment," with a book in hand, reclining on the forest floor with his feet up on a tree. "He Read all of histry that he Could Get hold of," including biographies of Jefferson, Washington, Clay, and Webster.[10] When he decided to become a lawyer, Lincoln did not attend a college or study in a law office but rather read legal books that he borrowed when he could spare the time from his work. Even after he established himself as a lawyer and politician, Lincoln continued his self-education throughout the rest of his life.

Despite the hardships, his education afforded Lincoln many advantages. As many have noted, very few books were available to him. Still, those that trickled into the frontier were considered the finest in the English language, like the King James Bible, the plays by Shakespeare, and the poetry by Robert Burns and Lord Byron. Furthermore, except for a few brief periods when he attended school, his education was entirely self-driven, as Lincoln never spent a moment on anything unless he saw a direct benefit. Even though most commentators see his farmwork as a hindrance to his education, it must not be seen this way. Most of the manual labor he performed was not very mentally taxing, providing the young Lincoln extended time to meditate on all that he was reading. An hour immersed in Shakespeare before breakfast followed by hours in the fields gave him the time to think deeply about the lessons and language of Shakespeare.

In 1832, at twenty-three, the young Lincoln knew exactly what he wanted—a career in politics—and ran unsuccessfully for the Illinois legislature. However, two years later he ran again and was successful. Lincoln served four terms in the Illinois legislature and one in the U.S. House of Representatives from 1847 to 1849. Still, his principled yet unpopular opposition to the Mexican War diminished his chances of being elected to office in Illinois for the foreseeable future. He spent the next five years dedicated solely to his law career and improving his mind, which he attempted to do by mastering the principles of Euclid.

Lincoln came out of political retirement when agitation over slavery erupted in 1854. Lincoln had opposed and debated Bancroft's favorite politician off and on since the 1830s. Still, it was his challenge to Douglas in recent years, especially the senatorial debates of 1858, that brought him national attention. In a speech a few months before arriving at Brady's studio, Lincoln disparaged Douglas's lengthy article on the history of popular sovereignty, which Bancroft had helped research, stating that Douglas's "explanations explanatory of explanations explained are interminable."[11] Although a master of imitation and mockery, Lincoln had come to New York to respond to Douglas's article with something more substantial than a sneer.

Bancroft and Lincoln shared a brief and pleasant conversation before Lincoln went before Brady's camera. Although the meeting was of little significance in and of itself, it represented in some ways a type of a passing of the guard. That evening Lincoln was scheduled to deliver his first speech in front of New York's high society at Cooper Union. Although people knew him to be an excellent western stump speaker who could hold his audience's attention for hours with his extemporaneous addresses, he had spent months carefully researching and crafting this lecture, and in these months of preparation he had armed himself with the facts of history. Unlike Bancroft and his champion Douglas, Lincoln centered his history on slavery, primarily the national government's actions to restrict its spread. Arthur Schlesinger Jr. once described Bancroft as a man "who both wrote and wrought American history."[12] How much truer this would be of Lincoln. This night he would astonish his East Coast audience, making him, in their minds, a viable candidate for the presidency. Hundreds of thousands of copies of his speech, paired with the picture Brady had taken that day, introduced him to the nation. As Harold Holzer argued, this was the speech that made Lincoln president, and this was a speech, more than anything else, about history.[13] No one doubts that Bancroft was a historian. However, Lincoln also deserves such a title if we consider someone a historian who, regardless of formal training or lack thereof, has performed extensive research on a historical topic to produce a well-reasoned argument supported with the best evidence available. That was precisely what Lincoln produced in his address at Cooper Union. This historical performance was no aberration but rather the culmination of more than two decades of using history in his political career; he would continue to utilize his skills as a historian well into his presidency. Lincoln's belief in a usable past had deep roots.

Prairie Roots and Memory

When Lincoln left Illinois for good in 1861, he sped across the state "on the wing," as the *Chicago Daily Tribune* phrased it, in the Presidential Special, a train fitted out for him to begin his journey to the White House.

The *Tribune* described his journey across the state as an almost continual "ovation," as "at every station and crossing and cabin, near the road, the people gathered . . . to see the train and strive to catch a glimpse of one who bears the hopes of so many." Even the roar of the "flying train" could not "drown the cheers and 'God speed you'" of the crowds.[14]

When Lincoln first arrived in Illinois more than three decades earlier, in 1830, there had been no ovations or cheers when he stepped off the boat, trudging through the muddy shores of the Wabash River. Instead of riding in a special train powered by coal and steam that glided across the plains, Lincoln had driven an ox-drawn wagon, powered only by muscle and sinew, through the river-bottom muck. The Illinois that Lincoln goaded the ox team across to his new home in some mosquito-infested woods west of the tiny village of Decatur was not yet the quilt-patterned landscape of corn and wheat fields made up of small family farms that Jefferson had envisioned but rather an open and undulating landscape of long bluestem and native wildflowers.

One Boston reporter, J. H. Buckingham, left an evocative account of his impressions of this prairie from the back of a stagecoach south of the central Illinois village of Tremont in 1847, writing something of a travelog of Illinois for the *Boston Courier*. Buckingham marveled at how "the tall grass, interspersed occasionally with fields of corn, looked like the deep sea; it seemed as if we were out of sight of land, for no house, no barn, no tree was visible, and the horizon presented the rolling of the waves in the far-off distance." He was "enchanted" at the polychromatic flush of summer wildflowers: "All the colors of the rainbow were exhibited on all sides . . . as if the sun were shining upon the gay and dancing waters." As the stagecoach moved farther south into new settlements, Buckingham marveled at the fecundity of the farms as they "passed through miles and miles of tall corn, the bright and beautiful green of which was almost dazzling in the sunlight; some acres of wheat, tall as an ordinary man; and many fields of oats, with some of barley—all of which appeared ready for the sickle."[15]

When Lincoln moved to Illinois in 1830, the prairie was still wild, and it still had not been fully tamed after thirty years of settlement when he boarded the Presidential Special in 1861. By the 1850s bears, elk, and panthers had been hunted to extinction, but other game was still abundant, like deer, turkey, partridges, and prairie chickens. In these days before barbed wire, farmers sometimes drove their hogs in the winter more than a hundred miles across the open plains to market in Saint Louis or Chicago. Well into the 1850s wolves posed dangers to both man and livestock.[16]

Visitors like Buckingham were often just as intrigued with the people who inhabited this grand prairie as they were with its physical beauty. To Buckingham's amusement, two of his fellow stagecoach passengers were not only great wits but also members of Congress returning to their home districts from a convention in Chicago. Even though they were political enemies, they were personal friends. While one kept the passengers in hysterics with his stories and jokes, the congressman from Alton, Illinois, got off the best one of them all, joking that his campaign strategy in his home district was to bow to all the men, kiss all the children, and make love to all the women. Based on the reporter's account, this congressman was "much disposed to play the amiable to several rather pretty girls" at stops along the way, calling into question just how much he really was joking. Buckingham, the sophisticated Bostonian, wryly concluded that "the character of the Western people is in every respect different from ours."[17]

For nearly three decades, Lincoln crisscrossed the state to visit and live among these people of the county seats of the eighth judicial circuit. These villages could be as untamed as the prairies that surrounded them, especially on court days. While the trials were usually solemn and prosaic, sometimes crowds in this entertainment-starved era packed into these timber courthouses to hear their neighbors' lurid private details aired in public. One example comes from an 1851 trial in Urbana, the county seat of Champaign County and home to just a few hundred settlers. Here Lincoln prosecuted a prominent resident, A. G. Carle, for "seduction" (impregnating a woman out of wedlock). During the trial, Lincoln's friend Judge David Davis wrote to his wife commenting sarcastically on the "beautiful State of morals, amongst the young men & young girls of this Grove." The defendant does not appear to have argued that he did not sleep with the woman but rather that just about every other man in the neighborhood had also slept with her, attempting, as Davis wrote, to "blacken her character desperately."[18] The defense called witnesses to corroborate Carle's claim, including Simeon Busey, a wealthy farmer who would later found a successful bank with his brother. Judge Davis wrote that the defense's attacks on the woman angered Lincoln and that he "bore down savagely" on Carle and his witnesses as the trial became "heated" and "very, very sore." Still, Davis declined to provide his wife details.[19] Lincoln's performance left quite the impression on Davis as, years later, he recounted to Lincoln's former law partner how Lincoln "went at" the witnesses and "crushed them" but did not specify how. Even though he almost certainly did not attend the trial, Henry C. Whitney, who was Lincoln's lawyer friend from Champaign (Urbana's neighboring town), was still retelling the tales of the case in 1887. These stories align with all the surviving documentary evidence. Further, his account gives some insight into how Lincoln *bore down savagely* on one witness. He reported, "There is Busey—he pretends to be a great heart smasher—does wonderful things with the girls—but I'll venture that he never entered his flesh but once & that is when he fell down & stuck his finger in his—."[20] Decades later, with unintended irony, the city of Urbana placed Lorado Taft's famous sculpture *Lincoln the Lawyer* in Carle Park, named in honor of the man Lincoln successfully prosecuted for seduction.

People not only came to see the trials but also to watch the traveling shows and play early forms of baseball in empty village lots. At night visitors packed into rustic taverns, with the men usually sleeping two to three to a bed. People played cards, drank whiskey, and told stories around the fire.

Many of Lincoln's friends recounted that he, with certain abstentions, participated in this fun as much as anyone. Whitney remembered once that when he opened the door to the sleeping quarters in a tavern, he saw two grown men, one the six-foot-four and skinny-as-a-rail Lincoln and the other the shorter and exceedingly rotund Judge Davis, in their night clothes bouncing around the room in a pillow fight. Whitney also remembered Lincoln and Davis, along with many of the "local wits" in the tavern, frequently "talking politics, wisdom & fun."[21] Lincoln loved this atmosphere, and as many friends on the circuit recalled, nearly everything reminded Lincoln of a story, which people would gather around to hear him tell.

For example, one friend, John B. Weber, recounted one of Lincoln's stories about judging people before getting to know them. Lincoln told him about the time he was living in New Salem and working as a surveyor shortly after his failed first run for the Illinois legislature when he was only twenty-three. According to Weber, Lincoln recalled that there was a German living a few miles away, and the rumor was that he was an old miserable "miser." One day the German hired Lincoln to survey some land, which Lincoln and a few other men performed. When the work was done, the German invited them to his home and served them an excellent supper, and after dinner the men gathered around the fire telling stories. Lincoln told one, and everyone applauded, after which the German offered his own story, which "was approved by an uproar of laughter." After several hours of this rustic conviviality, it was time for Lincoln and his men to leave. Before departing, Lincoln told his host, "I wish to show how easy persons may be deluded by forming conclusions upon ideas not based upon facts." He confessed that he had heard he was "an old miserly Dutchman" but was "happy to acknowledge that [he had] been very agreeably disappointed." The host thanked him for the honor and said that he, too, would like to share how meeting the young Lincoln had disabused him of his first notion of Lincoln. He had heard that Lincoln had been a candidate for the state legislature; so when Lincoln first arrived, he too had been disappointed because he expected to see a "smarter looking man." After telling this story to Weber, Lincoln "laughed heartily." Weber felt indignant, telling Lincoln that the man had treated him unjustly after he had paid him a compliment. Lincoln said, "No, No . . . He meant all he said, for it was before I was washed." The thought of not yet being washed reminded Lincoln of another story, and he proceeded to tell it to Weber to give him "some idea of the fix" he had been in:

> When I was a little boy, I lived in the state of Kentucky, where drunke-ness was very comon on election days, At an election . . . in a village near where I lived, on a day when the weather was inclement and the roads exceedingly muddy, A toper named Bill got brutally drunk and staggered down a narrow alley where he layed himself down in the mud, and re-mained there until the dusk of the evening, at which time he recovered from his stupor, Finding himself very muddy, immediately started for a pump . . . to wash himself. On his way to the pump another drunken man was leaning over a horse post, this, Bill mistook for the pump and at once took hold of the arm of the man for the handle, the use of which set the occupant of the post to throwing up, Bill believing all was right put both hands under and gave himself a thorough washing, He then made his way to the grocery for something to drink, On entering the door one of his comrades exclaimed in a tone of surprise, Why Bill what in the world is the matter Bill said in reply, G-d you ought to have seen me before I was washed.[22]

This was typical for Lincoln, as one man later recalled that he "appeared to have an endless repertoire" of stories that were "always ready, like the successive charges in a magazine gun, and always pertinently adapted to some passing event."[23] Lincoln's mind was a storehouse of humor-ous anecdotes, some that he had heard, some that he had made up, and others that he experienced, and he always seemed to have the perfect story for every occasion. As this series of stories shows, Lincoln had a remarkable memory, but it was not limited simply to frontier humor. J. H. Buckingham, the Boston reporter who set out to explore the prai-rie in 1847, marveled at the exceptional memory of one of his traveling companions, identifying him only as "our Whig congressman" (Lincoln was the only Whig congressman from Illinois at the time). Buckingham reported that as they headed south from Delevan into Lincoln's home district, Lincoln "knew, or appeared to know, every body we met, the name of the tenant of every farm-house, and the owner of every plat of ground. Such a shaking of hands—such a how-d'ye-do—such a greeting of different kinds, as we saw, was never seen before; it seemed as if he knew every thing." What's more, "he had a kind word, a smile and a bow for every body on the road, even to the horses, and the cattle, and the swine." Buckingham left perhaps the earliest written account of what people later said most startled and astonished them about Lincoln: both his sense of humor (although many politicians, in all earnestness, probably ought to bow before swine) and his remarkable memory.[24]

Silences and Memory

Lincoln impressed his friends with his exceptional memory, often surprising them with how he could recall even minor events from years or decades prior. As one friend observed, "His memmory was remarkably tenacious."[25]

People tend to think that having a good memory is a natural trait, which is undoubtedly true but not necessarily the whole truth. Lincoln's friends and associates left clues as to how Lincoln's exceptional memory was something that he worked at.

With nearly remarkable consistency many people who knew him at different stages in his life noted a peculiar feature, his meditations—or his deep and extended silences—where he had the time to think about and process his memory. One old settler from Kentucky remembered that his most noticeable trait was that "he alwas appeard to be very quiet during play time Never Seemed to be rude Seemed to have a liking for Solitude." His stepmother, Sarah Bush Lincoln, who lived with him for twelve years, recalled, "Abe, when old folks were at our house, was a silent & attentive observer—never speaking or asking questions till they were gone and then he must understand Every thing—even to the smallest thing—Minutely & Exactly—: he would then repeat it over to himself again & again—sometimes in one form and then in another & when it was fixed in his mind to suit him he became Easy and he never lost that fact or his understanding of it." According to Mrs. Lincoln, "What he thus learned he stowed away in his memory which was Extremely good—what he learned and stowed away was well defined in his own mind—repeated over & over again & again till it was so defined and fixed firmly & permanently in his Memory." James H. Matheny, Lincoln's best man and friend for decades, remembered him regularly spending much of the day "abstracting" and "glooming," consuming much more time thinking than reading. Stating that he became more abstracted and silent as he got older, Matheny said that Lincoln had two sides—one the public man who craved attention and renown and the other the secretive and private man who would rather "Stick his head in a hollow log, & see no one." Lincoln's sister-in-law Frances Todd Wallace recalled visiting her sister at home while Lincoln would "lean back—his head against the top of a rocking Chair—sit abstracted," and only break his extended silence with a joke, "though his thoughts were not on a joke." She remembered him as a sad and "abstracted" man.[26]

Lawyers who traveled the circuit recalled how peculiar the man was that could hold a whole audience wrapped up in his stories one moment and then completely withdraw within himself the next. Judge David Davis said that Lincoln was "as happy as *he* could be" traveling the circuit with his fellow lawyers and that he was not a "social man" but rather told his jokes and stories to "whistle off sadness." Lincoln's law partner of sixteen years, William Herndon, likely knew him better than anyone else besides his wife. Herndon wrote that Lincoln "could sit and think without rest or food longer" than any other man he knew. Herndon remembered meeting and greeting him in the street without Lincoln noticing as he walked past him locked deep in thought. In the law office, Lincoln was little better as he would lay reflecting on the sofa with his legs propped up on chairs. Remarking on his colleague's "eternal silences," Herndon said Lincoln "embodied reflection itself." According to Herndon, Lincoln was "the most secretive—reticent—shut-mouthed man that Ever Existed."[27]

Two astute observers believed that these silences and meditations, however gloomy they could be at times, were the key to his success. Adolphe de Chambrun, a French diplomat, was frequently with Lincoln in his final two months of life. In this brief time he observed Lincoln's extended silences. He hypothesized that Lincoln, in his earlier years, had "formed himself by [the] difficult and powerful process of lonely meditation."[28] While de Chambrun formed his opinion after only an acquaintance of a few weeks, Joshua Speed, who had known Lincoln for nearly three decades, reached the same conclusion. Lincoln lived with Speed when he first moved to Springfield, and after Speed moved back to his home in Kentucky, Lincoln wrote him the most revealing personal letters of his that survive. Speed visited Lincoln in the White House several times, and if Lincoln ever had a best friend, Speed was it. According to Speed,

> Lincoln studied and appropriated to himself all that came within his observation. Everything that he saw, read, or heard, added to the store of his information—because he thought upon it. No truth was too small to escape his observation, and no problem too intricate to escape a solution, if it was capable of being solved. Thought; hard, patient, laborious thought, these were the tributaries that made the bold, strong, irresistible current of his life. Lincoln drew his supplies from the great storehouse of nature. Constant thought enabled him to use all his information at all times and upon all subjects with force, ease, and grace.[29]

The importance of Lincoln's extended silences cannot be overstated. In popular perception, Lincoln made himself by reading books, but just as important was his silent reflection. While in his early life solitude was easy to come by, by the time he became a busy lawyer, family man, and politician he was still wrapping himself up in solitude, oblivious to those around him. These extended silences were not merely a quirk but rather essential to the man he was and the man he would become.

During these extended silences, Lincoln reflected deeply on the past. Memories may be born in the hustle and bustle of active life but can only be sustained and made meaningful in silence and meditation. Without reflection, these events are, as Lincoln's favorite author would state, nothing but "sound and fury, signifying nothing."[30] For Lincoln, the memory of the past possessed an almost sacred nature.

Early in his legal and political career, Lincoln developed the analytical and investigative skills of a historian, but what preceded was a strong emotional attachment to the past, aided by his memory. This emotional attachment is the antecedent of rational investigation, and they then work concurrently. Just as a sense of wonder at Manhattan skyscrapers precedes the desire of an architect to design buildings or one marveling at the stars precedes a desire to become an astronomer, a mystical attachment to the memories of the past can precede the desire to study it analytically as a historian.

Of course, it is impossible to know everything Lincoln was meditating on in these silences. However, he left enough of a written record to grant insight into these early reflections. From the written records, it is evident that Lincoln formed a mystical and almost sacred attachment to the past and a melancholic fascination with the relentless passage of time. Furthermore, he believed that these memories were not just meant to be pondered; instead they were essential sources of wisdom to guide his personal life and public career.

Ciphering Book

"Abraham Lincoln is my nam/And with my pen I wrote the same/I wrote in both hast and speed/and left it here for fools to read."[31] The earliest document to survive in Lincoln's handwriting, which contains the preceding doggerel, is his "Ciphering Book." Since workbooks were too expensive for every student to own, Lincoln stitched together several pieces of paper to create one of his own so that he could copy math problems from his teacher. There are word problems for calculating interest and long division problems up to four digits throughout the surviving sheets. While doing his calculations, his mind must have wandered as he wrote, "Abraham Lincoln his hand and pen he will be good but god knows When." He evidently took pride in his book as he wrote "Abraham book," "Abraham Lincoln book," and "Abraham Lincolns book" throughout.[32]

His stepmother, Sarah Bush Lincoln, reported that the young Lincoln would use his workbook to write down anything that particularly "struck him."[33] In one heavily damaged page survives the following:

> Time What an emty vaper
> tis and days how swift they are swift as an indian arr [. . .]
> fly on like a shooting star the presant moment Just [. . .]
> then slides away in [. . .] that we [. . .]ever say they [. . .]
> But [. . .] th[. . .]'re past[34]

These lines are from the two opening stanzas of Isaac Watts's "Hymn 58: The Shortness of Life and the Goodness of God." The misspellings and irregular line breaks that do not match the original publication point to the likelihood that the young Lincoln was writing from memory. The correct first two stanzas are below:

> Time, what an empty vapor 'tis!
> And days, how swift they are!
> Swift as an Indian arrow flies,
> Or like a shooting star.
>
> [The present moments just appear,
> Then slide away in haste,
> That we can never say, "They're here,"
> But only say, "They're past."][35]

The hymn continues by praising the mercy of God, man's only safe refuge. In the age of the Second Great Awakening, many frontier settlers memorized hymns like those of Isaac Watts, and Dennis Hanks, a family member who lived with Lincoln for a time in Indiana, recalled that Lincoln was fond of singing Watts's hymns.[36]

Lincoln's memorization and appreciation of these verses can be seen as the earliest evidence of several larger patterns in Lincoln's sentiments and thus prove significant. First, it is noteworthy that the only lines that survive from this hymn describe the "Shortness of Life" but not the "Goodness of God" of the later verses. These first few lines may correspond to the sentiments of Ecclesiastes, but by themselves they certainly have no redeeming grace of the Gospel. His close friends in young adulthood knew that Lincoln did not subscribe to any form of orthodox Christianity, and his stepmother reported that even in childhood Lincoln "had no particular religion" and "he never talked about it."[37] Secondly, these lines mark the beginning of the written record of Lincoln's fascination with time, the past, and wisdom. Lincoln would repeatedly return to the themes of the fleeting nature of the present, the mystical nature of the past, and the chastening humility that can be derived from this understanding.

It's debatable whether Lincoln held scripture to be holy, but he certainly possessed a mystical and almost sacred attraction to the past, and that sense of mysticism derived from personal memory. Furthermore, Lincoln rarely mentioned his past in the surviving documents, but when he did, it was usually to describe some lesson he had derived from it.

Communication to the People of Sangamo County

"Every man is said to have his peculiar ambition. Whether it be true or not, I can say for one that I have no other so great as that of being truly esteemed of my fellow men, by rendering myself worthy of their esteem."[38] Thus wrote the twenty-three-year-old Abraham Lincoln in 1832, announcing his candidacy for the Illinois legislature. While at this point in his life he hoped to be esteemed in the present, he would later express his hope to live on, in memory, in the future.

Lincoln referred to his personal memory several times in this first campaign address. He described in detail his investigations, in the preceding year, into the navigability of the Sangamon River and how his memory informed what practical actions the state could take to make it more navigable. Lincoln, who had only lived in New Salem for about a year, wrote to his constituents, "I was born and have ever remained in the most humble walks of life." He closed with, "If the good people in their wisdom shall see fit to keep me in the background, I have been too familiar with disappointments to be very much chagrined."[39] Like his comments on his humble origins, he did not elaborate on these disappointments but focused instead on the lesson he learned from them, namely that he should not take setbacks too hard, nor should he get his hopes too high. In his first campaign address, he was already showing that his personal memory of the past could inform the construction of public policy as well as give him wisdom to prepare for the inevitable setbacks of a political career.

According to Lincoln, however, personal memory was not the sole or most important source of wisdom that could be derived from the past. Lincoln wrote that education was "the most important subject which we as a people can be engaged in." The reason it was so important was because a man would "thereby be enabled to read the histories of his own and other countries, by which he may duly appreciate the value of our free institutions," which was of a "vital importance." Likewise, Lincoln argued that the political positions he held were supported by "time and experience" (i.e., history).[40] It is remarkable that from the very beginning, in Lincoln's first campaign speech, he shows how he felt that if this history was broadly cultivated, it would provide the wisdom Americans would need to remain a free people.

Address before the Young Men's Lyceum of Springfield

Francis McIntosh, a free Black man who worked on a riverboat as a porter and cook, was walking on the Saint Louis landing after his boat had docked on April 28, 1836, when he witnessed two police officers chasing two men. Accounts differ as to what happened next, but the police arrested McIntosh, either for helping the other two get away or for not aiding the police when they ordered him to help. As the two police officers were leading McIntosh up the hill to prison in the bustling downtown Saint Louis, he pulled out a knife and stabbed one officer in the chest and the other in the neck, killing one and severely wounding the other. McIntosh ran, but an angry crowd chased him, caught him, and put him in jail. As news spread and more people saw the bloody and lifeless body of the police officer McIntosh had killed lying in the street, an angry mob gathered outside the jail, demanding possession of McIntosh to lynch him. The sheriff refused and kept McIntosh's cell locked, but believing he could not fend off the mob, he took the jail's keys and his family and fled. McIntosh sat silently while some mob members left to get tools and worked for an hour to try and pry his door open. Once they got in, the mob dragged him out of the cell and took him a few blocks to the outskirts of town. They tied him to a locust tree, stacked rails, planks, and logs around him, and lit it on fire. McIntosh begged for someone to shoot him, but no one heeded his plea. McIntosh prayed and sang hymns until he finally died ten to twenty minutes later within the flames.[41]

During a grand jury hearing, Judge Luke Lawless urged the jurors not to charge anyone that had committed the lynching because mob violence had been known since time immemorial and the law could not restrain it. Instead of the murderers, Lawless blamed the entire affair on abolitionists, specifically Elijah Lovejoy, a Presbyterian pastor and publisher of the *St. Louis Observer*. Regarding abolitionists like Lovejoy, Lawless said, "[They] fanatisize the negro and excite him against the white man." After he read the aptly named Judge Lawless's comments, Lovejoy replied that he would rather "be chained to the same tree as McIntosh and share his fate" than accept such sophistry. According to Lovejoy, the judge, rather than protect the law, subverted it, making mob violence more likely in the future.[42]

Lovejoy's prediction proved prophetic, as a mob destroyed his Saint Louis office and printing press. Lovejoy moved his family out of the slave state of Missouri to what he believed was a safer location, Alton, a small but growing town in the free state of Illinois. Located upriver from Saint Louis, Alton was situated on limestone bluffs near the confluence of the Mississippi, Missouri, and Illinois rivers. There Lovejoy started the *Alton Observer* and continued publishing his abolitionist views.[43] Lovejoy outlined his beliefs in an article published in the *Observer* on July 20, 1837. He wrote, "Truth is eternal, unchanging . . . And truth will prevail, and those who will not yield to it must be destroyed by it." He then cataloged the reasons why abolitionists were against slavery. For Reverend Lovejoy, the first reason was not inspired by the Bible but rather the Declaration of Independence. Lovejoy wrote that "abolitionists hold that 'all men are born free and equal, endowed by their Creator with certain inalienable-rights, among which are life, *liberty*, and the pursuit of happiness'" and that these rights are not "abrogated, or at all modified by the color of the skin." He also criticized the hypocrisy of the slave-owning apologist John Calhoun who threatened nullification and secession if Congress did not repeal the tariffs. Alluding to Genesis 3:19, Calhoun wrote, "He who earns the money, who digs it from the earth with the sweat of his brow, has a just title to it against the universe. No one has a right to touch it without his consent, except his government, and this only to the extent of its legitimate wants; to take more is robbery." After quoting Calhoun, Lovejoy argued, "Now, this is precisely what slaveholders do, and abolitionists do but echo back their own language when they pronounce it 'robbery.'"[44]

Even though Alton was in a free state, Lovejoy would not enjoy peace in this town with many proslavery sympathizers. Mobs smashed and threw three of his printing presses into the river, and when the fourth one arrived in a warehouse, Lovejoy and his supporters armed themselves to defend it. When residents learned that the press was there on November 7, 1837, a mob gathered, and a pitched battle ensued. When the attackers attempted to set fire to the roof, Lovejoy rushed out to tip over the ladder. However, the mob shot him five times, and he died moments later. The defenders then relented, and the mob tore apart the printing press and gleefully threw it into the Mississippi. The next morning onlookers jeered and taunted the body of Lovejoy as it was carried through the streets to his home. As the body passed, one doctor shouted, "I would like to kill every damned abolitionist fanatic in town." No one was ever punished for his murder.[45]

These events, if not all these specifics, were still fresh in the memory of Springfield residents seventy miles away when, in January of 1838, the twenty-eight-year-old Abraham Lincoln delivered an address to the Young Men's Lyceum of Springfield, a public speaking organization, in the Second Presbyterian Church of Springfield, a one-story wooden structure that measured only twenty by twenty-five feet.[46] In this humble setting, Lincoln delivered his most ambitious speech to date, and it was the first in which he made extensive appeals to the past, especially to the memory of the Founding Founders.

Lincoln announced that the topic of his speech was "the perpetuation of our political institutions" and began with a paean to the Founders.[47] While Lincoln, in many ways, would make appeals to the past that did not include the memory of the American Revolution, the Founding Fathers would nonetheless prove to be a powerful source of inspiration and wisdom for his era. When Lincoln was born in 1809, the touchstone of national memory was the American Revolution. Accounts of the war were not the domain of historians but instead of those with a living memory of it. Washington, Franklin, and Hamilton were in their graves. However, Jefferson was in the Executive Mansion, Madison would soon succeed him, and Adams was in retirement in his Peacefield home with nearly two more decades yet to live. When Lincoln was born, the youngest veterans of the Revolution were not yet fifty, and while firsthand memory of that war would fade during his lifetime, it would not wholly flicker out until after his death.[48] Every sizable community would have had someone who had fought in it, not to mention the noncombatants who had lived through it. During a time when many people were illiterate, especially on the Kentucky frontier, the spoken word formed much of the understanding of that war. This revolutionary past was something sacred to be revered, cherished, and preserved as a source of inspiration.

Lincoln praised their common heritage and the importance of protecting their inheritance against what he saw as the biggest threat to those
institutions—namely, the rising mob violence throughout the country.
Lincoln argued that no foreign power could destroy the nation; rather it
was the growing anarchy that could prove fatal: "If destruction be our lot,
we must ourselves be its author and finisher. As a nation of freemen, we
must live through all time, or die by suicide." He gave several examples
to provide evidence of this lawlessness, including the murders of McIntosh and Lovejoy. He argued that the lynching of McIntosh was among
"the most dangerous in example, and revolting to humanity" as it was
"highly tragic." Aside from the length of time he mentioned, Lincoln
got McIntosh's story correct: "A mulatto man, by the name of McIntosh,
was seized in the street, dragged to the suburbs of the city, chained to a
tree, and actually burned to death; and all within a single hour from the
time he had been a freeman, attending to his own business, and at peace
with the world." Lincoln argued that this "mobocratic spirit" threatened
the "attachment of the People" to that government and thus endangered
its existence. In a clear reference to Elijah Lovejoy, Lincoln maintained
that "whenever the vicious portion of population shall be permitted to
gather in bands of hundreds and thousands, and throw printing presses
into rivers, shoot editors, and hang and burn obnoxious persons at pleasure, and with impunity; depend on it, this Government cannot last."[49]

Lincoln offered the cure for their present troubles:

> Let every American, every lover of liberty, every well wisher to his pos-
> terity, swear by the blood of the Revolution, never to violate in the least
> particular, the laws of the country; and never to tolerate their violation
> by others. As the patriots of seventy-six did to the support of the Declara-
> tion of Independence, so to the support of the Constitution and Laws, let
> every American pledge his life, his property, and his sacred honor;—let
> every man remember that to violate the law, is to trample on the blood
> of his father, and to tear the character of his own, and his children's lib-
> erty. Let reverence for the laws . . . become the *political religion* of the
> nation; and let the old and the young, the rich and the poor, the grave
> and the gay, of all sexes and tongues, and colors and conditions, sacrifice
> unceasingly upon its altars.[50]

Here he is appealing to the memory of the nation's founders and deliberately arguing for a *political religion* supporting the rule of law that would
imbue every aspect of the society's culture and embed itself thoroughly
in the collective consciousness of the nation.

For Lincoln the Founding Founders had earned undying glory: "They
were to be immortalized; their names were to be transferred to counties and

cities, and rivers and mountains; and to be revered and sung, and toasted through all time." However, Lincoln worried that all the glory had been "harvested" by the founding generation. He argued that there would be some in later generations who would seek their own paths to glory:

> This field of glory is harvested, and the crop is already appropriated. But new reapers will arise, and *they*, too, will seek a field. It is to deny, what the history of the world tells us is true, to suppose that men of ambition and talents will not continue to spring up amongst us. And, when they do, they will as naturally seek the gratification of their ruling passion, as others have *so* done before them.

He continued to appeal to the wisdom of the past ("the history of the world tells us"), arguing that the "towering genius" of the likes of Caesar or Napoleon (both men who tore down republics):

> sees *no distinction* in adding story to story, upon the monuments of fame, erected to the memory of others. It *denies* that it is glory enough to serve under any chief. It *scorns* to tread in the footsteps of *any* predecessor, however illustrious. It thirsts and burns for distinction; and, if possible, it will have it, whether at the expense of emancipating slaves, or enslaving freemen."[51]

Lincoln would "thirst" and "burn" for distinction throughout his life, but we must not read too much into this last statement because we know his future in a way he could never foresee.

He hoped that the revolutionary generation would live on in memory for all coming time, but it would necessarily fade and not hold the same strong influence as it had in the past. This is because a *"living history was* to be found in every family—in the limbs mangled, in the scars of wounds received, in the midst of the very scenes related—a history, too, that could be read and understood alike by all." This *"living history"* was necessarily a strong support for the institutions they created. There was a danger to the republic's survival as the revolutionary generation passed and this memory faded. According to Lincoln, "They were the pillars of the temple of liberty; and now, that they have crumbled away, that temple must fall, unless we, their descendants, supply their places with other pillars," which, derived from reason, would be *"general intelligence, morality* and, in particular, *a reverence for the constitution and laws."* By doing so Lincoln's generation would be able to perpetuate their institutions by protecting the memory of Washington and the Revolution. He closed by alluding to Matthew 16:18, stating the rock that their freedom was built on was not that of the apostle Peter but rather the continued reverence of the past and commitment to reason to support it.[52]

Even though he made a passionate appeal to reason, he did not create a rational argument based on historical research. Most of the speech is an emotional appeal to the memory of the recent past and that of the Founders. Two enemies threatened the government, anarchy and tyranny, with the former frequently begetting the latter. These dangers, he warned, would likely increase over time if the memory of the Founders faded. He appealed to the nation's cherished heritage and to reason to combat the growing lawlessness in the country. For Lincoln, memory and reverence for the past had the power to help protect the country from undoing everything the Founders had done and to provide an endless source of wisdom for the future.

A few scholars have also noticed some striking similarities between Lincoln's Lyceum Address and the most widely respected work of history at that time, Edward Gibbon's *The Decline and Fall of the Roman Empire*. Lincoln is said to have read Gibbon's book around the same time that he prepared the address, and the similarities in the opening sentence of each work are almost too similar for it to be a coincidence. Gibbon began his first chapter by stating, "In the second century of the Christian era, the Empire of Rome comprehended the fairest part of the earth, and the most civilised portion of mankind."[53] Compare this to the opening two sentences of Lincoln's lyceum address: "In the great journal of things happening under the sun, we, the American People, find our account running, under date of the nineteenth century of the Christian era. We find ourselves in the peaceful possession, of the fairest portion of the earth, as regards extent of territory, fertility of soil, and salubrity of climate."[54] Lincoln scholar Robert Bray has noted that "the language, tone, and sense of Gibbon's passage echo Lincoln's worry in the Lyceum Address." Both described the greatest dangers to the polity as coming from within rather than without. Both reviled demagogues that stirred the passions of the people rather than appealing to their reason. While Gibbon praised the civic religion of the Romans, Lincoln sought to create one where the American people would revere the Founding Fathers the same way the Romans cherished the memory of their great leaders.[55] Likewise, shortly after delivering this speech, Lincoln began to copy not just the message but also the mode of Gibbon—namely, he created a reasoned narrative about the past after conducting deep historical research.

Conclusion

Lincoln's earliest surviving documents illuminate his belief in the importance of the past. They show his powerful attachment to the Founders, but they also show that he believed that memory of the past in general, including his own, was useful in achieving a greater understanding of the present. When Lincoln referenced their national past in his early life, he only referred to aspects of the past that any well-informed citizen, literate or not, would already know. However, Lincoln began to develop a new understanding of history in the following years. He would no longer be simply content to rely on the knowledge of others. As we shall see, Lincoln began to do what historians do, investigate what evidence survives in the present to construct a narrative about the past to make meaning or, as Lincoln would see it, provide wisdom.

Chapter 2

The Emerging Historian (1839)

A Mind Full of Terrible Inquiry

In order to understand Lincoln the historian, we must first understand Lincoln the man.[1] Throughout his life, Lincoln was uncommonly inquisitive. From his investigation of the navigability of the waterways when he first arrived in Illinois to his research into military tactics in the White House, Lincoln was never one to accept something based solely on authority or what he heard. One friend said that Lincoln's "mind was full of terrible Enquiry" and "was skeptical in a good sense." Another friend wrote that he "analysed every proposition with startling clearness."[2]

One of Lincoln's lawyer friends on the circuit, Henry Clay Whitney, left the following account of Lincoln's inquisitive nature:

> While we were traveling in anti-railway days, on the circuit, and would stop at a farm-house for dinner, Lincoln would improve the leisure in hunting up some farming implement, machine or tool, and he would carefully examine it all over, first generally and then critically; he would "sight" it to determine if it was straight or warped: if he could make a practical test of it, he would do that; he would turn it over or around and stoop down, or lie down, if necessary, to look under it; he would examine it closely, then stand off and examine it at a little distance; he would shake it, lift it, roll it about, up-end it, overset it, and thus ascertain every quality and utility which inhered in it, so far as acute and patient investigation could do it.

Whitney wrote that this inquisitiveness was not simply limited to the mechanical world. Lincoln, according to Whitney, "would bore to the center of any moral proposition, and carefully analyze and dissect every layer and every atom of which it was composed, nor would he give over the search till completely satisfied that there was nothing more to know, or be learned about it." According to Whitney, "Lincoln would not take anything on faith or trust; that he would not walk in any beaten path; that he must make his own analysis; that he considered and tested all things as if he was the first man and totally without guide or precedent."[3] Joshua Speed, perhaps Lincoln's closest friend, likewise recalled Lincoln's innate inquisitiveness. According to Speed, Lincoln worked diligently to "study and understand all he saw. No matter how ridiculous his ignorance upon any subject might make him appear, he was never ashamed to acknowledge it; but he immediately addressed himself to the task of being ignorant no longer."[4] From inspecting farm implements during his days traveling the circuit to testing the new Spencer repeating rifle on the White House lawn, Lincoln had a deeply inquisitive mind.

Lincoln's curiosity and relentless questioning and testing were essential elements of his nature. When Lincoln wanted to understand something, he did not blindly accept someone else's testimony, but he first questioned and investigated it. Lincoln understood that only by examining and testing a proposition could he genuinely understand it.

Lincoln possessed what author and cofounder of the Center for Applied Rationality Julia Galef coined as the "scout mindset," the desire to explore and see the world as it is rather than what we would want it to be. This sensibility contrasts with the "soldier mindset," in which a person uses motivated reasoning to interpret the world. While the soldier seeks to protect and defend a position and attack and destroy an enemy's position, a scout's job is to explore and attempt to create a more accurate map of reality so that better decisions can be made. According to Galef, "Our judgment isn't limited by knowledge nearly as much as it's limited by attitude." However, people are people, and no person will seek to explore rather than attack or defend a position in all situations. As Galef writes, "The scout and the soldier are archetypes. In reality, nobody is a perfect scout, just as nobody is a pure soldier. We fluctuate between mindsets from day to day, and from one context to the next." As we shall see, this was undoubtedly true of Abraham Lincoln. However, the more one can adopt the sensibility of a scout rather than a soldier, the better one's decision-making process can be.[5] Along with his extensive meditations, Lincoln's inquisitiveness and desire to see the world as it was were keys to his success. Lincoln also practiced this attitude when trying to make sense of history.

Lincoln believed that wisdom could be derived from the past and that to discover this wisdom, it was necessary not to rely solely on common understandings of the past but to investigate it through critical analysis. Memory, while it may have a powerful emotional appeal, by itself is insufficient to understand the past fully and derive the greatest wisdom from it.

To better understand why this is, it is good to contrast memory with history. Memory is born in recall. History is born in inquiry. Memory begins with *knowing*. History begins with *not knowing*. Memory is born in confidence. History is born in humility. Memory deals with the lowest order of thinking. History is a higher-order thinking skill. Memory, in some sense, is the ending point of thought about the past. History is the beginning. Memory begins with a statement. History begins with a question. Memory is declarative. History is interrogative. Memory is proclamation. History is investigation. History understands that our own current understanding is not sufficient. It is a quest for truth, a search with no end. Memory and history may be different but not necessarily antagonistic categories. Memory, whether personal or collective, can be a powerful motivation to investigate the past.

While many historians today believe that only those who are professionally trained in universities deserve the title of historian, the autodidactic Lincoln used many of the skills necessary for the study of history in his reconstructions of the past. The work of history is a complex process, but historians can construct reasonably accurate interpretations of the past by beginning with inquiry. The historian then investigates and researches, looking for answers to these questions. In the process of investigation, new questions arise and are explored. Historians develop a thesis, which they present in some form with evidence to support it. They analyze the evidence and provide warrants to show how the evidence given supports their claims. Historians seek corroboration for any evidence they find and provide sources and context information. Whenever possible, they use primary, rather than secondary, sources. Historians acknowledge the limits to understanding, using hedges and addressing alternative viewpoints. They define key terms and seek to provide clarity rather than mystify and muddle. They explain the significance of the thesis and argue why it is relevant. They seek to increase the understanding of fellow historians and the general public. While he never received a second of professional training in the study of history, in some of his most important speeches, Lincoln used all of these skills of a historian while making arguments about the past.

At times Lincoln only appealed to what already existed within the memories of his audience and the voting public. At other times, Lincoln made arguments not by appealing to what was already common knowledge but by basing on his research in the past to bring these new aspects into a better understanding of the community.

Although Lincoln naturally possessed some of the habits of a historian, such as his inquisitive nature, these skills, the tools of the historian, are those that he worked at not through formal training to become a historian but rather through his legal training and practice. Joseph F. Roda, author of *Abraham Lincoln and Making a Case*, argues that "Lincoln's almost twenty-five years in the courtroom—in hundreds of trials and appeals—so shaped his approach to persuasion that he never stopped being the courtroom lawyer even outside the courtroom, in politics and the presidency."[6] In order to better understand how Lincoln made arguments about the past, we need to gain a better understanding of his legal career.

Lincoln the Lawyer

There are few who practice both law and history, but to be successful in one field, one must practice many of the essential skills in the other. By the very nature of their work, lawyers must research past events, ask questions, develop theses, and construct narratives with evidence to support their theses. As historians, they must make their arguments convincing or they will not have a long career in their field.

Lincoln learned about and developed these skills in his legal training. Just as Lincoln never studied history in college, he never attended law school. He read on his own all the legal books he could acquire, and these works provided insight into skills that could be used by both the lawyer and the historian. Two of these books were especially beneficial to the study of history, William Blackstone's *Commentaries on the Laws of England* and Simon Greenleaf's *A Treatise on the Law of Evidence.*

Blackstone's Commentaries

In the minds of early Americans, no greater authority on the law existed than William Blackstone. An eighteenth-century British jurist, Blackstone was best known for his *Commentaries on the Laws of England.* Many of Lincoln's New Salem friends and acquaintances reported seeing him reading it, and in his later years Lincoln advised other aspiring lawyers to master it if they sought professional success. While much of this work deals with arcane minutiae that would prove of little use to Lincoln, several aspects of the *Commentaries* would be beneficial for both a lawyer and a historian.

The most salient feature of the *Commentaries* for the historian is its focus on the importance of defining key terms. Blackstone, throughout his *Commentaries*, defined dozens of words, usually at the very beginning of each chapter. From commonly understood words like *law* and *title* to complex and more obscure legal terms such as *defeasance* and *lineal consanguinity*, Blackstone defined every term he deemed important.[7] Throughout his political career when making arguments about the past, Lincoln would define key terms to provide clarity for his audience.

Blackstone also taught that if there was any confusion or controversy over the law, it was essential to ascertain the original intentions of those who crafted and passed the legislation. Blackstone wrote, "The fairest and most rational method to interpret the will of the legislator is by exploring his intentions at the time when the law was made, by signs the most natural and probable. And these signs are either the words, the context, the subject matter, the effects and consequence, or the spirit and reason of the law." Blackstone argued that it was important to understand "the cause which moved the legislator to enact it" in the past in order to determine how it applies in the present, a principle Lincoln would apply in his historical arguments.[8]

To present evidence to support one's claim, Blackstone wrote that the records should be consulted in order to search for the proper precedent. "Public repositories" should be utilized "when any critical question arises in the determination of which former precedents may give light or assistance." The court's records were of "such high and super eminent authority that their truth is not to be called in question" and have been preserved for "perpetual memorial and testimony." The evidence found in these records was "that which demonstrates, makes clear, or ascertains the truth of the very fact or point in issue, either on the one side or on the other." The evidence allowed one to ascertain relevant precedents, which were of the utmost importance because people of the present must "abide by former precedents, where the same points come again in litigation." According to Blackstone, "we owe such a deference to former times as not to suppose that they acted wholly without consideration." Latter generations should only overturn precedent when "the former determination is most evidently contrary to reason" or "clearly contrary to the divine law." For Blackstone the only evidence that the courts should admit was that which was directly relevant to the issue at hand. Blackstone also taught that corroborating evidence was important because "one witness (if credible) is sufficient evidence to a jury of any single fact, though undoubtedly the concurrence of two or more corroborates the proof."[9] Each of these principles would prove helpful in making sense of the past.

Finally, Lincoln read in Blackstone a principle that he would hold fast to—that the law was "always ready to catch at anything in favor of liberty."[10]

Greenleaf's Evidence

Another law book that Lincoln read and recommended is Simon Greenleaf's three-volume work, *A Treatise on the Law of Evidence*. Greenleaf, a professor at Harvard's nascent law school, wrote his *Treatise* to use as a textbook in his classroom and published his first edition in 1842.[11] Like Blackstone in his *Commentaries*, Greenleaf defined dozens of terms and demonstrated the importance of precedents by citing hundreds of them. However, the bulk of his work explores the nature of evidence and how it can be used in the courtroom.

He began, of course, by defining *evidence*, which he described as being "all the means, by which any alleged matter of fact, the truth of which is submitted to investigation, is established or disproved." Since much of what we "know" is not derived from our own senses and experiences but instead learned from what others have sensed and experienced, it is essential to be able to determine what constitutes "competent" or "satisfactory" evidence and to use it properly. "Reason," especially that which is gained through "experience and observation," can aid in determining the veracity of a claim. According to Greenleaf, we can never determine what happened in the past with the certainty that a mathematician may prove an axiom, and it is necessary to a certain extent to rely on faith. This faith, however, is not blind because we can determine what happened in the past with sufficient certainty (with at least enough certainty in order to take action) by analyzing the evidence, searching for corroborating testimony, considering source and context information, and using human reason aided by experience.[12]

Greenleaf stressed that only evidence directly related to the issue at hand was permissible and that the evidence presented should be the best available. It must not distract the court from the central issue but directly address the charge. By best evidence available, Greenleaf meant "that no evidence shall be received, which is merely substitutionary in its nature, so long as the original evidence can be had. The rule excludes only that evidence, which itself indicates the existence of more original sources of information." According to Greenleaf, "This rule naturally leads to the division of evidence into Primary and Secondary. Primary evidence is . . . the best evidence," which is the "kind of proof which, under any possible circumstances, affords the greatest certainty of the fact in question." In certain circumstances, secondary sources are permissible. However, in order to best reconstruct a narrative of the past, one must never settle for a secondary source when a primary source is available. What is essential, according to Greenleaf, is that whenever possible, "all information must be traced to its source."[13] By "primary sources" Greenleaf did not mean transcribed copies of original documents but rather the original documents themselves. While Lincoln rarely had access to the original documents, he always tried to get as close to the original source as possible, as far as we can tell from on our limited knowledge of which sources Lincoln used. He rarely relied on secondary sources written by historians but rather attempted to use information from official journals, collections of speeches and letters, and contemporary newspaper accounts when available.

Taking context and source information into account, according to Greenleaf, can be essential to deciding the issue under contention. Human actions occur in a highly complex environment. In order to understand them, it is necessary to determine the "surrounding circumstances," because they "necessarily make a part of the proofs of human transactions." Furthermore, to a certain extent, the court must determine the truth based on its confidence in the testimony of witnesses. This confidence is "sanctioned by experience," which allows the court to believe the testimony of "men of integrity" who are devoid of "apparent influence, from passion or interest." This faith in their testimony "is strengthened by our previous knowledge of the narrator's reputation for veracity; by the absence of conflicting testimony; and by the presence of that, which is corroborating and cumulative." The court must consider the "interest" of the witness, which can help determine the veracity of their testimony. Applying the criterion of embarrassment, if a witness testifies against what appears to be their interests, that witness holds more credibility than one who testifies in what appears would support their interests.[14] While Lincoln would be weaker in the areas of contextualizing and sourcing than he would be in other methods of the historian (he frequently would quote something with attribution but with little to no information about the author or the time period), he could usually assume that his audience would have been reasonably familiar with these details (i.e., citing Jefferson during any period of his lifetime). He nevertheless would include context and source information when he felt it relevant. Furthermore, Lincoln frequently used the principle that a person testifying against their perceived interests was more credible than one testifying who did not. For example, later in his career, when he would make arguments that slavery was wrong, he never explicitly quoted abolitionists but rather cited the authority of prominent slave-holders like Washington, Jefferson, Madison, and Clay. To Lincoln, the statements of these slaveholders against the morality of slavery were more powerful than any arguments made by abolitionists because they, unlike abolitionists, testified against their apparent economic interests.

Lincoln may not have received any formal training in history, but the research he performed in his ongoing legal studies did much to give him a solid grounding in the skills needed to investigate the past analytically over the coming decades.

Law Career

While Lincoln practiced many skills that would be useful as a historian in his legal studies, the following question naturally arises: When Lincoln was making arguments about history, was he simply treating the past as a lawyer would, spinning the version of the truth his side wished to tell, regardless of whether it was right or wrong? One aspect of his legal career sheds some light on this. While all his colleagues recognized that Lincoln was one of the best lawyers in the state, his greatest weakness was his inability to effectively argue a case when he did not believe his party was in the right. One lawyer, Orlando B. Finklin, wrote that when "he had the right none could surpass him." Another lawyer, Samuel C. Parks, wrote that "when he thought he was wrong he was the weakest lawyer I ever saw," sometimes allowing other lawyers on his team to make the arguments because he felt the jury would see through him. Likewise, Judge David Davis said that Lincoln was "great in court anywhere if he thought he was right," but he one time refused to make an argument after hearing the testimony of witnesses, believing his client guilty. Lincoln's friend Joshua F. Speed, who sometimes hired Lincoln for his legal services, wrote, "He must believe that he was right and that he had truth and justice with him or he was a weak man—But no man could be stronger if he thought that he was right."[15] When Lincoln believed his cause just, as his law partner William Herndon wrote, he was a "hoss" of a lawyer.[16] This tendency must be kept in mind when considering his use of the past in his political career. While one should critique various aspects of his use of history, few would doubt his sincerity or belief that he was on the side of truth and justice.

One further aspect of his legal career that would affect his use of history is how he argued cases. To one lawyer, Lincoln advised, "In law it is good policy to never *plead* what you *need* not, lest you oblige yourself to *prove* what you *can* not."[17] Joshua Speed reported how Lincoln the lawyer applied this in practice:

> His analytical powers were marvelous. He always resolved every question into its primary elements, and gave up every point on his own side that did not seem to be invulnerable. One would think, to hear him present his case in the court, he was giving his case away. He would concede point after point to his adversary until it would seem his case was conceded entirely away. But he always reserved a point upon which he claimed a decision in his favor, and his concession magnified the strength of his claim.[18]

A few lawyers corroborated Speed's account of how Lincoln put this principle into action, but the most evocative account was made by Lincoln's lawyer friend Leonard Swett. According to Swett,

> As he Entered the Trial, where most lawyers object, he would say he "reckoned" it would be fair to let this in or that and sometimes, where his adversary could not quite prove what Lincoln Knew to be the truth he would say he "reckoned" it would be fair to admit the truth to be so & so When he did object to the Court after it heard his objection answered he would say "Well I reckon I must be wrong. Now about the time he had practised this ¾ through the case if his adversary didnt understand him he would wake up in a few minutes finding . . . himself beat. He was wise as a serpent in the trial of a cause but I have got too many scars from his blows to certify that he was harmless as a dove. When the whole thing is unravelled, the adversary begins to see that what he was so blanly giving away was simply what he couldnt get & Keep. By giving away 6 points and carrying the 7th he carried his case and the whole case hanging on the 7th he traded away every thing which would give him the least and in carrying that. Any man who took Lincoln for a simple minded man would very soon wake with his back in a ditch[19]

In making his claims about the past in his political career, he would accept the arguments of his adversaries, even if he did not fully believe them to be true if he felt they were not necessary to convince his audience. However, he held fast to the one essential line of argument he felt would persuade his listeners.

Thoughts on a Useable Past

Almost all of those who reported on what Lincoln read in his youth mentioned Lincoln's love of reading history. Some of these books, such as Parson Weems's biography of George Washington, would today be characterized more as myth, while others could be considered the best works of history then available, such as Edward Gibbon's *The History of the Decline and Fall of the Western Empire*. However, he rarely cited works of history or biography in his speeches about the past, and two men who knew him well in his adulthood, Joseph Gillespie and John T. Stuart, claimed that Lincoln didn't read much history. According to Stuart, Lincoln's former law partner, Lincoln "read hard works—was philosophical—logical—mathematical—never read generally—didn't know anything about history—had no faith in it nor biography." Gillespie, a fellow lawyer, a colleague in the Illinois legislature, and a friend, commented on Lincoln's thoughts on works of history,

> Mr Lincoln never I think studied history except in connection with politics with the exception of the history of the Netherlands and of the revolutions of 1640 & 1688 in England and of our revolutionary struggle he regarded it as of triffling value as "teaching by example" Indeed he thought that history as generally written was altogether to unreliable[20]

According to Gillespie, it was not the *past* but rather the *history*, as it was then written in many of the books he had read, that was so fruitless. Lincoln valued good history so much that when he wrote it himself, he sought to get it right by going to the original sources and using his own reason to create his narrative of the past. As his friend and law colleague Henry Clay Whitney wrote, "His clear perception and vigorous reasoning faculties forbade him from taking anything at second-hand; he must grind everything through the mill of his own logic."[21]

Although Lincoln may have doubted the utility of many of the histories then available, he never doubted his belief in a usable past. Experience, especially his years in the White House, caused him to modify some of his early ideas, but he never wavered from his belief in its utility.

Lincoln expressly stated both in letters and speeches in his early political career why the past was important. As mentioned earlier he argued in 1832 that education was necessary so that people would be able to "read the histories" in order to "duly appreciate the value of our free institutions," which was of "vital importance." Furthermore, in one letter, he wrote about the past, stating that "we dare not disregard the lessons of experience." In a speech to the Springfield Scott Club, he said, "History is philosophy teaching by example." In two separate speeches, one in front of the U.S. House of Representatives and one in Peoria, Illinois, Lincoln, when dealing with a controversial topic, told his audience that they should be "judging of the future by the past" in order to determine the best course in the present. In his 1839 speech on the Sub-Treasury, Lincoln mused on the value of "the experience of the past," which he "rel[ied] chiefly upon experience to establish" an argument. He continued:

> How is it that we know any thing—that any event will occur, that any combination of circumstances will produce a certain result—except by the analogies of past experience? What has once happened, will invariably happen again, when the same circumstances which combined to produce it, shall again combine in the same way. We all feel that we know that a blast of wind would extinguish the flame of the candle that stands by me. How do we know it? We have never seen this flame thus extinguished. We know it, because we have seen through all our lives, that a blast of wind extinguishes the flame of a candle whenever it is thrown fully upon it. Again, we all feel to *know* that we have to die. How? We have never died yet. We know it, because we know, or at least think we know, that of all the beings, just like ourselves, who have been coming into the world for six thousand years, not one is now living who was here two hundred years ago.
>   I repeat then, that we know nothing of what will happen in future, but by the analogy of experience.

For Lincoln studying the past had a clear and direct purpose—to guide the present and predict the future. According to the thirty-year-old Lincoln, envisioning the future based on previous experience was relatively uncomplicated, as simple as knowing from experience that a gust of wind will extinguish a candle. The wisdom of the past was there and readily available for anyone to find it. All one had to do was "examine it."[22]

Of course, Lincoln was not speaking and writing in a vacuum but was reflecting current trends on the value of studying history. His ideas about the past, and even some of his wording, were not original. For example, Lincoln probably learned the phrase "judging of the future by the past" from Patrick Henry's "Give Me Liberty or Give Me Death!" speech in which Henry proclaimed, "I have but one lamp by which my feet are guided, and that is the lamp of experience. I know of no way of judging of the future but by the past."[23] The expression "history is philosophy teaching by example," traditionally ascribed to the Greek historian Thucydides, was well-known during Lincoln's era. While not Thucydides's exact words, they are true to the spirit of what he wrote in

The Peloponnesian War: "If it be judged useful by those inquirers who desire an exact knowledge of the past as an aid to the interpretation of the future, which in the course of human things must resemble if it does not reflect it, I shall be content."[24] People of Lincoln's era revered the Founding Fathers and the ancient Greeks, and it is not surprising that Lincoln would draw inspiration from their thoughts on history.

More generally, the nineteenth century has been called the "Golden Age of History" as many historians in the Western world attained real political power for themselves and helped forge new national identities and gave individuals a sense of meaning in a collective process greater than the individual. The professionalized academic field of history, as we've come to know it, would not be fully realized until after Lincoln's death. Those who wrote history in antebellum America were usually college educated but made their living in some other profession. One study from 1959 found that 70 percent of American historians active from 1800 to 1860 had "attended college" (versus 99 percent in 1959) at a time when only 1 percent of their contemporaries had done so. Only one of these historians (George Bancroft) had earned a PhD. Unlike today's historians, the vast majority of these men (besides Mercy Otis Warren they were almost entirely male) did not have positions in academia. The leading profession for historians was "clergy" followed by "law and politics" and "printer, editor, bookseller." Many were retired or had no professional vocation whatsoever but were "gentlemen" who had the leisure to pursue their interests. While many were antiquarians whose works were little more than compilations of documents and accounts, the more renowned historians wrote for the general public and crafted their narratives to suit their tastes and interests.[25] Leading American historians such as George Bancroft, Francis Parkman, William Prescott, and John Motley wrote didactic histories, believing their field to be vital in maintaining and perpetuating the freedoms earned by their fathers and grandfathers.[26] Quite often these works overtly reflected the political views of their authors, something that their readers expected but that would be eschewed by later professionally trained historians who aimed to make their narratives "scientific." Unlike later generations, there was no firm dividing line between the practices of history and politics. For centuries many of the greatest historians in the Western tradition served in politics in some form, some reaching the highest positions of power, such as Coluccio Salutati, Leonardo Bruni, Niccolo Machiavelli, Edward Gibbon, and Thomas Macaulay. This tradition carried over into early America, with figures including John Marshall, Josiah Quincy III, David Ramsay, and George Bancroft. What is odd is not how many Western historians had served in government in the past but rather how few historians serve today. Furthermore, antebellum politicians who did not publish separate works of history nevertheless made frequent and abundant appeals to the past, sometimes based on their research, to shape the present and guide the future, which would become even more true in the years following the Kansas-Nebraska crisis of 1854.

The best example of an American statesman before Lincoln who turned to the wisdom of the past to guide the present was James Madison. In preparation for the Constitutional Convention, Madison closeted himself and engaged in deep historical study to seek wisdom from the past into how governments could be best organized, research and wisdom that became evident in the convention itself and the ratification debates that followed. However, enslaved labor afforded Madison the luxury to investigate the past at ease. Lincoln, the busy professional who worked to support others, and not vice versa, had to hustle for every moment of study.

Like many others of his era, Lincoln saw no reason to separate history and politics. While much of it has been lost to the irrecoverable past, there is still enough surviving evidence to give us insight into how Lincoln practiced the skills of the historian during his early political career.

Searching for Primary Sources

Compared with the surviving writings from his later years, the extant documents from Lincoln's early political career are paltry. Nevertheless, an interesting pattern does emerge from the few that do survive, namely Lincoln's search for the original sources of information. In January of 1840, the thirty-year-old Lincoln wrote to his senior law partner, John T. Stuart, for help. Lincoln, then serving in the Illinois legislature, had risen to be one of the leading Whig politicians in the state. Stuart was then serving in the U.S. House of Representatives as a Whig. Preparing for the coming presidential election that fall, Lincoln wrote to Stuart, "Be verry sure to procure and send me the Senate Journal of New York of September 1814. I have a newspaper article which says that that document proves that Van Buren voted against raisin troops in the last war." Likewise, later that spring Lincoln wrote to his friend Dr. Richard F. Barrett, asking him to procure newspaper articles from 1821 during his visit to New York City and, specifically, the journal of the New York Senate for the fall session of 1812. Lincoln had seen references to these sources, and he wanted to verify the secondhand information he had. He was so eager to get them that he told his friend to go to Albany if they were not available in New York City. He said, "[I] would not miss your getting them for a hundred dollars."[27] Before launching himself into the political battles of the election year, he wanted to arm himself with the facts that he had personally verified.

Like Stuart before him, Lincoln himself was, by 1847, both a senior law partner and a Whig member of the U.S. House of Representatives. While in Washington he wrote to his junior law partner, William Herndon, that he would start sending him issues of the *Congressional Globe*, which was the official record and journal of the U.S. Congress. Herndon could read them if he pleased, but most important for Lincoln was that he "be careful to preserve" them all to "have a complete file" of them.[28] They would be of little use to Lincoln in his Springfield law office while he was in Washington, but even though he had already forsworn running for reelection, he hoped that his political career would not be over, and he wanted a careful preservation of the records for the future.

While serving in Congress, Lincoln experienced firsthand why careful preservation of records was important. In 1848 the Whig congressman Lincoln and Democratic congressman James H. Thomas petitioned Secretary of State James Buchanan for a translated copy of a letter sent by Santa Ana to Andrew Jackson concerning agreements between Mexico and Texas. They found reference to it in official Senate documents, but they could not find copies of it after searching diligently. Lincoln and Thomas asked Buchanan if the State Department still had the record.[29] Buchanan replied that while the letter had been in the department temporarily for the purpose of translating it, the letter had been returned to the president, and no copies were preserved in the department.[30] One document Lincoln was able to locate was the 1836 Treaty of Velasco, which he transcribed in its entirety and used for a speech he delivered before Congress in 1848.[31]

These few records that survive corroborate the testimony of Lincoln's friends and colleagues, which said that Lincoln adhered to his legal training in that he should not settle for secondhand testimony when primary sources were available.

In searching for these documents, Lincoln was not solely looking to construct a narrative as accurately as possible. In his letter to Stuart, after asking him to track down old newspapers, Lincoln wrote, "Send me every thing you think will be a good 'war-club.'"[32] In analyzing Lincoln's speeches on history, it is necessary to determine if he was making disciplined arguments about the past that consider different viewpoints, in the mode of Julia Galef's scout mindset, or if his speeches were nothing but a series of *war clubs* to bludgeon his opponents in the soldier mindset.

The Emergence of the Historian: The Sub-Treasury Speech of 1839

The earliest surviving example of Lincoln using the tools of the historian in a significant address is his 1839 speech on the Sub-Treasury. However, besides the work done by Dr. Daniel E. Worthington and the editors of the *Papers of Abraham Lincoln Digital Library*, very little scholarly research has been done on this important early speech. Typically if historians bother to mention it, it is solely to comment on his melodramatic, self-righteous peroration (full of demons, evil spirits, imps, "belching" volcanoes, and such), comparing it unfavorably with the restrained tone of his later addresses.[33] It remains little known because it does not deal with the most pressing issues of the nineteenth century (slavery and national union) but rather with arcane economic problems that every year, to paraphrase Winston Churchill, seem ever more distant and prosaic.[34] However, a careful analysis of this speech is essential for our purposes because it is the first surviving example of Lincoln using the tools of the historian to make arguments about the past. After months of research into this one address, I have been able to find documentary evidence from sources likely available to him in Springfield in 1839 to test the validity of all but three of the dozens of historical claims he made. I have found a few errors in his speech, some immaterial and others of consequence, the largest being an accounting error. While his first attempt at historical analysis was the work of an amateur, it shows that it was the work of a highly diligent and thoughtful amateur whose primary assertions about the past were essentially correct.

The circumstances of the speech, according to Lincoln's friend Joshua Speed, were that during one evening in 1839 the leading young politicians of the state, including Lincoln and the future senators Stephen Douglas and Edward Baker, had gathered in Speed's store in downtown Springfield and "got to talking politics" when things "got warm," "hot," and "angry." Then, according to Speed, "Douglas Sprang up and Said—Gentlemen, this is no place to talk politics" and proposed to debate those issues publicly. Thus began the first great debates between Lincoln and Douglas, nearly two decades before the more famous ones of 1858.[35] While several of the top Whigs and Democrats participated in the discussions, they were dominated by a series of speeches by Lincoln and Douglas in November and December. The most contentious issue was the subtreasury system proposed by the Democrats that was meant to replace the national banking system Alexander Hamilton had initially founded in 1791. Officially called the "Independent Treasury System," the plan called for the Treasury Department to create a series of "sub-treasuries" throughout the country to handle the government's money, a system that would operate entirely independent from banks altogether. Lincoln and his fellow Whigs opposed the Democrats' plan and wished to return to the original national banking system.[36] To accomplish this, Lincoln diligently researched the history of various aspects of this issue and delivered his address on December 26, 1839.

Lincoln's thesis is that Congress should not adopt the proposed sub-treasury system and that they should return to the old national banking system. He supported this thesis with three specific reasons: that the subtreasury system would hurt the value and circulation of the currency, that it would be more expensive than the national bank, and that the money entrusted to the subtreasury would be less secure than the money deposited with the national bank. He used logic to support the first assertion, arguing that since the proposed system would lock money away for months at a time until disbursement, it would limit the circulation of the currency compared to the national bank that would lend out deposits frequently. This, along with the proposal of paying in specie, would cause deflationary pressures that would hurt the economy. He believed his second argument to be self-evident: that while the national bank paid the government an average of $75,000 annually for the privilege of handling its money, the subtreasury, according to its proponents, would cost tens if not hundreds of thousands of dollars a year. He used logic to support his third assertion, arguing that the proposed subtreasury system would encourage, rather than deter, corruption. Lincoln noted that the interests of a bureaucrat in the subtreasury went against his official responsibilities because he could never grow rich by merely doing his duty, personally storing the public's money until it came time for disbursement, but he would have both the opportunity and the interest to abscond with this money if he was dishonest. He appealed to the audience's memory of those government officials who had done that very thing, detailing precisely how much of the people's money each of the many defalcators had absconded with.[37]

To those who would argue that the administration would only pick honest officials, Lincoln appealed to the wisdom of the Bible, noting, "The Saviour of the world chose twelve disciples, and even one of that small number, selected by super-human wisdom, turned out a traitor and a devil. And, it may not be improper here to add, that Judas carried the bag—was the Sub-Treasurer of the Saviour and his disciples." Conversely, the interests of a banker were aligned with his duty, as one could grow wealthy by discharging one's duties faithfully, as a bank will prosper only when the public deems it trustworthy.[38] Lincoln primarily used reason and common sense, as he saw it, to support his thesis.

In the second part of his speech, Lincoln addressed contrary viewpoints, and in this section Lincoln demonstrated that he was using the tools of the historian. Some argued that the national bank was unconstitutional, but Lincoln noted that a majority of the Founders who acted on this issue voted in favor of it, and it was deemed constitutional by subsequent administrations, Congresses, and a definitive Supreme Court ruling. Lincoln did not provide detailed evidence to support this assertion. Still, it is noteworthy because, in many of his later speeches, he would more fully develop this method, namely the assertion that some proposed action in the present was not only constitutional but also expedient based on a detailed analysis into how the Founders voted on the same issue in their day.

Lincoln then used history to show how damaging the Jackson and Van Buren administrations were, arguing that government expenditures had increased rapidly and unnecessarily under their watch. After Lincoln noted that he analyzed all the relevant documents, he made four assertions: (1) the ten years under Jackson and Van Buren had cost more than the previous twenty-seven years combined, years that included the expensive War of 1812, (2) in the final year of the last Whig president, John Quincy Adams, the federal expenditures were roughly $13 million while the previous year of the Democratic Van Buren presidency had cost $40 million, (3) during the final year of the War of 1812, the national government spent only $30 million, even with all the additional expenses attendant to conducting that war, while Van Buren during a year of relative peace had spent $40 million, and (4) Van Buren had spent more in one year ($40 million) than was spent under George Washington's eight years combined ($16 million). Lincoln did note that population increases will necessitate increases in expenditures, but even keeping this in mind, expenses had still proportionately increased much more rapidly under Van Buren.[39]

What he did not note is the fluctuation in the value of money that would have altered these figures in real terms. Had there been significant inflation, it would have undermined Lincoln's arguments because, in real terms, the expenses under Madison could have been equal to that of Van Buren despite the nominal difference. However, the opposite is true, as the United States had experienced *deflation* and not *inflation* in those years. According to the Bureau of Labor Statistics, average prices fell between 1814 and 1838 by 47.16 percent, meaning that $100 in 1814 had the same purchasing power of $52.84 in 1838.[40] If Lincoln had these figures available to him, he could have shown that this deflation significantly enhanced rather than detracted from his argument.

Lincoln provided a warrant for these four pieces of evidence, namely "that there is no parallel between the *'errors'* of the present and late administrations, and those of former times, and that Mr. Van Buren is wholly out of the line of all precedents." Thus, Lincoln was implying, neither Van Buren nor his friends should be entrusted with any more financial responsibilities as they would be under the subtreasury system.[41]

To evaluate Lincoln's work, I searched only sources that could have been available to Lincoln in Springfield. At times, histories published more recently provide figures that differ from what Lincoln asserted in 1839, but it is unfair to judge him based on scholarship not available to him then. It is easy to determine some of the sources he used because he cited them directly. For example, in order to support his assertion that one reason for the rise in expenditures was the increase in corruption, Lincoln referred to a Senate hearing and told his audience not only what book the information could be found in but also the page number and where the book could be found: "Their report is found in the Senate Documents of 1833-'34—Vol. 5, Doc. 422—which Documents may be seen at the Secretary's Office, and I presume elsewhere in the State." When discussing the value of currency, he cited an official letter that could be found "in Senate Document, page 113, of the Session of 1838-'39."[42] Other assertions were more difficult to validate because he did not cite his sources. Still, it appears that almost all the evidence that Lincoln provided originated in the official records published by Congress, besides the executive documents he had explicitly cited. In this research, Lincoln may have consulted his personal library as it is probable that he owned the *Annals of Congress and Congressional Debates: From the First to the Twenty-fifth Congress inclusive excepting the Seventeenth and the First Session of the Eighteenth Congress*, which would have covered all of the congresses up until Lincoln's 1839 speech.[43] Lincoln also likely consulted the annual reports of the secretary of the treasury, the U.S. Statutes at Large, the 1832 *Legislative and Documentary History of the Bank of the United States* by David A. Hall and Matthew St. Clair Clarke, a copy of the Constitution, census records, and the accounts of receipts and expenditures of the federal government for various years. The preceding sources were both likely available to Lincoln in Springfield in 1839 and provide evidentiary support for Lincoln's claims. I have not been able to determine which of these sources Lincoln used directly and which of these he either read secondhand reports of or found the same evidence of in an entirely different source. While this speech is thick with assertions based on documentary evidence, the exception is when Lincoln attempted to prove that the Seminole War was costing more money than it should. He gave an account of government waste and noted that, "This fact is not found in the public reports, but depends with me, on the verbal statement of an officer of the navy, who says he knows it to be true."[44] He provided no corroborating evidence, but throughout the speech Lincoln mainly relied on primary source documents rather than hearsay. After months of research, I have determined that almost all the historical assertions Lincoln made were wholly or largely accurate, and it is essential to analyze these claims in detail.

Lincoln used history to prove that a national bank should be considered perfectly constitutional. To do so, Lincoln made the following assertions:

1. "A majority of the Revolutionary patriarchs, whoever acted officially upon the question, commencing with Gen. Washington and embracing Gen. Jackson, the larger number of the signers of the Declaration, and of the framers of the Constitution, who were in the Congress of 1791, have decided upon their oaths that such a bank is constitutional."
2. "The votes of Congress have more often been in favor of than against its constitutionality."
3. "The Supreme Court . . . has solemnly decided that such a bank is constitutional."

Unfortunately for us, Lincoln did not support these historical claims with specific evidence, telling his audience that he did not need to because he and other Whig speakers had already detailed the evidence before in earlier speeches during this great series of debates.[45] Sadly, nothing except a brief summary of one of these earlier speeches survives and says nothing about the constitutionality argument but does assert that Lincoln supported his "several propositions . . . not by rant, declamation and assertion, but by an array of documentary evidence, which could not be disputed."[46] However, using the sources likely available to him and methods of analysis he would adopt later in his career, it is possible to test the validity of his historical assertions.

Lincoln's first claim, that a majority of the Founding Fathers "decided upon their oaths that such a bank is constitutional," is complex because Lincoln defined these Founders in three distinct groups. Considering first the signers of the Declaration of Independence, who "acted officially upon the question" in 1791 on the First National Bank, this assertion is correct. In the House of Representatives, four signers of the Declaration of Independence (George Clymer of Pennsylvania, Elbridge Gerry of

Massachusetts, William Floyd of New York, and Roger Sherman of Connecticut) voted in favor of the bank while none voted against it. The bill passed the Senate by a voice vote, and it included four people who signed the Declaration of Independence (George Read of Delaware, Robert Morris of Pennsylvania, Richard Henry Lee of Virginia, and Charles Carroll of Maryland). The only signer of the Declaration of Independence who acted in his official capacity against the national bank was Thomas Jefferson, who as secretary of state advised President Washington to veto it. Secondly, considering the Framers of the Constitution who "acted officially upon the question" in 1791, this assertion is largely correct. While the measure passed the House thirty-nine to twenty, considering only "the framers of the Constitution," the vote was five to four in support of the legislation. (In favor: Roger Sherman of Connecticut, Elbridge Gerry of Massachusetts, Nicholas Gilman of New Hampshire, George Clymer of Pennsylvania, and Thomas Fitzsimons of Pennsylvania; Opposed: Abraham Baldwin of Georgia, Daniel Carroll of Maryland, Hugh Williamson of North Carolina, and James Madison of Virginia. If one only considers the Framers who signed the Constitution, the vote was 4 to 4, as Elbridge Gerry refused to sign). The bill passed the Senate by a voice vote, and it included nine Framers of the Constitution (Oliver Ellsworth and William S. Johnson of Connecticut, Richard Bassett of Delaware, George Read of Delaware, William Few of Georgia, Caleb Strong of Massachusetts, John Langdon of New Hampshire, Robert Morris of Pennsylvania, and Pierce Butler of South Carolina. Of these nine, Oliver Ellsworth and Caleb Strong did not sign).[47] The other two Framers of the Constitution who acted officially upon the question at that time were Alexander Hamilton, who as secretary of treasury proposed it, and George Washington who, as president, signed it into law in 1791. Although it was controversial, a majority of signers of the Declaration of Independence and the Constitution who had the opportunity acted in favor of the national bank in 1791. Thirdly, Lincoln argued that even President Jackson claimed that a national bank could be constitutional, which is true. Jackson, who famously won his war against the Second National Bank, still asserted in his veto message for a bill renewing the bank's charter that Congress could create new legislation for a national bank that could be constitutional if it had the right provisions.[48] However, the most prominent objectors to the bank's constitutionality were none other than the primary author of the Declaration of Independence, Thomas Jefferson, and the father of the Constitution, James Madison. While they, as secretary of state and representative in Congress, respectively, vehemently objected to the bank in 1791, they both acted differently when elected president.

Starting in 1801 the Jefferson administration faithfully administered the First National Bank for two whole terms, and Jefferson, who had a large majority of supporters in Congress, did not call for its repeal. Likewise, after the charter for the First National Bank expired, Madison changed his mind after experiencing the financial difficulties in fighting the War of 1812 without it, and he signed and defended legislation for the Second National Bank. While it had been controversial at all times, Lincoln was correct in his assertions about the opinions of the Founding Fathers on the constitutionality of the National Bank.

Next, Lincoln correctly asserted, "The votes of Congress have more often been in favor of than against its constitutionality."[49] Congress approved the First Bank of the United States in 1791. When the charter was up for renewal in 1811, the Senate voted seventeen to seventeen to renew the charter. Vice President George Clinton broke the tie when he voted to reject it, and thus the charter expired. In 1815 Congress passed a bill for a new national bank, but President Madison vetoed it. However, the very next year Congress again passed a bill for a national bank, which President Madison signed this time. Four years before its charter was to expire, Congress passed a bill to renew the bank in 1832, but President Jackson vetoed it.[50] Lincoln was correct that Congress ruled the contentious national bank to be constitutional more times than not.

Thirdly, Lincoln asserted "The Supreme Court—that tribunal which the Constitution has itself established to decide Constitutional questions—has solemnly decided that such a Bank is constitutional." In 1819 the Supreme Court unanimously decided that a national bank was constitutional in its famous *McCulloch v. Maryland* decision with an opinion written by Chief Justice John Marshall.

While in some ways Lincoln minimized the controversy surrounding the issue, he correctly asserted that a preponderance of authority figures in the early republic—the Founding Fathers, the various Congresses, and the Supreme Court—stated that a national bank could be constitutional.

However, Lincoln demonstrated in this early work of history that he was not content to rest his case solely on the opinions of authorities of the past, no matter how revered or learned. He would use the original documentary evidence to support his claims. Since the argument revolved around the constitutionality of a law, he would analyze the Constitution itself to prove his assertion. Lincoln's opponents argued that there is no "express" power granted in the Constitution for a national bank and that it is thus unconstitutional. Lincoln asserted that if that were the standard by which to judge the constitutionality of legislation, then the Democrats' plan for a subtreasury system was equally unconstitutional, as the Constitution does not expressly grant Congress the power to create one. Lincoln argued that that was the wrong way to read the Constitution. Quoting the Constitution, Lincoln stated, "One of the express powers given Congress, is 'To lay and collect taxes; duties, imposts, and excises; to pay the debts, and provide for the common defence and general welfare of the United States.'" Since "Congress is expressly authorized to make all laws necessary and proper for carrying this power into execution," Lincoln logically deduced "that *some* fiscal agent is *indispensably necessary*" in order to carry out these express powers. By carefully analyzing the Constitution, Lincoln concluded that the correct interpretation is that both a national bank and a subtreasury system are constitutional. The right question was not which one was constitutional but rather which one was "most '*proper*' on the grounds of expediency."[51] While this textual analysis closely aligned with Chief Justice Marshall's opinion in the *McCulloch v. Maryland* decision, Lincoln chose to rest the credibility of his argument on the words of the Constitution itself and on common sense, rather than on an appeal to authority.

Lincoln made a few minor factual errors in this speech, but he did make one significant mistake, and we can trace it to two contradictory statements he made in the speech about the sources of his evidence. Before making a detailed analysis of federal expenditures under various administrations, Lincoln stated that he was deriving his information from "authentic public documents, consisting of the regular series of annual reports, made by all the Secretaries of the Treasury from the establishment of the Government down to the close of the year 1838." He no doubt used some of them, and he may have consulted all of them, but I do not believe that these were his ultimate sources of information on federal expenditures. While these reports were a morass of minutiae of national revenue and expenditures, many, especially the earliest ones, lacked the redeeming feature of something approaching a clear bottom line. I calculated my own totals for national expenses from these reports, but some of these figures were nowhere near the ones Lincoln listed. However, he left a clue as to where he got these figures from. While before his analysis of historical federal expenditures he claimed he got his data from dozens of reports from the secretary of the treasury, immediately after his analysis Lincoln claimed that he got his information from a single "authentic document."[52] I believe the latter rather than the former claim to be accurate because, while there may be others out there, I found a single document likely available to him with figures that match precisely those Lincoln presented in his speech. This is Document 192 from the executive documents of the third session of the House of Representatives for the Twenty-Fifth Congress, which includes the "annual expenditures of the Government, exclusive of trust funds, and payments on the account of the public debt."[53]

The problem with this source is that it only includes federal expenditures until 1837.[54] To make the arguments he wanted to make, Lincoln needed the figures from 1838, which he likely got from the annual report of the finances for 1838 by Secretary of Treasury Levi Woodbury, which listed federal expenditures as being $40,427,218.68 for 1838; Lincoln rounded to $40 million. However, Lincoln said that all his spending figures excluded payments on the national debt, which is true of his numbers for all years up to 1837 but not for 1838. If you subtract "public debt" payments totaling $2,217.08 from the secretary's report from the original figure, we are still left with $40,425,001.60, meaning that Lincoln's rounding to $40 million was still reasonable. However, the report also lists "redemption of treasury notes," which totaled $8,089,440.64 for a payment on debt and which was excluded from the figures from earlier years Lincoln was using, thus making the total federal expenditures exclusive of debt payments to be $32,335,560.96, well below Lincoln's figure. That means Lincoln was comparing apples to oranges by using figures that excluded payments on debt for all the years from 1789 to 1837 but included these payments for 1838.[55]

Lincoln used these figures to prove that the Jackson and Van Buren administrations were recklessly spendthrift. While his accounting error did invalidate the calculations, it did not, close examination shows, invalidate his conclusion, merely the extent of it. For example, Lincoln argued that the government under Van Buren's administration in 1838 spent *twice and a half* as much in *one* year, as Gen. Washington did in *eight*."[56] From 1789 to 1796, which encompassed all but the final few months of Washington's second term in 1797, the federal government spent $15,880,698.58, an amount that Lincoln rounded up to $16 million. Excluding payments on debt, the federal government spent $32,335,560.96, not $40 million. Therefore, in Van Buren's first full year, the government spent *twice* as much as the entire two terms of Washington, not *twice and a half*.[57] Likewise, Lincoln claimed that in the last year of the John Quincy Adams administration, the government spent $13 million, or about a dollar per person. In comparison, the Van Buren administration had just spent $40 million in the previous year, which was approximately $2.50 per person.[58] According to the 1830 census, which is nearest to John Quincy Adams's last full year in office in 1828, the population of the United States was 12,858,670.[59] In 1828 the federal government spent $12,505,972.05. By using these figures, the government expended $0.97 per person. By rounding those two previous figures to the nearest million, Lincoln got $1 per person. While there was no recent census in the intervening years, Lincoln appears to estimate the population to have risen to sixteen million by 1838, a good hypothesis, giving him the figure of $2.50 then being expended by the federal government per person if that total had really been $40 million. However, using the correct figure that excludes debt payments, federal expenditures per person were $2.02.[60] While Lincoln's figures were not exactly correct, his larger point—that federal expenditures had rapidly increased—was correct because federal spending per person had doubled in the previous decade.

This accounting error, which is the second most significant one that he made about the past that I have been able to find, should not obscure what Lincoln accomplished in this address. In this speech, he correctly expounded on the history of how the national bank provided a stable currency while at the same time providing revenue for the government, a discussion of the recent history of defalcations among government officers, a detailing of corruption in the post office in the past, analysis of how respected authorities (presidents, Congresses, and the Supreme Court) all attested to the constitutionality of a national bank, a close analysis of the Constitution to prove the constitutionality of a national bank, analysis of the rapid increase in government spending in the past decade in comparison to earlier administrations, and an examination of issues then before Congress. To accomplish this, Lincoln spent an extensive amount of time researching the fiscal history of the United States.

Conclusion

Not only does this early speech prefigure those more extensive and mature addresses Lincoln would make later in his career but it also foreshadowed the more famous debates he would have nearly two decades later with Stephen Douglas about history. In this speech, Lincoln devoted seven paragraphs to refuting Douglas's assertions from an earlier address. Lincoln argued that Douglas's arguments were either patently untrue or, when accurate, had no just application for the uses Douglas attempted to make of them. After this analysis, Lincoln jeered that Douglas was "stupid enough to hope" that Lincoln "would permit such groundless and audacious assertions to go unexposed."[61] According to Lincoln, Douglas was *stupid* for thinking that Lincoln would not investigate his claims, and Lincoln would spend the next two decades conducting research to disprove the assertions of the "Little Giant." Perhaps as much as his natural inquisitiveness and his legal training, Lincoln's decades-long rivalry with Stephen Douglas drove him to research the past to counter a man he felt was manipulating history to achieve dubious political ends.

Although not without flaws, Lincoln would continue to use the tools of the historian to make these kinds of reasoned arguments until the very end of his life. For Lincoln, having a solid and well-informed knowledge of the past provided wisdom, especially in understanding human nature.

Chapter 3

History and Human Nature (1840–53)

Sharpened Perceptions

In many ways Lincoln was unusual for a man for his time and place. He did not smoke, drink, or chew. He did not gamble, and he rarely hunted. He neither was baptized nor joined a church, and infrequently attended any services. He did not participate in many of the social pastimes around him, even when he would have been under considerable peer pressure to do so. However, he was able to not only befriend but also inspire those who took part in all those activities.[1] How was he able to stand apart from and yet lead his community?

One explanation is that, even from an early age, Lincoln seemed to have an almost intuitive understanding of human nature. As a young boy he was able to read and write so well that not only would some adults ask him to read their correspondence and newspapers for them; they sometimes asked him to compose their letters as he could write in a clearer language than they were able to express verbally.[2] According to one friend, Lincoln told him that "his perceptions were sharpened" because "he learned to see other people thoughts and feelings and ideas by writing their friendly confidential letters."[3]

However he acquired this skill, Lincoln showed that he was able to understand the motives of those very different from him, a skill that would be useful in interpreting the past.

Temperance Address

The best early example of Lincoln's understanding of human nature in his early political career is his Temperance Address, delivered to the Washingtonians, a temperance organization, in Springfield on February 22, 1842, Washington's birthday. Founded two years prior, this group of former alcoholics had spread rapidly throughout the country, preaching the evils of alcohol as ones with the experience to know.[4]

In this speech Lincoln argued that the temperance movement had worthy goals and had made significant progress in the previous twenty years. However, many of those who had promoted the movement earlier had used poor tactics. If it were to achieve its ultimate objectives, it must have a better understanding of human nature, as with, he argued, the Washingtonians. Lincoln utilized several sources of wisdom to prove his point, including wisdom derived from the Bible, humor, hymns, history, and his own reasoning.

To show that those who drink alcohol should not be demonized, Lincoln described the history of drinking and the temperance movement. He argued that the movement was enjoying more success now than in earlier years because those who previously led the campaign—namely preachers, lawyers, and hired agents—were less sympathetic than those leading it now. The Washingtonians cannot be said to have had an ulterior motive. Their members were filled with "sincerity" and "sympathy" for those who drink, making their arguments more persuasive. Lincoln also gave a short account of drinking in the past, saying that the practice was "just as old as the world itself." Until about twenty years prior, it had been "recognized by every body, used by every body, and repudiated by nobody." From infants to the elderly, from preachers to the homeless, everyone used it. It was used at every "rolling or raising, a husking or hoe-down" and "any where without it, was *positively insufferable.*" He provided a hedge, stating, "It is true, that even *then*, it was known and acknowledged, that many were greatly injured by it; but none seemed to think the injury arose from the *use* of a *bad thing*, but from the *abuse* of a *very good thing.*" The point of this short account of the past was to argue that those who wish to convince those who drink, manufacture, or sell alcohol not to do so should not "assail, contemn, or despise" people engaged in such a universal practice.[5]

Even though a preponderance of evidence shows that Lincoln did not believe in any traditional form of Christianity at this stage in his life, he thought that there was an abundance of wisdom to be found in Christian scripture as well as in the hymns of Isaac Watts. After comparing the curse of alcohol to the angel of death, Lincoln quoted Ezekiel 37:9 to emphasize that those who have succumbed to this curse may still be saved: "Come from the four winds, O breath! and breathe upon these slain, that they may live." To show the authority of the testimony of former alcoholics, he quoted Mark 5:15 and Luke 8:34, describing the powerful effect of seeing these former madmen "clothed, and in his right mind" using "simple . . . language" that is full of "logic" and "eloquence" that "few, with human feelings, can resist." When he quoted "Hymn 88: Life the Day of Grace and Hope" by Isaac Watts, Lincoln argued that the Washingtonians are true to the original Christian message that all may be saved: "While the lamp holds out to burn, The vilest sinner may return."[6] Perhaps alluding to the Apostle Paul, who had persecuted Christians before converting, he said the Washingtonians "were the chief of sinners, now the chief apostles of the cause" who were casting out demons and the "drunken devils" so that the lost could be "redeemed from his long and lonely wanderings in the tombs" as the man was saved in Mark 5 and Luke 8. To those who would not support a society like the Washingtonians because these teetotalers had not suffered the sin of alcoholism, Lincoln appealed to their faith:

> Surely no Christian will adhere to this objection. If they believe, as they profess, that Omnipotence condescended to take on himself the form of sinful man, and, as such, to die an ignominious death for their sakes, surely they will not refuse submission to the infinitely lesser condescension, for the temporal, and perhaps eternal salvation, of a large, erring, and unfortunate class of their own fellow creatures. Nor is the condescension very great.[7]

At times he referred to Christian texts because they were a cultural touchstone for his audience and helped illustrate the points he was making more clearly, while at other times he was clearly using the Bible as a source of wisdom. He may have scorned the theology at this time in his life, but he did not shun its wisdom.

Lincoln did not solely rely on external sources of wisdom but also used his own reasoning and logic. Lincoln's Temperance Address is unique in his early speeches in that it contains many epigrams and aphorisms that his later addresses would be known for. For example, Lincoln criticized those who promoted a temperance system that some believed would take one hundred years to work: "Few can be induced to labor exclusively for posterity; and none will do it enthusiastically. Posterity has done nothing for us; and theorise on it as we may, practically we shall do very little for it, unless we are made to think, we are, at the same time, doing something for ourselves." He used humor to illustrate that it is human nature to not be too concerned with benefits or punishments in the distant future: "'Better lay down that spade you're stealing, Paddy,—if you don't you'll pay for it at the day of judgment.' 'By the powers, if ye'll credit me so long, I'll take another, jist.'" According to Lincoln at this stage of his life, for any system to work, its benefits must be much more immediate. He also argued that those who used recriminations to try and change the minds of those who produced and drank alcohol would not be successful because "it is not much in the nature of man to be driven to any thing; still less to be driven about that which is exclusively his own business; and least of all, where such driving is to be submitted to, at the expense of pecuniary interest, or burning appetite." Continuing his postulates on human nature, Lincoln argued, "To have expected them to do otherwise than as they did—to have expected them not to meet denunciation with denunciation, crimination with crimination, and anathema with anathema, was to expect a reversal of human nature, which is God's decree, and never can be reversed." Instead of denunciations, he said, "If you would win a man to your cause, *first* convince him that you are his sincere friend. Therein is a drop of honey that catches his heart, which, say what he will, is the great high road to his reason, and which, when once gained, you will find but little trouble in convincing his judgment of the justice of your cause, if indeed that cause really be a just one." According to Lincoln, "Such is man, and so *must* he be understood by those who would lead him, even to his own best interest." He also argued that positive peer pressure, or "moral influence," can also help promote temperance. To those who disagree with him, Lincoln offered the following thought experiment:

> Let me ask the man who would maintain this position most stiffly, what compensation he will accept to go to church some Sunday and sit during the sermon with his wife's bonnet upon his head? Not a trifle, I'll venture. And why not? There would be nothing irreligious in it: nothing immoral, nothing uncomfortable. Then why not? Is it not because there would be something egregiously unfashionable in it? Then it is the influence of *fashion*; and what is the influence of fashion, but the influence that *other* people's actions have actions, the strong inclination each of us feels to do as we see all our neighbors do?[8]

More than any other in his early career, this speech shows the young Lincoln using his own reasoning to create wisdom to help him make his case.

Lincoln closed his "Temperance Address" by appealing to the memory of the American Revolution, arguing that if the temperance movement were to achieve its ends, this moral revolution could have an even greater effect than the earlier political revolution.[9]

Lincoln the teetotaler showed that he had been meditating on how to convince those who act and think differently. Even though he makes many references to the past, Lincoln did not use any wisdom derived from historical research in this speech. However, he showed himself thinking about how to convince people, which is useful for anyone who would attempt to make a historical argument (history is a persuasive art), especially a contentious one.

Oh Memory! Thou Mid-way World/ 'Twixt Earth and Paradise: Lincoln the Poet

Lawrence Weldon, a lawyer who traveled with Lincoln on the circuit, remarked that Lincoln typically rose before the other lawyers. Weldon usually found him alone by the fire stirring the coals and staring silently into the embers. There, according to Weldon, Lincoln would "muse ponder and soliliquize wisper." Weldon remembered one time he found Lincoln in this position, reciting from memory the poem "Mortality" by William Knox. Lincoln, according to Weldon, told him that that poem "sounded as much like true poetry as any thing he had ever heard," especially the final two verses.[10]

Lincoln loved poetry, and his friends, family members, acquaintances, and colleagues all testified that they regularly found him reading it or reciting verses from memory. His favorite poets were well-known: Robert Burns, Lord Byron, and William Shakespeare. However, his favorite poem was by William Knox, who was a relatively unknown Scottish poet.

Knox's poem "Mortality" in many ways matched the sentiments of Watts's "Hymn 88," which Lincoln recorded in his ciphering book as a boy, and the poetry he himself would write as an adult. The poem begins:

> Oh! why should the spirit of mortal be proud?
> Like a swift-fleeting meteor, a fast-flying cloud
> A flash of the lightning, a break of the wave
> He passeth from life to his rest in the grave.[11]

Knox's thoughts on a mortal's life neatly matched Watt's thoughts on time. Both used the word *swift* to describe life and used similes to express this swiftness. For Watts time is "swift as an Indian arrow flies."[12]

For Knox human life is like a "meteor," a "fast-flying cloud/A flash of the lightning, a break of the wave."[13]

Knox's poem describes how beloved family members and fair maidens would all belong to the dust. These lines resonated with Lincoln, who had lost several close family members, along with the woman who was perhaps his first love (Ann Rutledge). Knox described how both the high and low had been felled by death, which is something that Lincoln, who knew both, would never forget. [14]

For two stanzas Knox argues that the living of the past are just like the living of the present:

> For we are the same our fathers have been;
> We see the same sights our fathers have seen;
> We drink the same stream, we view the same sun,
> And run the same course our fathers have run.
>
> The thoughts we are thinking, our fathers would think;
> From the death we are shrinking, our fathers would shrink;
> To the life we are clinging, they also would cling;
> But it speeds from us all like a bird on the wing.[15]

The idea that the people of the past were just like the people of the present—that they had the same thoughts, feelings, hopes and fears—was a powerful idea for Lincoln. Throughout his political career, Lincoln appealed to and researched history because he believed that since the people of the past were just like the people of the present, they could provide eternally relevant lessons on human nature. Lincoln especially loved the final stanza:

> 'Tis the wink of an eye—'tis the draught of a breath—
> From the blossom of health to the paleness of death,
> From the gilded saloon to the bier and the shroud:—
> Oh! why should the spirit of mortal be proud?[16]

According to Weldon, "The weird and melancholy association of eloquence and poetry had a strong fascination for Mr. L" because it "contrasted the realities of eternity with the unstable and fickle fortunes of time."[17] This poem provided Lincoln with the wisdom that the people of the past were just like the people of the present, and since they were now dust, his generation would be one day as well, and thus there was no reason for a mortal to be proud. This lesson would aid Lincoln in his political career, as he never would let his pride get in the way of his political goals as it would for his opponents and colleagues.

Lincoln reportedly wrote poetry in his childhood, but the only surviving poems he is proven to have written come from his adulthood; they were written in 1844, after he visited his boyhood home in Indiana while campaigning for Henry Clay. One, which he probably wrote in 1846, is divided into three cantos, which all relate to his personal memory of his youth in Indiana.

It is impossible to read Lincoln's "My childhood-home I see again" without seeing the influence of Knox's "Mortality." Lincoln's bittersweet reflection inspired him to write a paeon to memory:

> O memory! thou mid-way world
> 'Twixt Earth and Paradise,
> Where things decayed, and loved ones lost
> In dreamy shadows rise.
>
> And freed from all that's gross or vile,
> Seem hallowed, pure, and bright,
> Like scenes in some enchanted isle,
> All bathed in liquid light.[18]

Memory has the power to give one access to a sacred netherworld where the living commune with the dead. Lincoln continues in the fifth stanza:

> As leaving some grand water-fall
> We ling'ring, list it's roar,
> So memory will hallow all
> We've known, but know no more.[19]

The memory of everything that has been lost has the power to render the past sacred. As Lincoln visited those who remained and the landmarks of his childhood, he heard that time had felled half of those he had known and loved. For those still among the living, he saw "young childhood grown, strong manhood grey." Lincoln concluded this spiritual pilgrimage with the following two stanzas:

> I hear the lone survivors tell
> How nought from death could save,
> Till every sound appears a knell,
> And every spot a grave.
>
> I range the fields with pensive tread,
> And pace the hollow rooms;
> And feel (companions of the dead)
> I'm living in the tombs.[20]

Here Lincoln was silently wandering the scenes of his childhood, meditating on those who had been lost and the ephemeral nature of life. Lincoln implied that these memories were driving him to madness, alluding to the Gospels and the story of the demon-possessed man who lived in the tombs and would cry out and cut himself at all hours of both day and night. Many people who commented on his silences noted how "melancholy" he appeared when he withdrew within himself. In these silences, it is not much of a stretch to assume that he was at times communing with loved ones lost and "living in the tombs."[21]

The third and shortest canto further develops his meditations on the past and the passage of time:

> The very spot where grew the bread
> That formed my bones, I see.
> How strange, old field, on thee to tread,
> And feel I'm part of thee![22]

Many historians see the past as dead—that it is just too different to be of much practical value. As his poetry shows, Lincoln deeply felt that the past was not dead but rather lived within him.

Before leaving Lincoln's poetry, we should explore one minor controversy. After Lincoln's death, Lincoln's closest friend, Joshua Speed, wrote to Lincoln's law partner William Herndon that Lincoln had once written a poem on suicide and had it published anonymously in the *Sangamo Journal* around 1838. Herndon looked and claimed that he believed someone had cut out the poem from the back files, possibly Lincoln himself.[23] The poem was thought to have been lost, but historian Richard Lawrence Miller announced that he believed he found the missing poem entitled "The Suicide's Soliloquy" in the August 25, 1838, issue. Miller argued that he thought it was the missing poem because it was published at the correct time, it was about suicide, its theme matched those of other poems Lincoln wrote, and it possessed technical features that were similar to other poems he wrote. While it is unlikely that "The Suicide's Soliliquy" will ever be proved to be Lincoln's with any certainty, Miller's arguments are reasonable and compelling.[24]

Two further things could be said to support Lincoln's authorship. The poem contains an introduction stating that "the following lines were said to have been found near the bones of a man supposed to have committed suicide, in a deep forest, on the Flat Branch of the Sangamon, sometime ago." The Flat Branch enters the Sangamon in a forest just east of Taylorville, approximately twenty-five miles southeast of Springfield. Since he wished to remain anonymous, the author would not likely have given such a specific location in the poem if that had not been near where he lived, as that would threaten to remove their anonymity. However, the author would likely choose a location far from where they lived, yet one they were familiar with. Although the confluence of the Flat Branch and the Sangamon was far from Lincoln's home, he would have known the location, as it was located along the state road Lincoln frequently traveled as a legislator, connecting Springfield to Vandalia, which was then the state capital. Furthermore, another indication that Lincoln probably penned this poem is that, like his other extant poetry, the author of these verses seems to be fixated on memory. In the poem, the narrator details why he felt he must commit suicide:

> To ease me of this power to think,
> That through my bosom raves,
> I'll headlong leap from hell's high brink,
> And wallow in its waves.
>
> Though devils yell, and burning chains
> May waken long regret;
> Their frightful screams, and piercing pains,
> Will help me to forget.

Only death will cease his "power to think," and even hell with all its tortures would, in some ways, be a comfort because it "will help [him] to forget" whatever the memories are that are torturing him.[25]

If it was Lincoln who wrote this poem, he published it three years to the day after the death of Ann Rutledge. Friends and neighbors reported that after her death, Lincoln's memory of her drove him to insanity, and he became suicidal.

If we accept Lincoln's authorship, we have written proof of how powerful memory was, so powerful that Lincoln nearly ended his life. Memory has the power to destroy, but as we shall see, memory also has the ability to restore and drive one to spectacular feats of accomplishment.

History in the Halls of Congress

Since his youth, Lincoln had been an avid reader. When he did not have many options during his childhood, Lincoln seems to have read every book he could get his hands on. However, after he moved to Springfield and then later, in his two stays in Washington, he was never far from a library, and he became much more selective. Lincoln does not seem to have read *generally* but rather *purposefully*. According to his law partner Herndon, Lincoln explained his reading habits thusly:

> I don't love to read generally, and as I do not love to read I feel no interest in what is thus read. I don't, & can't, remember such reading. When I have a particular case in hand I have that motive, and feel an interest

in the case—feel an interest in ferreting out the questions to the bottom—love to dig up the question by the roots and hold it up and dry it
before the fires of the mind.[26]

In 1847 Lincoln began his first and only term in Congress, and he was
determined to leave a mark. In order to do so, he spent hours of diligent
research to prepare for speeches that he hoped would win him national
renown. Lincoln, who has lived on in history as a war president, sought
to make his mark as an antiwar congressman by directly challenging the
commander in chief, President James Polk.

Even today freshmen congressmen typically remain relatively silent
and learn from more experienced legislators, but little more than two
weeks into his congressional career, on December 22, 1847, Lincoln threw
down the gauntlet, seeking to challenge the morality of the Mexican War.
Lincoln analyzed President Polk's earlier messages justifying the war,
quoting Polk's argument that Mexico "invaded *our teritory*, and shed the
blood of our fellow *citizens* on *our own soil.*" Lincoln introduced a series
of resolutions determined to show that the war was based on false premises because the "spot" where fighting began was Mexican territory, and
thus America was guilty of unprovoked aggression and not vice versa.[27]
While these "spot resolutions," as they came to be known, were ignored
in Washington, the war was popular in Lincoln's home district, and for
years afterward he would be derisively called "Spotty" Lincoln.

Lincoln followed up these resolutions three weeks later, on January 22, 1848, with a tightly reasoned argument on the recent past, the
start of the Mexican War. Whereas previously he asked the president to
prove that the spot where the fighting started was American territory, he
would now attempt to use historical research to prove his thesis that the
location where fighting commenced was at best disputed and at worst
Mexican territory. In this address Lincoln referenced several of President
Polk's speeches, the Louisiana Purchase Treaty of 1803, the Adams-Onís
Treaty, an agreement that Lincoln had transcribed from *Niles' Register*
that Santa Anna had signed after his capture by the Texan Army in 1836,
the 1836 Constitution of the Republic of Texas, and the State Constitution of Texas of 1845. He argued that while the boundary was disputed
on paper, Mexico in fact exercised authority in some settlements north
of the Rio Grande. In contrast, the United States exercised authority in
some communities south of the Nueces, and thus the de facto border
was somewhere in between. Lincoln criticized President Polk for sending "the army into the midst of a settlement of Mexican people, who
had never submited, by consent or by force, to the authority of Texas or

of the United States" and thus leading the Mexican army to defend what it saw as its territory.[28] Although Lincoln did exaggerate the significance of certain things, such as the importance of the 1845 state constitution making no mention of its southern border, the argument was largely historically accurate. In fact, one scholar, in 1967, wrote that "Lincoln's analysis of the several aspects of the boundary question, and his appraisal of President Polk's responsibility for the initiation of the War in that address in the House, is superior to the treatment in any histories of the Mexican War now available."[29] However, during his day Lincoln's speech was not remembered for his tightly reasoned arguments at the beginning but rather the highly emotional and personal attacks on the president at the end. There Lincoln argued that Polk must have felt the "blood of this war, like the blood of Abel," which was "crying to Heaven against him," and that the president's last message was "like the half insane mumbling of a fever-dream."[30]

Lincoln believed that President Polk abused history not only in his justification of the war but also in his opposition to the national government funding internal improvements, and Lincoln challenged the president's interpretations of the past in his June 20, 1848, speech before the House. One of Polk's objections to these improvements was that it would lead to excesses. Polk noted that in one year there were proposals for funding various projects in excess of $200 million.[31] Lincoln argued, "Let us, judging of the future by the past, ascertain whether there may not be, in the discretion of congress, a sufficient power to limit, and restrain this expansive tendency." Lincoln asked why Polk cited the amount of money "*applied* for" and not "how much was *granted*." Lincoln asked, "Would not that have been better evidence?" After searching "authentic documents," most likely the reports of the secretary of the treasury, the aggregate total spent on internal improvements was less than $2 million, much less than the president's $200 million. Lincoln provided a warrant, stating that the past proved that the federal government could spend money on improvements without it necessarily leading to excess, contrary to Polk's assertion. He also criticized Polk's use of a quote by Thomas Jefferson. Polk correctly noted that Jefferson thought that government funding of internal improvements required an amendment to make it constitutional but did not acknowledge that Jefferson also believed these programs could benefit the country. Lincoln openly admitted that he disagreed with Jefferson on the constitutionality aspect and cited two legal experts to justify his opinion.[32] Lincoln agreed with Polk that the past can help guide the present but Lincoln also knew that it can also hinder our understanding rather than help if history is not done correctly. In these early speeches, Lincoln sought to challenge the most powerful man in the country, but even if Polk learned of Lincoln's speeches, he sensibly ignored them.[33]

Perhaps most remarkable about this last speech is that it demonstrates Lincoln's understanding of human nature and the limits of collective action. Lincoln noted that many had pointed out the problems that any internal improvement program would have, and he readily agreed. However, for Lincoln, this was not the real test of whether action should be taken. Lincoln argued:

> The true rule, in determining to embrace, or reject any thing, is not whether it have *any* evil in it; but whether it have more of evil, than of good. There are few things *wholly* evil, or *wholly* good. Almost every thing, especially of governmental policy, is an inseparable compound of the two; so that our best judgment of the preponderance between them is continually demanded.[34]

This shows Lincoln already held a deep understanding of human nature and public policy, and he would continue to use this wisdom to guide him in the future.

As noted earlier, Lincoln's friends and law colleagues Joseph Gillespie and John T. Stuart said that Lincoln had little faith in the biographies and histories written in his day, and a speech delivered in the House of Representatives in 1848 corroborates that assertion. Lincoln delivered a campaign speech supporting General Zachary Taylor, but much of it denigrated his Democratic opponent, Lewis Cass, and his supporters. Lincoln criticized "all his biographers (and they are legion)" for trying to turn Cass, despite his limited combat experience, into the type of military hero Andrew Jackson was. Lincoln mocked the myth growing around Cass's broken sword: "Some authors say he broke it, some say he threw it away, and some others, who ought to know, say nothing about it. Perhaps it would be a fair historical compromise to say, if he did not break it, he did n't do any thing else with it." Recalling his personal experience in the Black Hawk War, he mocked the military pretensions of the biographers who glorified Cass:

> By the way, Mr. Speaker, did you know I am a military hero? Yes sir; in the days of the Black Hawk war, I fought, bled, and came away. Speaking of Gen: Cass' career, reminds me of my own. I was not at Stillman's defeat, but I was about as near it, as Cass was to Hulls surrender; and, like him, I saw the place very soon afterwards. It is quite certain I did not break my sword, for I had none to break; but I bent a musket pretty badly on one occasion. If Cass broke his sword, the idea is, he broke it in de[s]peration;

I bent the musket by accident. If Gen: Cass went in advance of me in picking huckleberries, I guess I surpassed him in charges upon the wild onions. If he saw any live, fighting indians, it was more than I did; but I had a good many bloody struggles with the musquetoes; and, although I never fainted from loss of blood, I can truly say I was often very hungry. Mr. Speaker, if . . . they shall take me up as their candidate for the Presidency, I protest they shall not make fun of me, as they have of Gen: Cass, by attempting to write me into a military hero.

For good measure, Lincoln then added what he felt the biographers left out; namely, Cass's flip-flopping on the issue of the extension of slavery along with his ability to receive excessive amounts of governmental compensation for his work. He then provided detailed evidence based on what appears to be extensive research to support these assertions.[35] While not much of a work of history itself, it shows Lincoln's views on the importance of getting history right and was perhaps his most effective political speech in Congress.

Niagara Falls: The Indefinite Past

Despite all his experience with nature, Lincoln seldom celebrated its beauty. Even though he grew up in the age of Romanticism and loved its poetry, one will search Lincoln's *Collected Works* in vain for any Wordsworthian praises of the "jocund company" of daffodils or the like.[36]

However rarely he left his impressions in written form about nature, there are a few times when nature inspired him, and the best example is in his notes regarding Niagara Falls. After a series of speeches in Massachusetts in 1848, Congressman Lincoln stopped at Niagara Falls on his way home. Like so many before and since, Lincoln marveled at the falls as he jotted some private notes on the experience, possibly while riding on a steamer on the Great Lakes to Chicago. Typical for Lincoln, the Niagara Falls inspired him to meditate on the "indefinite past":

When Columbus first sought this continent—when Christ suffered on the cross—when Moses led Israel through the Red-Sea—nay, even, when Adam first came from the hand of his Maker—then as now, Niagara was roaring here. The eyes of that species of extinct giants, whose bones fill the mounds of America, have gazed on Niagara, as ours do now. Cotemporary with the whole race of men, and older than the first man, Niagara is strong, and fresh to-day as ten thousand years ago. The Mammoth and Mastadon—now so long dead, that fragments of their monstrous bones, alone testify, that they ever lived, have gazed on Niagara. In that long—long time, never still for a single moment. Never dried, never froze, never slept, never rested.

The Niagara Falls inspired him to contemplate the meaning of the infinite and *indefinite* past, the continuities they represented, and the wisdom of the ephemeral nature of life.

Furthermore, Lincoln wrote that "The geologist will demonstrate that the plunge, or fall, was once at Lake Ontario, and has worn it's way back to it's present position; he will ascertain how *fast* it is wearing now, and so get a basis for determining how *long* it has been wearing back from Lake Ontario, and finally demonstrate by it that this world is at least fourteen thousand years old." According to Lincoln, geologists can use what exists in the present ("how *fast* it is wearing now") to reconstruct what happened in the past ("so get a basis for determining how *long* it has been wearing back from Lake Ontario") in order to make meaning of that past ("finally demonstrate by it that this world is at least fourteen thousand years old").[37] For Lincoln, this process was not simply limited to the domain of geologists. Lincoln, finding inspiration all around him, was not merely content to rely on others to investigate what happened in the past. Lincoln would continue to do what historians do, analyze what evidence survives in the present to construct a narrative of the past in order to make meaning or, as Lincoln would see it, provide wisdom.

Clay Eulogy

Lincoln criticized Cass's biographers, but he was not above hagiography himself, as he demonstrated with his eulogy of Henry Clay. Clay died in 1852, a time when Lincoln was out of office and had no immediate hopes to attain any position, as his principled stand against the Mexican War left him unpopular with voters. Lincoln delivered a eulogy in the Illinois statehouse on July 6, 1852, one of the many given across the country. While much of this address could be considered hagiography, as most are, he showed in this speech how the past inspired him.[38]

Lincoln began by appealing to the memory of the nation's founding, noting that within a year of the signing of the Declaration of Independence, Henry Clay was born, and "the infant nation, and the infant child began the race of life together." For nearly five decades, Clay was a leading statesman who helped guide that young nation from weakness and obscurity to strength and prominence. Clay possessed many of the qualities that Lincoln admired, such as his lifelong self-education, sound judgment, strong will, love of liberty, wisdom, logic, the ability to inspire action in his fellow men, and eloquence that was born not of flowery oratory but rather from his "deeply earnest and impassioned tone, and manner, which can proceed only from great sincerity and a thorough conviction, in the speaker of the justice and importance of his cause."[39]

Until this time, Lincoln rarely spoke about slavery, focusing primarily on traditional Whig economic issues such as tariffs and internal improvements. While Lincoln would not make his opposition to the expansion of slavery the focus of his politics until 1854, his eulogy of Clay shows him already moving in that direction. Lincoln detailed Clay's positions on slavery, and it appears that he performed some research to do this. Lincoln argued that although Clay "was the owner of slaves," he "ever was, on principle and in feeling, opposed to slavery." He noted that one of his first and last acts in public life, events separated by nearly five decades, were the same—namely, supporting a proposal for the gradual abolition of slaves in Kentucky. Citing a Saint Louis newspaper, Lincoln worried that some were beginning to deny the beliefs laid out in the Declaration of Independence. Those who might do so would be betraying the principles the country was founded on and disagreeing with the most admired statesman in their history. Lincoln argued that Clay was against slavery not just because of practical considerations but rather moral ones. To prove this, Lincoln quoted at length a speech Clay delivered to the American Colonization Society in 1827:

> If they would repress all tendencies towards liberty, and ultimate emancipation, they must do more than put down the benevolent efforts of this society. They must go back to the era of our liberty and independence, and muzzle the cannon which thunders its annual joyous return. They must renew the slave trade with all its train of atrocities . . . They must blow out the moral lights around us, and extinguish that greatest torch of all which America presents to a benighted world—pointing the way to their rights, their liberties, and their happiness. And when they have achieved all those purposes their work will be yet incomplete. They must penetrate the human soul, and eradicate the light of reason, and the love of liberty. Then, and not till then, when universal darkness and despair prevail, can you perpetuate slavery, and repress all sympathy, and all humane, and benevolent efforts among free men, in behalf of the unhappy portion of our race doomed to bondage.[40]

Lincoln would return to these words repeatedly throughout the rest of his career, especially the phrase "blow out the moral lights around us."

Lincoln argued that slavery was the greatest threat to that Union that strove for liberty, and the two greatest American statesmen of the 19th century, Thomas Jefferson and Henry Clay, concurred. Lincoln quoted a letter Thomas Jefferson wrote in 1820 at the height of the Missouri crisis about whether it should be admitted as a slave state. Jefferson wrote:

I had for a long time ceased to read newspapers, or to pay any attention to public affairs, confident they were in good hands . . . But this momentous question, like a fire bell in the night, awakened, and filled me with terror. I considered it at once as the knell of the Union. It is hushed, indeed, for the moment. But this is a reprieve only, not a final sentence. A geographical line, co-inciding with a marked principle, moral and political, once conceived, and held up to the angry passions of men, will never be obliterated; and every irritation will mark it deeper and deeper. I can say, with conscious truth, that there is not a man on earth who would sacrifice more than I would to relieve us from this heavy reproach, in any *practicable* way. The cession of that kind of property, for so it is misnamed, is a bagatelle which would not cost me a second thought, if, in that way, a general emancipation, and *expatriation* could be effected; and, gradually, and with due sacrifices I think it might be. But as it is, we have the wolf by the ears and we can neither hold him, nor safely let him go. Justice is in one scale, and self-preservation in the other.[41]

Lincoln largely agreed with Jefferson's sentiments here. However, he cut Jefferson's quote short because, in the very next sentence, Jefferson espoused his theory that slavery would dissipate the more it spread and dispersed and lost its concentration in any one locality, an idea Lincoln could not have disagreed with more.[42] However, for Lincoln, Clay represented a bridge from the Founders like Jefferson and their highest principles to those of his own day.

Lincoln admired Clay, the statesman who opposed slavery but was able to compromise with his fellow slave owners to hold the country together with his Missouri Compromise and then with his leadership during the Nullification Crisis and the Compromise of 1850. Lincoln noted how God punished the Egyptians, the slave masters of the Hebrews. Lincoln hoped for the ultimate abolition of slavery so that a just God would not see fit to render judgment on the nation when it no longer had Clay's leadership to guide it. Through wisdom and compromise, Clay was able to sustain the Union that, according to Lincoln, was the world's champion of liberty.[43]

Clay's leadership as president of the American Colonization Society inspired Lincoln. Like Clay and Jefferson before him, Lincoln believed that gradual emancipation and the colonization of the freed slaves was the most humane and liberal policy feasible. He quoted Clay's support for this policy, stating:

There is a moral fitness in the idea of returning to Africa her children, whose ancestors have been torn from her by the ruthless hand of fraud and violence. Transplanted in a foreign land, they will carry back to their native soil the rich fruits of religion, civilization, law and liberty. May it not be one of the great designs of the Ruler of the universe, (whose ways are often inscrutable by short-sighted mortals,) thus to transform an original crime, into a signal blessing to that most unfortunate portion of the globe?[44]

Lincoln was never as eloquent as Clay in his support of the colonization of freed slaves. Still, it was an idea Lincoln professed for nearly the rest of his life until experience and changing circumstances led him to alter his views. It is curious to note that, while Lincoln's heroes (Washington, Jefferson, Madison, and Clay) did not live up to their public sentiments (that slavery was wrong) in their private actions, Lincoln seems to have acted more liberally in private than his publicly espoused views as, by all accounts, he appears to have treated African Americans as neighbors, at least as much as one could do at that time under the law.

However, Lincoln's eulogy of Clay shows the beginning of an important pattern; when Lincoln cited authorities on the moral evils of slavery, he would not quote abolitionists, no matter how eloquent, but instead slave owners like Jefferson and Clay. As Simon Greenleaf taught, a witness's testimony holds more credibility if it seems to go against one's personal interests. Lincoln held fast to this principle when using the arguments of prominent slave owners to argue against slavery.

Conclusion

After he left Congress in 1849, Lincoln was in the political wilderness with no immediate prospects for the future. He was no doubt a talented politician, but he was no statesman. In his Temperance Address Lincoln had shown his deep understanding of human nature. However, Lincoln did not effectively apply this understanding during his time in Congress, as his immature attack on Polk revealed a seriously misunderstanding of the president's character, such as it was, and was not well calculated to win support either at home or in Washington. However, the years following his term in Congress were a time of deep reflection, and when he would reemerge in 1854, Lincoln made much more effective use of his understanding of human nature and history in his speeches.

Finally, Lincoln's eulogy of Clay represents a dramatic shift in Lincoln's focus, partly due to his broader experience gained by serving in Washington and partly due to his reflections on the changing attitudes to slavery in nation. At that point, America was undergoing a radical paradigm shift in its views toward slavery, and credit for much of this change belongs to John C. Calhoun, a man whose early politics (support of tariffs and internal improvements) were very similar to Lincoln's and whose tight, logical rhetorical style Lincoln greatly admired.[45] With good reason, many of Calhoun's contemporaries, according to the historian Robert Elder, compared Calhoun to "Milton's eloquent, fallen archangel in *Paradise Lost*, in whose mouth the poet placed arguments so rational and appealing that they called into question the reliability of reason itself."[46] While earlier in his career he remained almost entirely silent on the issue, by the end of his life, Calhoun vocally and eloquently championed slavery. He had come to see that, rhetorically, abolitionists held an advantage over apologists for slavery so long as they defended it as a "necessary evil." For Calhoun, raced-based slavery was not a threat to White liberties but its bedrock, uniting all White men in a slave-owning society in an equality readily understood.[47] In his most infamous address delivered in 1837, Calhoun declared slavery not to be a "necessary evil" but rather a "positive good." Why? According to Calhoun, Africans were in a "low, degraded, and savage condition," having never established any kind of society capable of making Africans and their descendants "so civilized and so improved, not only physically, but morally and intellectually" as the "fostering care of our institutions." Furthermore, Calhoun believed that all societies were based on the exploiters and the exploited, and at least Southern slave owners were more honest about it than Northern industrialists. In fact, slave owners extracted comparatively less from their slaves than industrialists did of their workers. Slavery, Calhoun felt, was not an anachronism destined to die out but rather the wave of the future, immune to "disorders and dangers resulting" from labor strife of the North.[48]

Calhoun was neither the first nor the last to mistake the messiness of relative liberty as a weakness and to deem their society built on unfreedom as superior. Senator William Cabell Rives of Virginia, a fellow slaveowner, rebuked Calhoun for his speech, stating that even slaveowning Founders such as Jefferson and Madison (Rives had known both men personally) called slavery an evil and looked forward to its end, but Calhoun's message resonated with many young slave owners.[49] Late in life, in 1850, Calhoun, the ardent Jeffersonian, made his most explicit attacks on Jefferson's principles in the Declaration of Independence and what would become the Ordinance of 1787 forbidding slavery from the Northwest Territories. Jefferson "committed a great error" and was guilty of possessing "philanthropic, but mistaken views of the most dangerous character." According to Calhoun, Jefferson's claim that "all men are created equal" was "inserted in our declaration of independence without any necessity" because "it made no necessary part of our justification in ... declaring ourselves independent." For Calhoun, Jefferson's statement was worse than useless: "We now begin to experience the danger of admitting so great an error to have a place in the declaration of our independence. For a long time it lay dormant; but in the process of time it began to germinate, and produce its poisonous fruits." Jefferson, according to Calhoun, took an "utterly false view of the subordinate relation of the black to the white race in the South." Calhoun argued that Blacks were "utterly unqualified to possess liberty," yet Jefferson mistakenly believed they were "fully entitled to both liberty and equality." According to Calhoun this mistaken belief was causing "dangerous agitation which now thretens to engulf . . . our political institutions, and involve the country in countless woes."[50]

By the time Lincoln delivered his eulogy for Clay, Calhoun was in his grave, but his ideas, once extreme and rare, had metastasized and spread throughout the South. Inspired by Calhoun, the next generation of Southern statesmen became ever more overtly proslavery. The primary historical disagreement amongst themselves was how to interpret the meaning of the phrase "all men are created equal." There were some who would argue that the Declaration excluded all but White men, or as Senator Jefferson Davis would put in 1861, that it excluded all but "men of the political community," which in 1776 meant White men of property.[51] However, another strain of Southern thought concurred with Calhoun's, Clay's, and Lincoln's interpretation, arguing that Jefferson's assertion really did include all men. However, unlike Clay and Lincoln, Calhoun and many others believed that the Founders were mistaken. For example, in his infamous Cornerstone Speech the future vice president of the Confederacy, Alexander Stephens, proclaimed "the great truth that the negro is not equal to the white man; that slavery subordination to the superior race is his natural and normal condition."[52] These slavery proponents, in many ways, were responding to a growing abolitionist movement that believed the principles of the Declaration were the bedrock of their fight for human liberty.

As Lincoln rededicated himself to his legal career, it was becoming clear that America was pulling itself apart, and this conflict, as was evident beginning with Calhoun, was going to be a war over history and what the American project was to mean.

Chapter 4

We Are Not What We Have Been

(1854–56)

Lincoln Music

According to one story, a group of lawyers gathered in a tavern after a long day in court in 1854 and discussed the most controversial topic of the day, Senator Stephen Douglas's Kansas-Nebraska Act. Lincoln listened intently, engaged in the lively debate with his fellow lawyers, and continued the discussion upstairs in their overcrowded sleeping quarters. When the others slept, one lawyer noticed Lincoln was brooding on the edge of his bed, and when he woke up in the morning, Lincoln was still sitting on the edge of his bed, lost in thought.[1]

Lincoln left few written accounts of his feelings immediately after the passage of the Kansas-Nebraska Act, except for stating, "I was losing interest in politics, when the repeal of the Missouri Compromise aroused me again," or more graphically, that he had been "thunderstruck."[2] Whether apocryphal or not, one thing the preceding story does get right is that in the immediate aftermath of the passage of the Kansas-Nebraska Act, while the country was being roiled in conflict and people were debating the issue from coast to coast, Lincoln remained silent. For months after the passage of the Kansas-Nebraska Act, Lincoln studied in the state library, jotted down notes, pondered the issues about it, and tested his arguments in anonymously published articles in the local paper. Only after months of historical research, thought, and forming and reforming his ideas, did Lincoln speak. When Lincoln did reemerge, he was no longer the petty party politician promoting banks, roads, and the like, but rather a statesman, fighting for what he believed the American project to mean. In describing this change that became evident in his 1854 speeches, historian Shelby Foote wrote, "And now the Lincoln music began to sound."[3] This "Lincoln music," more than anything, was sung by the muse of history.

Kansas-Nebraska Act

Even though Stephen Douglas has been given the lion's share of the credit for the Kansas-Nebraska Act, and rightly so, it did not emerge as he wanted it. It has been remembered as the act that repealed the Missouri Compromise line, allowing slavery into new territories, if the residents so chose, where it had been prohibited for more than three decades. While the expansion of slavery became the preeminent issue in the country, slavery for Douglas was a sideshow, an irritating detail he would rather not deal with, besides collecting profits from the Mississippi plantation he inherited from his father-in-law. In fact, Douglas declared (without a hint of irony from one who earned bread from the sweat of the brow of others) back in 1851 that he had "determined never to make another speech upon the slavery question" because he was "heartily tired of the controversy."[4] Douglas was an ultranationalist and expansionist who wanted more land, more states, and more wealth. He pushed for a transcontinental railroad to unite the country permanently, and he wanted to take credit for the railway publicly and profit from it privately. As chairman of the Senate Committee on Territories, Douglas saw it as his responsibility to organize the West and find a way to build a transcontinental railroad. In 1853 he proposed a bill to create the Nebraska territory adhering to the Missouri Compromise, but southern Democrats balked at the notion of more new free territories that would become free states. In January of 1854 Douglas proposed a new bill that was essentially the same, except it remained silent on whether it was adhering to the Missouri Compromise. This was still not good enough for southern senators. As Senator David Rice Atchison of Missouri proclaimed, "I am free to admit that at this moment, at this hour, and for all time to come I should oppose the organization of the settlement of the territory unless my constituents and the constituents of the whole South . . . could go into it upon the same footing, with equal rights and equal privileges, carrying that species of property with them."[5] Douglas began to realize that he could not get his bill through Congress any other way. After a Kentucky senator formally proposed tacking on a repeal of the Missouri

Compromise, he relented, but not without misgivings. As he said, "I will incorporate it in my bill, though I know it will raise a hell of a storm."[6] By repealing the Missouri Compromise and allowing settlers to determine whether they would allow slavery in Kansas and Nebraska, Douglas could finally get the bill to pass both houses of Congress and signed into law on May 30, 1854.

Douglas knew there would be problems, but he made a virtue of necessity and argued that rather than being a flawed compromise that he never wanted, it was, in fact, consistent with the original American principles he professed to cherish. Douglas claimed that the Kansas-Nebraska Act was a reaffirmation of popular sovereignty, which was the belief that the majority of any locality had the right to determine how it was to govern itself without any interference by outside powers, eliding the rights of states with the rights of national territories. Furthermore, it promised to move the debate from the national level that threatened to tear the country apart to the local level, thus making it much less dangerous, so that the nation could focus on, as Douglas saw it, more important issues. Douglas was right about one thing: it did cause one hell of a storm, and it had consequences that neither Douglas nor his supporters could foresee.

Man of Self-Invention Reinvents Himself

For all intents and purposes, Lincoln seemed to have reached a dead end in his political career in 1849 when he left Washington after his one term in Congress. By prior arrangement, Lincoln had agreed not to run again, but had he chosen to, it is questionable whether the people would have reelected him because his opposition to the Mexican War was deeply unpopular. Stephen T. Logan ran in his place, but he lost in this Whig-leaning district to a Democratic contender. On his way out of office, Lincoln fought for patronage jobs for his supporters and unsuccessfully sought for himself a Land Office position. A likely contributing factor to this loss was the fact that a group of Springfield Whigs petitioned against him, citing his opposition to the war.[7] The winner of the coveted post, Justin Butterfield, had opposed the War of 1812 but had subsequently learned his lesson. When someone asked him if he was against the Mexican War, he replied, "No, by God, I oppose no wars. I opposed one war, and it ruined me, and henceforth I am for *War, Pestilence, and Famine.*"[8]

For the next five years, Lincoln did participate in Whig politics from time to time, but primarily he rededicated himself to his legal career, becoming one of the most sought-after lawyers in the state. When he could spare a moment, he did a curious thing: he took up studying Euclid, the ancient Greek "father of geometry." His former law partner, John T. Stuart, recalled that in the evenings after court on the circuit, "Lincoln would strip off his coat and lay down on the bed" and read "till late of night" by candlelight and then "reflect and digest."[9] Lincoln later recalled, in the third person with a sense of pride, "He studied and nearly mastered the Six-books of Euclid, since he was a member of Congress. He regrets his want of education, and does what he can to supply the want."[10] Euclid's *Elements* had no direct application to his legal career besides sharpening his already ultralogical mind.

However, with the advent of the Kansas-Nebraska Act of 1854, Lincoln redirected his mind and study. It is difficult for us in the present to fully understand why the law elicited such consternation in the North. After all, the Missouri Compromise of 1820 allowed for the continued westward expansion of slavery, and the Compromise of 1850 included a draconian fugitive slave law. In spite of this and the fact that slavery had already spread as far south as Florida and as far west Texas, Lincoln and others had professed, and not without cause, that they believed that slavery was still on the ultimate path of extinction. By looking at the maps of the United States in 1820 and 1850, we can understand why. Even though the Missouri Compromise and previous agreements allowed for slavery to spread into the southwestern territories of the land purchased from France in 1803, the Louisiana Purchase tilted heavily to the north. Without further expansion, the United States would have been dominated by free states. Likewise, even though the United States became more geographically balanced after the annexation of Texas and the acquisition of the Southwest after the Mexican War, it was still a reasonable position to assume that the North still held the advantage. With the admission of the state of California in 1850, a massive free state now extended down to America's southern border, thus blocking slavery's expansion. Likewise, while the territories in the desert southwest could potentially become slave states, most assumed that slave owners would not be able to make a profit in that environment. By 1854 slavery had spread about as far as it legally and practically could unless Congress repealed the Missouri Compromise. Unless the United States acquired more territory somewhere south, free states would soon come to significantly outnumber slave states, with all the potential power that entailed. That is why proslavery congressmen pushed so hard for the repeal of the Missouri Compromise—so that they could break out of the antislavery cordon that surrounded them. For all the gains that slave states had made in the past few decades before 1854, the free states had gained more, and

Southerners were not wrong when they perceived that the future of their peculiar institution was threatened. That is why they stubbornly fought to overturn the Missouri Compromise.

However, it was more than a geographical turning of the tables that upset Lincoln and others in the North. What was perhaps most disturbing was a growing change in principles in the country. Over the preceding few decades, more and more Southerners had gone from publicly admitting that slavery was an embarrassment that would hopefully someday end (as most of the Founding Fathers had professed) to publicly advocating the moral right of slavery and that it should be perpetuated forever (as Calhoun and his acolytes professed). Likewise, while there was an ever-increasing abolitionist movement in the North, there was also a growing amoral group in the North, led by Douglas, who didn't argue that slavery was right or wrong but rather shifted the moral question to focus on whether or not communities should be allowed to decide for themselves such a fundamental issue. From the 1760s until roughly the beginning of the next century, America had undergone the first of its great liberty movements. However, by 1854 the United States was experiencing a great anti-liberty movement. This movement could trace its origins back to the shifting attitudes of Jefferson and Madison in the 1790s, a time when the expansion of the recognition of the rights of man was being subsumed into the amoral pursuit of personal interest and private wealth. Both the geography (due to the repeal of the Missouri Compromise) and the spirit of the times seemed to be changing rapidly in favor of slavery, and that is why Lincoln, who had said publicly said little about slavery before, now felt "thunderstruck."

He could have chosen to remain silent. He had no obvious political position available to tempt him, his potential opponent was so formidable, and he was earning a comfortable living. As historian William Lee Miller wrote, "We tend to think of 'moral' choices as those that life forces upon us—quandaries, perplexities, choices among goods and evils that we cannot evade." This was not true of Lincoln in 1854. He could have easily avoided challenging Douglas, and no one, besides perhaps his wife, would have criticized him for it. As Miller argued, "There are also those latent possibilities lying all around us all the time if we bestir ourselves. Lincoln in 1854 bestirred himself."[11]

How did Lincoln *bestir* himself? He began with careful study. As the *Illinois State Register*, a hostile Democratic newspaper, put it, Lincoln that summer "had been nosing for weeks in the State Library pumping his brain and his imagination for points and arguments."[12] Lincoln's future secretaries in the White House, John G. Nicolay and John Hay, who would later be his biographers, wrote about Lincoln's study, "Where others were content to take statements at second hand, he preferred to verify citations as well as to find new ones" so that when he did speak out, his arguments would be "not only bold but original." Nicolay and Hay wrote that he was still the good-humored man his friends had known for years, "but it became noticeable that he was less among the crowd and more in the solitude of his office or his study, and that he seemed ever in haste to leave the eager circle he was entertaining."[13] At the same time he was conducting research, Lincoln was writing notes, testing his thoughts, and experimenting with his ideas—arming himself with logic and history for the coming political combat. When Lincoln finally emerged from this Aeschylean silence, he had transformed himself from a politician to a statesman. This man, who had consciously invented himself in his teens and twenties, reinvented himself in his forties. It was this moment of solitary study and silent reflection when Lincoln became *Lincoln*. This Lincoln transformed would be on full display at the Illinois State Fair.

Illinois State Fair

A crowd, "principally farmers and hard-fisted men, whose conversation smacked of huge apples, tall corn, and fine stock," gathered around the new Chicago and Mississippi Railroad depot in Alton on the evening of October 2, 1854, according to the *Missouri Republican* out of Saint Louis.[14] Their excitement was building for something relatively new in Illinois history: traveling by rail to Springfield (the line connecting the two cities opened only two years prior) to the second annual Illinois State Fair.[15] For these farmers, who had all driven wagons, hogs, and cattle across the sodden prairie on unpaved roads (as Lincoln had when his family first arrived in the state), gliding across the state on wrought-iron rails at thirty miles an hour with livestock in tow must have seemed nothing short of miraculous. The *Missouri Republican* reporter who witnessed this excitement was struck by the romance of the experience, appreciating not only the "broad prairies" softly lit by the moonlight but also the "slight sprinkling of very pleasing young ladies" among the "merry" passengers. They spent the four-hour trip "arguing, laughing, telling jokes, and the like" as they thundered towards the state capital.[16]

On the same evening, at the opposite end of the state in Chicago, the young Horace White, a cub reporter for the *Chicago Journal*, boarded a train to the state fair from the opposite direction. A thunderstorm lit up the night sky, making "frightful music overhead." However, the greatest danger was more terrestrial, as the train derailed at two in the morning

near Dwight when it struck two cows on the tracks. Besides being de-
layed for three hours, this was no major setback, according to White, as
nothing was "damaged except the cattle which were crushed into just
no shape at all."[17]

Despite recent growth, this burgeoning state capital could not house
all the arriving fairgoers, so many spent their nights sleeping on the
wooden floors at the depot or in a barroom. Even though a cold front
and severe hailstorm that night made it feel more like December than
October, the next morning, according to the *Republican* reporter, "the
streets were alive with people at an early hour, and soon, wagons, car-
riages, carts, and mongrel 'wehikles' of all sorts, were passing about, with
a sign inscribed in chalk upon them, 'to the Fair—10cts.'" The reporter
paid his fare, and once the farmer packed as many paying passengers
into his wagon as he could, they were off to the fairgrounds about a mile
west of the city. "Such hawing and jeeing by everybody, and bustling
and splashing of the slushy mud about," according to our reporter, "is
not witnessed every day," and he recalled how "the cold cutting wind
made our noses blue." However, despite the inconveniences, the people
maintained buoyant spirits in anticipation of what lay ahead.[18]

For those accustomed to the relative quiet of the farmstead, the sight
that greeted them at the state fair must have been something of a revela-
tion (of heaven or hell, depending on one's notion). The *Missouri Republican* remarked, "What a Babel of noise and confusion we hear and see
all about." The reporter cataloged the varied sources of this cacophony:
"Over yonder are the agricultural implements and other mechanical
inventions, and the noise caused by trials of them, mingling with the
neighing of horses, braying of donkeys, lowing of cows, and wheezing of
chronic Shanghai roosters, is most euphonious." The Missouri reporter
was impressed with the wealth of new agricultural machines, such as
the "double-geared plows and reapers, and mowers, and corn-shellers,
and straw-cutters, portable little older mills, &c., &c. It proves that the
Yankee genius sticks out prominently, even in Suckers [a mildly derog-
atory term for Illinoisians]." Just outside the fairgrounds were various
nineteenth-century tourist traps such as a circus held in a "dingy tent,"
gingerbread stands, a tent with live snakes (being of a "corpulent order"),
and "a negro dancer," along with plenty of music and a man auctioning
off his wares from the back of his wagon: "Thirty-seven-'naff,'naff,'naff—
will you now make it forty?"[19]

Back in the fairgrounds there were, according to the *Missouri Republican*, "politicians great and small, of every clique and party" plying their
trade amongst all the horse stalls and pigpens (perhaps at home in their

native environment). In the days before instant mass communication, wherever the voters flocked, politicians were sure to follow. Amongst the din of auctioneers, bellowing cows, and farm implement demonstrations, there was politics in the air. Horace White, the cub reporter from the *Chicago Journal*, wrote that "politics have been brewing in Springfield" with the politicians "working like famished tigers."[20] The whole nation, not just Springfield, was abuzz with the new Kansas-Nebraska Act, and the most famous man in America, Stephen Douglas, was in town to defend his policy.[21] For better or worse, it was these people, among the rough and tumble of a frontier state fair, with all their hard-earned common sense along with their fears and superstitions (some that were peculiar to that era and others that were more enduring), who were a microcosm of those who would ultimately be deciding the greatest issues in American history, first with their votes, then later with their blood.

On October 3, according to the *Missouri Republican*, "at half-past one, P.M., the cannon began to roar, announcing that Senator Douglas was about to make his great speech on the Nebraska act." To the consternation of the exhibitors, the fairgrounds began to empty as the people made their way to the capitol building.[22] Douglas delivered his speech in the House of Representatives to thunderous applause from his supporters as his political opponent of two decades, Abraham Lincoln, listened attentively in the lobby. When it was over, Lincoln stood on the stairway above the crowd filing out and announced that he would deliver a speech the next day. In the late summer of 1854 Lincoln had begun experimenting with his new ideas in public, with speeches in Winchester and Bloomington. However, his main test would come in front of this state fair audience on October 4. When it came time for Lincoln to speak, Douglas sat front and center. For two decades Douglas had listened to Lincoln's speeches against him, but even he had to be surprised at the new Lincoln.

The Springfield Speech

Horace White, the cub reporter fresh out of college, recalled his first impression of Lincoln and his speech more than five decades later: "He began in a slow and hesitating manner, but without any mistakes of language, dates, or facts. It was evident that he had mastered his subject, that he knew what he was going to say, and that he knew he was right."[23] Lincoln began with a carefully worded thesis: "The repeal of the Missouri Compromise, and the propriety of its restoration, constitute the subject of what I am about to say." He then proceeded to tell his audience what he would not do: "I do not propose to question the patriotism, or to assail the motives of any man, or class of men; but rather to strictly confine myself to the naked merits of the question." Perhaps thinking of the lessons of Blackstone and Greenleaf, Lincoln promised to stick solely to the subject at hand, the Kansas-Nebraska Act, and not to introduce irrelevant evidence or ad hominem attacks to confuse and mislead the audience. Like Blackstone and Greenleaf, he clarified key terms; namely, *slavery*: "I wish to MAKE and to KEEP the distinction between the EXISTING institution, and the EXTENSION of it, so broad, and so clear, that no honest man can misunderstand me, and no dishonest one, successfully misrepresent me."[24] In this introduction, Lincoln set the parameters for the arguments he would make.

In the second section of his speech, Lincoln provided "a short history" of the Missouri Compromise, which he thought would "perhaps be proper." Douglas and his supporters argued that popular sovereignty was the bedrock of the American Revolution. Any attempt to restrict this right, including the right to determine if slavery would be legal, trampled on those sacred rights. Lincoln would use history to prove the opposite was true. He began with a short history of the national government's attempts to limit the spread of slavery into new territories. Lincoln noted that the slaveholder Thomas Jefferson, from the slave state of Virginia, was the primary inspiration for the Ordinance of 1787, which prohibited slavery in the territories that the national government owned north of the Ohio River. Lincoln, with history, proved Douglas's views to be false: "Thus, with the author of the declaration of Independence, the policy of prohibiting slavery in new territory originated." According to Lincoln, this proved that his position concurred with the greatest authority on the original principles of America.[25]

Lincoln then paused his history to contrast the values of the past (the Founders) with the values of the present (the supporters of the Kansas-Nebraska Act). Lincoln proclaimed with withering sarcasm, "But *now* new light breaks upon us. Now congress declares this ought never to have been; and the like of it, must never be again. The sacred right of self government is grossly violated by it!" Lincoln believed that those who would make a virtue of the spread of slavery violate their heritage because this position "assaults upon all we have ever really held sacred."[26]

Lincoln then returned to his history lesson, tracing the spread of slavery and the compromises made from 1803 to the present day. He noted that even though slavery was spreading, the Missouri Compromise represented a continuity in principle since, in it, "the same language is employed as in the Ordinance of '87" in prohibiting slavery north of the parallel 36°30.' He provided an extended quote from a speech Stephen Douglas delivered in 1849 in which he argued that "this Compromise had been canonized in the hearts of the American people, as a sacred thing which no ruthless hand would ever be reckless enough to disturb." His historical research blended seamlessly with his personal memory as he alluded to his own experience in Congress in fighting to restrict the spread of slavery with his support of the Wilmot Proviso along with the national memory of recent events, such as the Compromise of 1850 and the passage of the 1854 Kansas-Nebraska Act. Above all, he highlighted how rapidly Douglas went from fully supporting the Missouri Compromise to remaining neutral about it to writing legislation to repeal it and finally to his full-throated justification of that repeal. Lincoln finished his short history lesson on the Missouri Compromise by providing a hedge: "The foregoing history may not be precisely accurate in every particular; but I am sure it is sufficiently so, for all the uses I shall attempt to make of it, and in it, we have before us, the chief material enabling us to correctly judge whether the repeal of the Missouri Compromise is right or wrong."[27]

After this short history lesson and hedge, Lincoln provided an extended warrant to explain why this history supports his thesis that the repeal of the Missouri Compromise was wrong. Those who supported ending it could only have done so because they supported or were indifferent to the spread of slavery. The young reporter in the audience, Horace White, remembered many years later: "Gradually he warmed up with his subject, his angularity disappeared, and he passed into that attitude of unconscious majesty."[28] Lincoln passionately proclaimed:

> This *declared* indifference, but as I must think, covert *real* zeal for the spread of slavery, I can not but hate. I hate it because of the monstrous injustice of slavery itself. I hate it because it deprives our republican example of its just influence in the world—enables the enemies of free institutions, with plausibility, to taunt us as hypocrites—causes the real friends of freedom to doubt our sincerity, and especially because it forces so many really good men amongst ourselves into an open war with the very fundamental principles of civil liberty—criticising the Declaration of Independence, and insisting that there is no right principle of action but *self-interest*.[29]

Time and time again, Lincoln would claim that the Revolutionary War stood for something higher than self-interest, that it was based on the bedrock of the "fundamental principles of civil liberties." According to Lincoln, his opponents were ignoring or abusing history to support their perceived interests in the present.

In the third section, the lengthiest of his speech, Lincoln addressed contrary viewpoints deliberately and meticulously. Just as he was heating up, he cooled it down. Before countering opposing arguments, he acknowledges his opponents had many valid points. Even when he might disagree with them, the fact that they hold those opinions matters and cannot be easily disregarded. Speaking of Southerners, Lincoln argued "They are just what we would be in their situation. If slavery did not now exist amongst them, they would not introduce it. If it did now exist amongst us, we should not instantly give it up. This I believe of the masses north and south." No group of people was innately morally superior to another, but context, interest, and inertia rendered a powerful hold over people's actions. Rather than proclaiming the guilt of his opponents, he acknowledged the collective complicity of the country in both the introduction and continuance of the sin of slavery: "When southern people tell us they are no more responsible for the origin of slavery, than we; I acknowledge the fact. When it is said that the institution exists; and that it is very difficult to get rid of it, in any satisfactory way, I can understand and appreciate the saying. I surely will not blame them for not doing what I should not know how to do myself." Even though he already stated how much he hated slavery, Lincoln granted that he believed that the Southerners were right in that there were abundant complications in attempting to end the institution. When he acknowledged that he and Southerners might be wrong in their feelings about denying political and social equality for Blacks, Lincoln argued that "A universal feeling, whether well or ill-founded, can not be safely disregarded." While many Northerners opposed the forcible return of fugitive slaves to their masters in the South, Lincoln acknowledged the constitutional rights Southerners had, which he would respect. Just like the lawyer Lincoln who would "reckon" that those opposing viewpoints "may" be true, Lincoln gave away all the points that he felt he could not prove to his audience's satisfaction, but he held fast to the one core point of his argument: "But all this; to my judgment, furnishes no . . . excuse for permitting slavery to go into our own free territory."[30]

After acknowledging that Southerners made what he believed to be many valid arguments, Lincoln cataloged a list of assertions of those that supported the repeal of the Missouri Compromise and proceeded to counter these arguments one by one. For several of them, Lincoln used the advice of Blackstone to look at the original intentions of those who wrote the law. For example, some argued that those who voted for the Wilmot Proviso were repudiating the Missouri Compromise. Lincoln spoke as an expert to the contrary, stating that he and his fellow legislators did not think that by voting to stop the spread of slavery into the new territories acquired from Mexico they were therefore voting to allow slavery to spread in the old territories acquired from France. Furthermore, if those who wrote the Missouri Compromise believed that the principle should apply to all future lands acquired, not just the land bought from the French, they would have said so. Lincoln argued, "An intention to extend the law is not only not mentioned in the law, but is not mentioned in any contemporaneous history. Both the law itself, and the history of the times are a blank as to any *principle* of extension; and by neither the known rules for construing statutes and contracts, nor by common sense, can any such *principle* be inferred." [31] To imply that legislators who wrote and approved the Missouri Compromise meant the line to extend to lands that it did not mention corrupts history, and to insist that those who voted for the Wilmot Proviso were repudiating the Missouri Compromise corrupts logic.

Some argued that the repeal of the compromise was a nonissue because the lands of Kansas and Nebraska were not conducive to slavery and thus would remain free territories. Lincoln acknowledged that he relied on hearsay to argue that "there are more slaves, in proportion to whites, in the north western county of Missouri, than within any county of the State." Assuming he meant Atchison County, in Missouri's extreme northwest, this claim was not correct, as he would have seen if he had consulted the 1850 census. In 1850 1,678 people lived in Atchison County, thirty of them slaves, meaning the proportion of people enslaved in the far northwestern county was 1.8 percent, far from the highest proportion in the state. However, had Lincoln looked further south, to the counties of Platt, Jackson, and Clay, which lie in the central region on Missouri's extreme western border abutting Kansas, he would have discovered that the percentage of people enslaved there were 17 percent, 21 percent, and 27 percent, respectively, some of the highest proportions in the state.[32]

Even if Lincoln was *mistaken* in the specifics, he was not wrong in his overall argument that "slavery pressed entirely up to the old western boundary of the State," and that it would surely spread to the west bank of Missouri River into Kansas because it had the same climate and would likely be populated by the same kinds of people who lived on the east bank. Some argued that Missouri residents would not cross over into Kansas because there was no law to protect the right to slaves. Using the wisdom of history, Lincoln argued, "Wherever slavery is, it has been first introduced without law. The oldest laws we find concerning it, are not laws introducing it; but regulating it, as an already existing thing." Furthermore, some argued that it did not matter if some Missouri residents brought their slaves to Kansas because more antislavery people could move there and thus outlaw it. Lincoln countered that experience had shown how difficult it is to remove slavery once it is firmly rooted in society. To those that argued that a restriction would make no difference because people would still bring their slaves in, Lincoln replied that they should look at history. When the United States acquired the lands that would become Illinois and Missouri, there were already slave-owning French residents living on both sides of the Mississippi River. However, because of the Ordinance of 1787, slavery was prohibited in Illinois, where it slowly died out, while in Missouri, where there was no law against it, slavery grew exponentially. The only difference between the two cases was that the U.S. government outlawed slavery in one territory while in the other it did not. Some argued, as Thomas Jefferson once did in a private letter, their belief in the "diffusion theory," the idea that since the importation of slaves was illegal, the spread of slavery across the country would diffuse and weaken the Slave Power as it would not be as strong as it was if it centralized in any locality. While not responding to Jefferson by name, Lincoln countered that the increase in the slave population could not be wholly accounted for by natural reproduction, that the slave trade had not been adequately suppressed, and that the increasing of territories that allowed slavery would only increase the demand and rewards for those who would traffic in this illicit trade.[33] By using both history and logic, Lincoln showed that the repeal of the prohibition of slavery in Kansas and Nebraska did matter and that they must take steps to reverse it.

Some argued that Northerners should neither be concerned with the repeal of the Missouri Compromise nor object when Southerners took their slaves to new territories, just as Southerners would not object to where Northerners took their hogs. Lincoln believed that this point would have been valid if there were no difference between slaves and hogs, both being mere property. Rather than quoting the arguments of Northern abolitionists to demonstrate the common humanity of Blacks, Lincoln used the behavior of Southern slave owners themselves to show that they too believed that they were something more than mere property. Referring to history, Lincoln noted that in 1820 Congress, with near unanimous Southern support, declared that kidnapping people from Africa to be sold in the slave trade to be the equivalent of piracy and thus punishable by death. Lincoln noted, "But you never thought of hanging men for catching and selling wild horses, wild buffaloes or wild bears," showing that Southerners thought that Africans were something more than beasts to be owned. Lincoln, who had ample social experience with slave owners, noted that respectable people would not associate with slave dealers if they could help it, but they had no qualms with those who traded in "corn, cattle, or tobacco." Probably using census records, Lincoln noted that there were more than four hundred thousand free Blacks in the country, and if one calculated their value at $500 a person, then there was more than $200 million worth of "property" going unowned. Lincoln asked rhetorically, "How comes this vast amount of property to be running about without owners?" While he does not account for those who liberated themselves, Lincoln correctly pointed out that many were legally freed because there was "SOMETHING which has operated on their white owners, inducing them, at vast pecuniary sacrifices, to liberate them." Lincoln provided the warrant: "In all these cases it is your sense of justice, and human sympathy, continually telling you, that the poor negro has some natural right to himself—that those who deny it, and make mere merchandise of him, deserve kickings, contempt and death."[34] Lincoln could have relied on the authority of well-known abolitionists to argue the humanity of Blacks, but he adhered to the advice of Greenleaf, that the most powerful testimony comes from those who testify against their apparent self-interest, and Southerners, against their pecuniary interests, had testified through their actions that they, too, believed in the humanity of Blacks.

Lincoln argued that Northerners should also be concerned about the spread of slavery because it hurt their own personal interests. Those who wished to move west to start over would be at a severe economic disadvantage if they had to compete against slave labor. Those who did not wish to emigrate would be at a political disadvantage if more slave states came into the union. Because of the Three-Fifths Compromise in the Constitution, slave states received a greater proportion of representatives in Congress relative to their free citizens than free states. Probably using census records, Lincoln showed that even though there were twice as many Whites in Maine as there were in South Carolina, they received the same number of representatives in Congress. Although he did not challenge the Constitution itself, he argued that its effects made it the interest of free people to arrest the spread of slavery.[35]

Many orators and politicians will content themselves to attack the weakest link of their opponent's arguments (if they even bother to address any of them at all), adhering to the fallacy that if part of the argument can be shown to be false, then all of it is so. Lincoln did not do that, and he went after the strongest argument that Stephen Douglas had, namely the Kansas-Nebraska Act was merely upholding the essential principle of democracy, that of popular sovereignty. Lincoln began by stating that he, too, believed in popular sovereignty, noting, "My faith in the proposition that each man should do precisely as he pleases with all which is exclusively his own, lies at the foundation of the sense of justice there is in me." This was a proposition he believed was true for both individuals as well as communities. He agreed with Douglas on this point, but the disagreement was merely on how to apply popular sovereignty. Lincoln professed:

> The doctrine of self government is right—absolutely and eternally right—but it has no just application, as here attempted. Or perhaps I should rather say that whether it has such just application depends upon whether a negro is *not* or *is* a man. If he is *not* a man, why in that case, he who *is* a man may, as a matter of self-government, do just as he pleases with him. But if the negro *is* a man, is it not to that extent, a total destruction of self-government, to say that he too shall not govern *himself*? When the white man governs himself that is self-government; but when he governs himself, and also governs *another* man, that is *more* than self-government—that is despotism. If the negro is a *man*, why then my ancient faith teaches me that "all men are created equal"; and that there can be no moral right in connection with one man's making a slave of another.

Here he returned to first principles, claiming that the despotism of monarchy rests on the same principle as the despotism of slave ownership, that some people, by the nature of their birth, are to enjoy the right to rule others. Douglas had argued that Whites in Nebraska were fully capable of governing themselves as well as "a few miserable negroes." Lincoln responded:

> What I do say is, that no man is good enough to govern another man, *without that other's consent*. I say this is the leading principle—the sheet anchor of American republicanism. Our Declaration of Independence says: "We hold these truths to be self evident: that all men are created equal; that they are endowed by their Creator with certain inalienable rights; that among these are life, liberty and the pursuit of happiness. That to secure these rights, governments are instituted among men, DERIVING THEIR JUST POWERS FROM THE CONSENT OF THE GOVERNED."

As no person or group would willingly consent to their enslavement, slave ownership and popular sovereignty cannot exist consistently in principle. Lincoln noted that slave owners could appeal to necessity as there was no way, as they saw it, to immediately free all the slaves without serious difficulties, but it must not be considered a moral right. Lincoln provided the warrant: "I have quoted so much at this time merely to show that according to our ancient faith, the just powers of governments are derived from the consent of the governed."[36] Here Lincoln appealed to their shared heritage, the Declaration of Independence and the Revolution, to argue that they must preserve all that was best with their inheritance.

Douglas argued that his policy was the true popular sovereignty supported by the Founding Fathers because several states would only support independence from Britain if they were allowed to regulate their domestic concerns without outside interference. Lincoln was more than happy to let the opinions of the Founders be the test: "I am glad he has done this. I love the sentiments of those old-time men; and shall be most happy to abide by their opinions." Lincoln noted that the idea that slavery should be quarantined did not originate with his generation but rather the Founders:

> This same generation of men, and mostly the same individuals of the generation, who declared this principle—who declared independence—who fought the war of the revolution through—who afterwards made the constitution under which we still live—these same men passed the ordinance of '87, declaring that slavery should never go to the north-west territory. I have no doubt Judge Douglas thinks they were very inconsistent in this . . . But there is not an inch of ground left for his claiming that their opinions—their example—their authority—are on his side in this controversy.[37]

Lincoln was never one to accept that something should be done in the present solely because it had been done in the past, but he believed that precedents were powerful, especially if they adhered to reason, and he clearly believed that history and reason were on his side on this issue.

Some argued that those who opposed slavery should not agitate against it because they were threatening the Union over something that did not directly involve them. Lincoln said that this went against basic human nature:

> Slavery is founded in the selfishness of man's nature—opposition to it, is his love of justice. These principles are an eternal antagonism; and when brought into collision so fiercely, as slavery extension brings them, shocks, and throes, and convulsions must ceaselessly follow. Repeal the Missouri compromise—repeal all compromises—repeal the declaration of independence—repeal all past history, you still can not repeal human nature. It still will be the abundance of man's heart, that slavery extension is wrong; and out of the abundance of his heart, his mouth will continue to speak.[38]

While he did paraphrase Matthew 12:34 and Luke 6:45 to sanctify his words, Lincoln primarily used his own reasoning to show that agitation against slavery would not cease until slavery ended. As Lincoln was delivering this speech, the young reporter Horace White recalled, "Sometimes his manner was very impassioned, and he seemed transfigured with his subject. Perspiration would stream from his face, and each particular hair would stand on end. Then the inspiration that possessed him took possession of his hearers also."[39]

In the fourth section of his speech, Lincoln provided prophecies of what would happen if the people did not repudiate the Kansas-Nebraska Act. If they allowed Douglas's popular sovereignty plan to proceed, Lincoln foresaw bloodshed:

> Through all this, bowie-knives and six-shooters are seen plainly enough; but never a glimpse of the ballot-box. And, really, what is to be the result of this? Each party WITHIN, having numerous and determined backers WITHOUT, is it not probable that the contest will come to blows, and bloodshed?

If the question of slavery in Kansas was to be determined not by ballots but by bullets, Lincoln foresaw only one outcome: "And if this fight should begin, is it likely to take a very peaceful, Union-saving turn? Will not the first drop of blood so shed, be the real knell of the Union?"[40] Blood, once shed, was not likely to remain contained in one locality but to spread and metastasize, threatening the Union.

From this dire prospect, Lincoln moved to the fifth section of his speech, highlighting what should be done and why. First, he reiterated his thesis, namely "that the Missouri Compromise ought to be restored," which he believed was the best way to save the Union. Even if an immediate repeal would be difficult, a victory of Anti-Nebraska candidates in the 1854 election would repudiate the principle and could sway some senators not up for reelection who initially supported it to vote for its repeal. Those who opposed the Kansas-Nebraska Act could not let their different party affiliations divide them. They must "stand with anybody that stands RIGHT. Stand with him while he is right and PART with him when he goes wrong."[41]

They should also restore the original views of the Founders toward slavery, not as a positive good that must be protected but as a moral evil that at best would be tolerated to maintain the Union. It could not be reiterated enough—slavery was evil and should be treated as such. Lincoln proclaimed:

I object to it because it assumes that there CAN be MORAL RIGHT in the enslaving of one man by another. I object to it as a dangerous dalliance for a few people—a sad evidence that, feeling prosperity we forget right—that liberty, as a principle, we have ceased to revere. I object to it because the fathers of the republic eschewed, and rejected it. The argument of 'Necessity' was the only argument they ever admitted in favor of slavery; and so far, and so far only as it carried them, did they ever go.[42]

Lincoln portrayed himself as a conservative, as he sought to uphold what he believed to be the highest ideals of the revolutionary generation.

He provided a short history of their attitudes to slavery to support this assertion. The Founders did not invent the institution of slavery but rather "found the institution existing among" them and sought to limit its influence as much as possible. Before the Constitution was signed, they forbade the spread of slavery into the Northwest Territory. When they drafted the Constitution, they did not use the word *slave* but referred to the institution obliquely. Lincoln used an analogy to explain why they did this: "Thus, the thing is hid away . . . just as an afflicted man hides away a wen or a cancer, which he dares not cut out at once, lest he bleed to death; with the promise, nevertheless, that the cutting may begin at the end of a given time." He then detailed how they took several actions after the adoption of the Constitution to restrict slavery—namely, abolishing the exportation of slaves in 1794, banning the importation of slaves in the slave territory of Mississippi in 1798, outlawing American participation in the slave trade among foreign nations in 1800, restricting the internal slave trade "in aid of one or two State laws" (here Lincoln may be referring to the 1804 act that organized the lands purchased from France in 1803 that placed limitations on the internal slave trade into those territories), prohibiting the African slave trade immediately when it was constitutional to do so in 1808, and passing a law that equated the slave trade with piracy and instituting the death penalty for the crime. For Lincoln, this history showed that "the plain unmistakable spirit of that age, towards slavery, was hostility to the PRINCIPLE, and toleration, ONLY BY NECESSITY."[43] Lincoln did not argue that the Founders were unanimous in their condemnation of slavery or always enacted their public professions in their private lives but rather that there was a generalized feeling if not unanimity amongst the Founding generation that slavery was wrong in principle and should be treated as such in their national life.

Just as at the beginning of the speech, Lincoln contrasted the principles of the revolutionary generation with his more degenerate age:

> Little by little, but steadily as man's march to the grave, we have been
> giving up the OLD for the NEW faith. Near eighty years ago we began
> by declaring that all men are created equal; but now from that begin-
> ning we have run down to the other declaration, that for SOME men to
> enslave OTHERS is a 'sacred right of self-government.' These principles
> can not stand together. They are as opposite as God and mammon; and
> whoever holds to the one, must despise the other.

Lincoln used history to show that Douglas and the Kansas-Nebraska Act
supporters represented a fundamental break with the past, rather than a
continuity with the Founders. He warned his audience, "Let no one be
deceived. The spirit of seventy-six and the spirit of Nebraska, are utter
antagonisms; and the former is being rapidly displaced by the latter."[44]
The study of history is always an important check on those who would
seek to pervert the understanding of the past to sanctify the perceived
interests of the present.

Lincoln closed with a peroration that challenged his audience to a
renewed commitment to original principles:

> Let us turn slavery from its claims of 'moral right,' back upon its exist-
> ing legal rights, and its arguments of 'necessity.' Let us return it to the
> position our fathers gave it; and there let it rest in peace. Let us re-adopt
> the Declaration of Independence, and with it, the practices, and policy,
> which harmonize with it. Let north and south—let all Americans—let
> all lovers of liberty everywhere—join in the great and good work. If we
> do this, we shall not only have saved the Union; but we shall have so
> saved it, as to make, and to keep it, forever worthy of the saving. We shall
> have so saved it, that the succeeding millions of free happy people, the
> world over, shall rise up, and call us blessed, to the latest generations.[45]

In his peroration Lincoln not only appealed to the memory of the past
but reminded his audience that they themselves can live on in memory
forever.

Judging by the reaction it generated, Lincoln's speech was an unqualified success. The next day the *Illinois Daily Journal* noted:

> Mr. Lincoln was frequently and warmly applauded . . . We venture to say
> that Judge Douglas never, in the Senate Chamber or before the people,
> listened to just such a powerful analysis of his Nebraska sophisms, or
> saw such a remorseless tearing of his flimsy arguments and scattering
> them to the winds, as he endured yesterday from Mr. Lincoln.

According to the *Journal*, "Mr. Lincoln closed amid immense cheers.
He had nobly and triumphantly sustained the cause of a free people, and
won a place in their hearts as a bold and powerful champion of equal

rights for American citizens, that will in all time be a monument to his honor."[46] The speech had moved them so much that the paper continued to rhapsodize over it days later: "This anti-Nebraska speech of Mr. Lincoln was the profoundest, in our opinion, that he has made in his whole life. He felt upon his soul the truths burn which he uttered, and all present felt that he was true to his own soul." He spoke "with emphasis, feeling, and true eloquence;—eloquent, because true, and because he felt, and felt deeply, what he said . . . He quivered with feeling and emotion. The whole house was as still as death," as he spoke. According to the *Journal*, the reporters gathered there from the slave states of Missouri and Kentucky were impressed, arguing that Lincoln's antislavery speech was better than anything that William Seward, Charles Sumner, or Salmon Chase had ever delivered.[47] One of these papers, the *Missouri Republican*, occupied ambiguous ground during this great moment of political realignment—it was a Whig paper that nevertheless supported the Democrat Stephen Douglas's Kansas-Nebraska Act in hopes that slavery could spread beyond Missouri's western border. Even though its reporter thought Douglas gave a masterful performance at Springfield, he found much to praise in Lincoln's speech, stating that it "was the best historical display of facts upon that side of the question that I have ever listened to."[48] At the other end of the political spectrum was Horace White, who came to idolize Lincoln for the rest of his life after first hearing him speak in Springfield. While at the time he wrote, "Abraham Lincoln is a mammoth," White recalled, more than five decades later, that this speech "made so profound an impression on me that I feel under its spell to this day." This was because "his speaking went to the heart because it came from the heart. I have heard celebrated orators who could start thunders of applause without changing any man's opinion. Mr. Lincoln's eloquence was of the higher type, which produced conviction in others because of the conviction of the speaker himself."[49] Lincoln's biographers Nicolay and Hay note the abrupt change in Lincoln:

> Men were surprised to find him imbued with an unwonted seriousness. They heard from his lips fewer anecdotes and more history. Careless listeners who came to laugh at his jokes were held by the strong current of his reasoning and the flashes of his earnest eloquence, and were lifted up by the range and tenor of his argument into a fresher and purer political atmosphere.

According to Nicolay and Hay, his audience especially appreciated "the overwhelming current of his historical arraignment" that "extorted the admiration of even his political enemies." For Nicolay and Hay, Lincoln's

Springfield speech transformed his political career: "Lincoln had hitherto been the foremost man in his district. That single effort made him the leader on the new question in his State."[50]

While the reactions to his history were overwhelmingly positive, it is essential to look at it critically to determine how he constructed his historical arguments. While the overwhelming majority of his historical assertions were correct, he made a few errors, some inconsequential (like the exact location of the Missouri counties with the highest percentage of slaves) and others more serious. For example, he asserted that Jefferson convinced the Virginia legislature to cede its claims to the Northwest Territory conditional on "the prohibition of slavery therein." While Jefferson certainly wanted slavery prohibited in that territory, Virginia did not approve the cessation of its claims upon those terms. Several years later, Lincoln wrote to John L. Scripps, who was writing a biography of Lincoln for his 1860 presidential campaign, informing him that he had made a mistake six years earlier in his speech delivered at Springfield. He wrote that his claim was "an error." He continued, "Such prohibition is not a condition of the deed; and in any reprint of the speech, the text should be preserved, but there should be a note stating the error." That same year Lincoln wrote a pair of letters to James O. Putnam, and in one of them, Lincoln corrected a historical mistake Putnam made about John Adams. When Putnam wrote back apologizing, Lincoln replied:

> You must not lay much stress on the blunder about Mr. Adams; for I made a more mischievous one . . . I stated that the prohibition of slavery in the North West Territory was made a condition in the Virginia deed of cession . . . while, in fact, it was not. Like yourself, I have since done what I could to correct the error.[51]

We do not know how Lincoln discovered his mistake, but he readily admitted it when he did. Furthermore, rather than going back and correcting the earlier record, Lincoln made a point to tell Scripps that he must retain the mistake and have it noted as such.

The Pulitzer Prize-winning historian Eric Foner has criticized Lincoln's address not for factual errors but rather for faulty interpretations. Foner writes that Lincoln had a "highly selective reading of history," and this argument is not without merit. For example, Foner writes that Lincoln made Jefferson's antislavery record "far more consistent than it actually had been." This is correct. In this speech, Lincoln named Jefferson as the author of the "egalitarian preamble" of the Declaration of Independence and the inspiration for what would become the Northwest Ordinance of 1787 that banned slavery in the territories north of the Ohio

River. However, while Lincoln did discuss Jefferson's 1820 "diffusion" theory that slavery should be allowed to spread to new territories (which Jefferson believed would hasten the day of abolition) to refute it, Lincoln did not name Jefferson as a supporter of that theory. Nor did Lincoln discuss any of the manifold inconsistencies of Jefferson in the intervening years. Likewise, Foner argued that "Lincoln's account of history in effect erased proslavery Americans from the nation's founding."[52] While Lincoln would say there were Founders who had opposed immediate emancipation on practical grounds, he did not mention a single leader during the revolutionary generation who thought of slavery as a moral good. For example, James Jackson, a Revolutionary War veteran and a representative from Georgia, declared during the first session of the First Congress in 1789 that slaves "were better off in their present situation than they would be if they were manumitted." According to Jackson, they would do no work but rather would become "common pickpockets" and "petty larceny villains" if they were freed. In fact, he suggested, they were better off as slaves in America than living free in Africa. Jackson was not alone in expressing views like this, which were quite popular in Georgia and South Carolina during the Revolutionary era, and indeed Lincoln did not mention them. However, Lincoln can be forgiven for this omission because even Congressman Jackson acknowledged that his views on slavery were in the minority. As he put it in 1789, it is the "fashion of the day to favor the liberty of slaves."

Furthermore, it was James Madison, the slave owner from Virginia, who delivered a lengthy reply to Jackson on the floor of the House, arguing, "It is to be hoped, that by expressing a national disapprobation of this trade, we may destroy it, and save ourselves from reproaches, and our posterity the imbecility ever attendant on a country filled with slaves."[53] In one way or another, all the most prominent Founding Fathers expressed some disapproval of slavery and looked forward to the day of its eradication (even though they mistakenly convinced themselves that it could be accomplished relatively painlessly, to them, with time). Lincoln did not argue that the Founding Fathers were primarily abolitionists but rather that there was a general consensus that slavery was morally wrong. While they differed in how much they were committed to that principle or how best to enact this sensibility, Lincoln was not wrong to say the general feeling was there during the Revolutionary era. This generation had had more than feelings about it. It was during this era that half of the states either ended or began the process of ending slavery in places where people of European descent had practiced it for more than a century. Likewise, they outlawed the practice in the Northwest

Territory. This land that, to some extent, had already been infected with slavery, as there were French, American, and Native owners of slaves there. They also outlawed the slave trade as soon as they were constitutionally able to. Lincoln was not writing this speech about the history of slavery from the perspective of the twenty-first century but rather from the perspective of how slavery looked in 1854, when there was a growing number of people who argued that enslaved people were nothing but property, that there was nothing wrong with the institution, and that the idea the federal government could restrict slavery in the territories violated the Constitution's guarantee to people's natural right to property. Using history, Lincoln successfully proved that a preponderance of the revolutionary generation, whom they all revered, did not hold those views. Foner is correct in that Lincoln did not portray the full complexity of that generation. However, this weakness should not blind us to the fact that Lincoln, after careful research, stated that the Founding Fathers asserted that slavery was immoral and could be restricted in federal territories. In this primary assertion, Lincoln was not wrong.

In his Springfield speech Lincoln professed that he could not swear that every detail was accurate, but that the facts, in general—namely, that the Kansas-Nebraska Act was a dangerous break from precedent—were correct to prove his argument. Furthermore, while this speech shows Lincoln making errors, it also indicates Lincoln's commitment to the truth and his willingness to bring embarrassment upon himself to protect the pursuit of truth. It shows how Lincoln believed that the truth about the past was too precious to be abandoned by expedients to meet the perceived interests of the people of the present. Lincoln's remarkable speech at Springfield was the starting point for all the great speeches before his presidency, which in one way or another, would explore the same historical themes. Finally, it shows Lincoln growing in his ability to present an accurate depiction of that past, a skill that was not static but that he would keep honing for years to come.

The Peoria Speech

Confusingly, the speech Lincoln delivered in Springfield on October 4, 1854, is not known today as his "Springfield Speech" but rather as his "Peoria Speech." Even though the *Daily Journal* provided an accurate summary of his address in Springfield, it was not published verbatim until after he delivered essentially the same speech in Peoria.[54] In the transcript of his Peoria Speech, Lincoln noted that he was ending the words that he spoke in Springfield and had a few words that he would like to add to address points made by Stephen Douglas subsequent to his initial address.[55] As with the original Springfield speech, this short addendum centered on history.

An example of how Lincoln continued to rework and refashion the same arguments based on more research can be seen in his Peoria Speech, where he provided a more detailed argument on slavery in Illinois than he had done twelve days earlier in Springfield. Douglas argued that it was not the Northwest Ordinance of 1787 that restricted slavery north of the Ohio River but rather the popular sovereignty of each individual state that did it. Douglas also contended that when Illinois was admitted into the Union, it was done so as a slave state. Lincoln called this "quibbling all the way through." Without defining what was meant by a "slave state," Lincoln admits there were some slaves held legally in Illinois when it became a state in 1818. Lincoln correctly noted that the French introduced race-based chattel slavery in what would become Illinois long before the United States took possession of the territory. They settled in the fertile floodplain of the Mississippi between Kaskaskia in the south and Cahokia in the north and were allowed to retain possession of their slaves after the United States took control. While the first state constitution did not outlaw slavery outright in Illinois, Lincoln correctly noted that it forbade any new slaves from being brought into the state, and it banned the practice of quasi-slavery through indentured servitude while still honoring prior contracts. Lincoln contrasted Illinois with Missouri, since both states already possessed slavery when acquired by the United States and there was no significant natural difference between them besides which side of the Mississippi they lay on. While slavery died out in Illinois, it thrived and multiplied in Missouri, and Lincoln argued that was because of the Northwest Ordinance of 1787, which outlawed slavery in Illinois and not in Missouri. To support this assertion, he provided evidence from the census figures: "Between 1810 and 1820 the number of slaves in Missouri INCREASED 7,211; while in Illinois, in the same ten years, they DECREASED 51. This appears by the census returns." Lincoln noted that a little more than a year after the signing of the 1818 Illinois Constitution, there were only "117" slaves compared to a total population of "55,094," which according to Lincoln was a ratio of "about 470 to one." His warrant was that "During this time, the ordinance forbid slavery to go into Illinois; and NOTHING forbid it to go into Missouri. It DID go into Missouri, and did NOT go into Illinois. That is the fact. Can any one doubt as to the reason of it?"[56]

Had Lincoln's numbers been accurate, his reasoning would have been sound, but he seems to have made one error in his figures that threw his calculations off and would have weakened his argument had anyone caught it. Lincoln said that the 1820 census showed that 117 slaves were residing in Illinois, when in fact, the census records show that there were 917. Lincoln is unlikely to have deliberately altered this number. Besides his reputation for honesty, he was willing to go out of his way to point out the factual errors he made in the past. Likewise, Lincoln told everyone exactly where he found his evidence, making it easy to contradict him. A more likely scenario is that he either misread it or the copy he used contained a misprint. Some figures from this era, even when printed, can be difficult to discern because of poor printing quality, making it likely that the 9 in 917 could have been easily mistaken for a 1, thus making it appear to be 117. With bad printing, it can be challenging to decipher the numbers because, unlike text, there are no context clues to help determine the correct meaning. Without the original copy Lincoln used, it is impossible to know with certainty. Whatever the cause, the error is significant because he used the figure to show that slavery was diminishing in Illinois from 1810 to 1820, when in fact it was increasing rapidly. The census figures show that in 1810 there were 168 enslaved persons living in Illinois, making it 1.37 percent of the total population of 12,282. In 1820 the number of slaves jumped to 917, making it 1.7 percent of the total population of 55,211 (still a vastly lower percentage than those found in what have been commonly known as "slave states"). Rather than a *decrease* of 51 slaves during that decade, as Lincoln asserted, this means there was an *increase* of 749 slaves. There was a 446 percent increase in the number of slaves, which outpaced both the total population increase in Illinois (350 percent) and the increase of the enslaved population in Missouri during that decade (240 percent).[57] Furthermore, these figures do not include the number of slaves registered in other states who nonetheless labored in Illinois. There is no accurate data for their numbers, but Lincoln omitted their existence in this discussion. The reality of slavery during this decade was much more complex than Lincoln asserted, and having correct figures certainly would have allowed him to present a more accurate argument.

Even though his evidence was faulty, it does not necessarily invalidate his overall premise that the Ordinance of 1787 was the primary reason Illinois was a free state and Missouri was a slave state. Lincoln correctly noted that slavery had been introduced in Illinois before there were any laws to prohibit it. If there were no laws to restrict slavery from going into Kansas, it would go there too.[58] Like Missouri, Illinois, when it applied for statehood, not only had a preexisting French population that had owned slaves for more than a century but also was predominantly settled by people born in southern slave states, especially Kentucky. However, the federal ban on slavery likely discouraged many slave-owning Kentuckians from moving to Illinois; these Kentuckians would instead have chosen Missouri, understanding correctly that their "property" would be more secure. When Illinois applied for statehood, it copied much of the language of the prohibition of slavery from the Northwest Ordinance of 1787 in its constitution, while Missouri, on the other hand, insisted on protecting slavery, remaining defiant even when their admission as a slave state threatened to tear the country apart in 1820. Congress nearly rejected Missouri's admission as a slave state where there were no prior federal prohibitions against slavery, even at the risk of disunion. It is nearly impossible to conceive of a scenario where Congress, two years prior, would have admitted Illinois if the residents petitioned to join the Union as a slave state under the guise of popular sovereignty in defiance of the Northwest Ordinance. Furthermore, while slavery did increase in the 1810s (both numerically and proportionally), it decreased every decade thereafter until there were no slaves reported in 1850. Meanwhile, Missouri's slave population had risen to more than eighty-seven thousand.[59] While Lincoln acknowledged that Illinois did not entirely follow the Ordinance of 1787 when it became a state, it adhered to it enough by adopting its language in its constitution so that slavery would dwindle in the coming decades and eventually be outright abolished in 1848. The only meaningful difference between Illinois and Missouri in their early years of statehood was that the Northwest Ordinance of 1787 applied to the former and not the latter, thus resulting in vastly different outcomes.

In the rest of his speech in Peoria, Lincoln more effectively countered several other of Douglas's claims. While Douglas believed popular sovereignty led to the abolition of slaves living in the original Northern states, Lincoln noted that they all abolished slavery either during or shortly after the Revolution, and no more slave states had voted to abolish slavery in more than five decades. For Lincoln, "it was the principle of the REVOLUTION, and not the principle of Nebraska bill, that led to emancipation in these old States," ideas he delineated earlier in his address. Douglas argued that God himself endorsed popular sovereignty since He allowed man to choose between good and evil. Lincoln, using Biblical wisdom, responded, "God did not place good and evil before man, telling him to make his choice. On the contrary, he did tell him there was one tree, of the fruit of which, he should not eat, upon pain of certain death. I should scarcely wish so strong a prohibition against slavery in Nebraska." When Douglas argued that free states held an electoral advantage over slave states because, while in most cases Blacks could not vote, they still counted free Blacks as one whole person while enslaved Blacks were only counted as three-fifths of a person for representation purposes, Lincoln correctly noted that slave states had thirty-three thousand more free Blacks than free states did and that they were counted in the same way as they were in the North.[60] When Stephen Douglas denied that the Compromise of 1850 was a "compromise" because it was made up of a series of separate acts, Lincoln defined key terms by reading the definition from *Webster's*. He argued that what Congress did in 1850 met the exact definition of compromise because the legislators understood that those bills were a mutually dependent and packaged deal. When Douglas argued that the 1853 act to establish the territory of Washington repealed both the Northwest Ordinance of 1787 and the prior ban on slavery when it was part of the Oregon Territory, Lincoln scornfully replied, "Now I had seen the Washington act before; and I have carefully examined it since; and I aver that there is no repeal of the ordinance of '87, or of any prohibition of slavery, in it. In express terms, there is absolutely nothing in the whole law upon the subject—in fact, nothing to lead a reader to THINK of the subject." Stephen Douglas took the positions that he did because he had "no very vivid impression that the negro is a human; and consequently . . . no idea that there can be any moral question in legislating about him." He continued, "[While] the great mass of mankind . . . consider slavery a great moral wrong; and their feelings against it, is not evanescent, but eternal. It lies at the very foundation of their sense of justice; and it cannot be trifled with. It is a great and durable element of popular action, and, I think, no statesman can safely disregard it."[61] In his response to Lincoln, Douglas had thrown up a litany of charges and counterarguments that Lincoln was able to effectively disprove with wisdom derived from history, the Bible, and his own reasoning.

The most remarkable aspect of his Peoria addendum is the peroration where Lincoln assaults Stephen Douglas's misuse of history:

> This is no other than a bold denial of the history of the country. If we do not know that the Compromises of '50 were dependent on each other; if we do not know that Illinois came into the Union as a free state—we do not know any thing. If we do not know these things, we do not know that we ever had a revolutionary war, or such a chief as Washington. To deny these things is to deny our national axioms, or dogmas, at least; and it puts an end to all argument. If a man will stand up and assert, and repeat, and re-assert, that two and two do not make four, I know nothing in the power of argument that can stop him. I think I can answer the Judge so long as he sticks to the premises; but when he flies from them, I can not work an argument into the consistency of a maternal gag, and actually close his mouth with it.[62]

While Lincoln provided numerous hedges and acknowledged that not everything may be completely accurate in his speech, he argued passionately that there were historical truths that were knowable and should be faithfully adhered to. He was against what would become a later interpretation of history, that it is not the written facts but rather power that matters. For Lincoln, there was no conflict between truth and power.

Lincoln continued to deliver essentially the same speech throughout the campaign of 1854, and even though he was only on the ballot for the relatively minor position in the Illinois House of Representatives, he had emerged as the leading Anti-Nebraska man in the state. In fact, he received a plurality of votes on the first ballot for U.S. senator in 1855, but Lincoln released his supporters to vote for Lyman Trumbull because he was the only Anti-Nebraska candidate who could earn a majority. Many of Lincoln's supporters were understandably upset, but Lincoln, who had known not to be prideful since his childhood, graciously congratulated Trumbull. Those who supported Trumbull would then become ardent Lincoln supporters, helping unite the nascent Illinois Republican Party around Lincoln.

We Are Not What We Have Been

Even though Lincoln's political star was rising in Illinois, privately, he grew pessimistic about the direction in which the country was heading. This is evident in a letter he wrote to George Robertson in 1855. Robertson had provided legal work for Lincoln in Kentucky, and he was a former member of Congress. The purpose of Lincoln's letter was to thank him for giving him an inscribed copy of his recently published book, *Scrap Book on Law and Politics, Men and Times*, which was a collection of his papers and speeches.[63]

Lincoln praised the work, especially Robertson's account of his experience with the Missouri crisis while in Congress as a representative from Kentucky, writing, "[It] afforded me much of both pleasure and instruction."[64] He praised one speech Robertson delivered in 1819 in opposition to Congress limiting the spread of slavery into the Arkansas Territory, arguing instead that it should be left to the residents of Arkansas to determine if slavery should be legal or not.[65] Even though Robertson professed opinions in 1819 that were nearly identical to Douglas's popular sovereignty opinions in 1855, Lincoln wrote to Robertson, "Your short, but able and patriotic speech upon that occasion, has not been improved upon since, by those holding the same views;

and, with all the lights you then had, the views you took appear to me as very reasonable."[66]

Unlike Douglas, Robertson, in 1819, expressed his belief that one day America would see a "peaceful extinction of slavery," but Lincoln, at least in this letter, disagreed with this assessment. He wrote:

> Since then we have had thirty six years of experience; and this experience has demonstrated, I think, that there is no peaceful extinction of slavery in prospect for us. The signal failure of Henry Clay, and other good and great men, in 1849, to effect any thing in favor of gradual emancipation in Kentucky, together with a thousand other signs, extinguishes that hope utterly. On the question of liberty, as a principle, we are not what we have been. When we were the political slaves of King George, and wanted to be free, we called the maxim that "all men are created equal" a self evident truth; but now when we have grown fat, and have lost all dread of being slaves ourselves, we have become so greedy to be *masters* that we call the same maxim "a self-evident lie" The fourth of July has not quite dwindled away; it is still a great day—*for burning fire-crackers!*

For Lincoln, experience had shown that rather than working toward a gradual abolition, slavery was becoming more entrenched in American society. Lincoln continued:

> That spirit which desired the peaceful extinction of slavery, has itself become extinct, with the *occasion*, and the *men* of the Revolution. Under the impulse of that occasion, nearly half the states adopted systems of emancipation at once; and it is a significant fact, that not a single state has done the like since. So far as peaceful, voluntary emancipation is concerned, the condition of the negro slave in America . . . is now as fixed, and hopeless of change for the better, as that of the lost souls of the finally impenitent. The Autocrat of all the Russias will resign his crown, and proclaim his subjects free republicans sooner than will our American masters voluntarily give up their slaves.

Lincoln exaggerated here as the spirit had not become extinct, but he is right in noting that it was the men of the revolutionary generation who had abolished slavery in half of the states, and since then not only had no single state followed suit but slavery had also spread into entirely new regions. This degeneration of common principles is a theme Lincoln would continue to refer to in the coming years. Showing that Lincoln was already brooding over ideas he would discuss in his famous "House Divided" speech three years later, Lincoln wondered, "Can we, as a nation, continue together *permanently—forever*—half slave, and half free?"[67]

Lincoln would never express sentiments this pessimistic in public. Both before and after this letter, Lincoln voiced his hope that by limiting the spread of slavery, one day it could be peaceably abolished, even if he had no definite plan for how or when this would be accomplished. However, in this letter, Lincoln argued that history had shown that Americans were rapidly losing the spirit of the revolutionary generation. This history led him to believe that they could never peaceably abolish slavery.

Princeton: The Supremacy of Divine Law

One man present at Lincoln's 1854 Springfield address was no stranger to history. He had worked, lived, and studied under Elijah Lovejoy in Alton. He stood guard at Lovejoy's home the night he Elijah was murdered several blocks away, and he watched the next day when crowds jeered at the lifeless corpse as it was brought home by his friends.[68] He recalled that his body "looked perfectly natural, but little paler than usual, and a smile still resting upon his lips."[69] This witness to history was Elijah's younger brother, Owen Lovejoy. He had sworn over his brother's lifeless body that he would dedicate his life to continuing his brother's work to end slavery.[70]

Like his brother before him, Owen Lovejoy went into the ministry and became an outspoken abolitionist leader but did it from the relative safety of a small town in north-central Illinois, Princeton. Unlike Alton, which bordered Missouri and was filled with Southerners with proslavery sympathies, Princeton was 125 miles from Missouri and largely settled by abolitionist-minded Northerners. Even though it was still a small frontier village when Lovejoy arrived, it was not an uncultured community. Several of the brothers of poet William Cullen Bryant settled in Princeton, and the most prominent of them, John Bryant, was a decent poet himself.[71]

The Hampshire Colony Church called Owen Lovejoy to be their minister in 1838, the year after his brother's death. Congregationalists had founded the church in 1831 in Northampton, Massachusetts, and traveled west via the Erie Canal and the Great Lakes to plant the seeds of their faith on new soil.[72]

Lovejoy took up the mantle of his fallen brother and quickly earned a reputation as the most eloquent abolitionist in Illinois, as evidenced by his 1843 sermon entitled "Supremacy of Divine Law." In it Lovejoy proclaimed that the fugitive slave clause in the Constitution was "null and void" and ought to be "disregarded and disobeyed," and he urged his congregants to "trample in the dust" any law that breaks God's laws. First and foremost, they must not fear men and their laws but fear God and obey his commands. He cataloged a list of those in the past who obeyed God by defying earthly authority, from the midwives who subverted

Pharaoh's command to kill Hebrew baby boys to the three Jewish captives who refused to bow down to the statue of King Nebuchadnezzar of Babylon to early martyrs of the Christian church who defied Rome to their Protestant ancestors who defied earthly authority. He reminded them that their nation was founded by rebels who shed their blood rather than submit to the tyranny of a king and parliament. They must preserve their heritage of defiance of unjust laws. To those who might feel that breaking the law was wrong, Lovejoy pointed out that "human legislation does not make right and wrong . . . that it cannot do—it's only aim is, or at least ought to be, to establish and secure right; to prevent and suppress wrong." To determine what is right, they "must have some other standard besides the ever varying and contradictory enactments of Congresses, Legislatures and Parliaments." Even though the authorities had the power to take their liberty and property, should they give aid to the fugitive slave, and even though extralegal mobs had the ability to take their lives, they must, like their forebearers before them, fear God and not men. Turning to his mother in the congregation he asked, "Mother, can you not spare another son?" He closed by making meaning of the memory of his brother's martyrdom: "Beside the prostrate body of that murdered brother, while the fresh blood was oozing from his perforated breast, on my knees while alone with the dead and with God, I vowed never to forsake the cause that was sprinkled with his blood. The oath was written in blood. It must stand."[73]

Lovejoy practiced what he preached, and he was skilled in hiding and defending fugitive slaves in his home, which was a station on the Underground Railroad. For example, in 1849 Missouri men kidnapped a Black man, John Buckner, in Princeton and attempted to take him to Missouri. They were arrested for kidnapping, and Buckner was arrested for being a fugitive slave. A crowd of both proslavery and antislavery men crowded the courthouse to witness the drama. Sympathizers secreted Buckner out, and he fled to Lovejoy's home. A race ensued with proslavery men chasing him and antislavery men running to defend him. Buckner, Lovejoy, and some of their abolitionist friends arrived first. Lovejoy, a powerfully built man, guarded the gate to the house and slammed it on someone who attempted to break in. Meanwhile, the crowd saw a man take off running from the Lovejoy property into the field and chased after him. When they finally caught him, they realized he was a decoy, as Buckner had hidden in the empty bottom of a wagon that had been carted off and was a safe distance away before the mob discovered the ruse.[74]

Lovejoy, to the dismay of many in Illinois and throughout the country, was elected to Congress in 1856, and he openly declared on the House floor not only his opposition to the fugitive slave clause but also his open defiance of it:

> I do assist fugitive slaves. Proclaim it, then, upon the house-tops; writ upon every leaf that trembles in the forest; make it blaze from the sun at high-noon, and shine forth in the milder radiance of every star that bedecks the firmament of God; let it echo through all the arches of heaven, and reverberate and bellow along all the deep gorges of hell where slaver-catchers will be very likely to hear it. Owen Lovejoy lives at Princeton, Illinois, three-quarters of a mile east of the village and he aides every fugitive that comes to his door and asks it. Thou invisible demon of Slavery! Dost thou think to cross my humble threshold, and forbid me to give bread to the hungry and shelter to the houseless? I BID YOU DEFIANCE IN THE NAME OF GOD![75]

While Lincoln was typically cool and dispassionate and counseled strict adherence to the law, Lovejoy burned with the zeal of righteousness that no law could restrain.

Even though of a widely disparate temperament and holding a differing view on the Fugitive Slave Law, Lovejoy greatly admired Lincoln after listening to his 1854 Springfield speech. While in Springfield, Lovejoy attempted to enlist Lincoln in the nascent Republican Party, but Lincoln was not yet willing to abandon the Whigs, which he had loyally supported for two decades. However, when the party finally disintegrated, Lincoln joined Lovejoy's Republicans and traveled throughout Illinois and the Midwest in 1856, campaigning for its first nominee for president, John C. Fremont.

Typical of these campaign speeches was the one Lincoln delivered in Princeton on July 4, 1856. The Independence Day rally was held in Bryants Woods, a grove south of town that John Bryant owned. According to the *Tiskilwa Independent*, approximately eight thousand to ten thousand people attended the rally. One of those was Owen Lovejoy, who would deliver his own address immediately after Lincoln.[76]

According to the *Independent*, Lincoln gave a lengthy history lecture that included a discussion of the Declaration of Independence, the Ordinance of 1787, the Missouri Compromise, the nullification crisis, the Texas controversy, the organization of the Utah and Washington territories, and the Kansas-Nebraska Act. When he finished, "Mr. Lincoln took his seat amid loud and enthusiastic cheers."[77] Despite their differences, Lovejoy and Lincoln would become both personal friends and political allies. As he did to Lovejoy in 1854 in Springfield, Lincoln would continue to inspire his audiences in 1856 with his campaign speeches that were, like those in 1854, primarily lectures on history.

Election of 1856

To Lincoln's surprise, he received a significant number of votes to be the Republican vice-presidential nominee, which was a sign of how he was beginning to earn a national reputation. Just as at Princeton, Lincoln traveled throughout the Midwest, campaigning for the Republicans, making logical arguments derived from history.

On July 19, Lincoln delivered a speech at Dearborn Park on Lake Michigan in Chicago (today along Michigan Avenue between Washington and Randolph Streets). The Chicago *Democratic Press* reported that Lincoln's address was about the "indisputable facts in our political history" and drew conclusions from those facts that were "unanswerable." The *Democratic Press* reported, "We have never seen an audience held for so long a time in the open air to listen to an argumentative speech." At the same time, the Peoria *Weekly Republican* wrote that his speech could not "fail to produce a telling effect upon the political sentiment of Chicago."[78]

On August 27, Lincoln delivered an address in Kalamazoo, Michigan, that was warmly received. Perhaps referring to the charge from Jefferson's first draft of the Declaration that did not make it into the final, Lincoln declared that slavery had been "deplored" by the founding generation, who blamed Britain for its introduction and maintenance. Britain had rejected colonial petitions before the Revolution to ban the slave trade. Lincoln argued that James Buchanan was now taking the position not of Jefferson but rather King George III, allowing slavery to spread anywhere where people desired it. When Lincoln finished, the crowd saluted him with "great cheering."[79]

Lincoln's rapport that he was building with his audiences can be best seen in his address in Vandalia on September 23 in south-central Illinois. It was less of a speech than a public conversation with his friend "Long Jim" Davis, a Democrat, with significant input from the audience. Davis recalled that when Lincoln was in Congress, he had "abused" Lincoln for his vote for the Wilmot Proviso, yet he applied to Lincoln to get a government job, and to the crowd's delight, according to the reporter, "he got it!" Davis bragged that he delivered the first speech that was printed in Illinois against the Kansas-Nebraska Act and, referring to Republicans, added, "If any of these little men want a speech on the subject I will send them one of mine." Lincoln replied that he "thought it must be a *very* little man who could learn anything from that speech," which elicited laughter from the crowd. When Lincoln delivered his speech, he advocated walking down the "old paths" of Washington, Jefferson, and Clay, quoting them extensively. Republicans in south-central Illinois communities like Vandalia were much less popular than they were in the north, and they were derogatively referred to as "Black Republicans." This explains the comment one Democratic doctor made when he interrupted Lincoln's speech to exclaim, "I must be a woolly head!" Lincoln challenged this racial prejudice indirectly through humor: "Very well, shave *off* the wool then." A reporter noted an "unlucky twist in the doctor's hair and whiskers," and that the cut "was evidently enjoyed by the audience more than by himself." After finishing his history lecture on the prominent Americans opposed to slavery, Lincoln asked the doctor, "What more than this has Fremont said, that you call him a woolly head? I ask you, sir?" When the doctor struggled to find words to respond, Lincoln quipped, "You can make this charge, and yet, when called upon to justify it, your lips are sealed." After the doctor huddled with some friends for a few moments, he replied, "He found the woolly horse and ate dogs," referring to the myths surrounding Fremont's exploration of the West. Lincoln replied that it was not true, but even if that was, "how does it prove that Fremont is a *woolly head*—how?" According to the reporter, the doctor, "wearing the expression of a man standing on a bed of live coals, did not get off any answer." After a long pause, Lincoln, using the language of the fox hunt, exclaimed, "You're *treed*, my friend!" and the audience erupted into laughter. According to the reporter, even though it was a "hand-to-hand fight," he praised "the self-possession, wit, and unflagging good nature of the speakers," which "made the discussion *tell* on the sober, honest men who listened."[80] Even in presumptively enemy territory thick with racial prejudice, Lincoln was able to win over his audiences with both humor and history.

Conclusion

Although he had not held political office in seven years, by 1856 Lincoln had become, outside of Stephen Douglas, the leading politician in Illinois. He had done it through his lectures that were primarily about the past. From his extended address in Springfield in 1854 to his campaign speeches in 1856, Lincoln used these historical arguments to build a movement. Lincoln had shown exceptional growth to become the man he was at that time, and he was marshaling all his intellectual and rhetorical strength to confront the "Little Giant" in the Senate race of 1858.

Chapter 5

The Logic of History

Personal Memory

In the silence of his private ruminations, Lincoln picked up his pen sometime after the election of 1856 and jotted down some thoughts about his past:

> Twenty-two years ago Judge Douglas and I first became acquainted. We were both young then; he a trifle younger than I. Even then, we were both ambitious; I, perhaps, quite as much so as he. With *me*, the race of ambition has been a failure—a flat failure; with *him* it has been one of splendid success. His name fills the nation; and is not unknown, even, in foreign lands. I affect no contempt for the high eminence he has reached. So reached, that the oppressed of my species, might have shared with me in the elevation, I would rather stand on that eminence, than wear the richest crown that ever pressed a monarch's brow.[1]

Typically for Lincoln, he concluded these private musings on the past with the lesson to be learned, that all the power and glory in the world is but a trifle if one cannot benefit one's fellow man.

When people tend to think about Stephen Douglas and Abraham Lincoln, they think of the senatorial debates of 1858. However, their competition was more than a quarter century long. People even tend to overlook the dozens of speeches during the year 1858 that took place outside of their formal debates that they delivered as they crisscrossed the state. Some of Lincoln's campaign addresses are more praiseworthy than his debate speeches, even if they lose somewhat of their dramatic appeal of the head-to-head contest. While in the 1830s and 1840s their disagreements centered on tariffs and banks, Lincoln renewed his challenge to Douglas in 1854, based on his opposition to Douglas's Kansas-Nebraska Act. However, history did not pause, events moved swiftly, and Lincoln and Douglas would have new issues to debate, including the Dred Scott decision.

The Plainest Print Cannot Be Read through a Gold Eagle: Lincoln's 1857 Springfield Speech

Lincoln delivered only one major address in 1857, and it was primarily about the Dred Scott decision and how to correctly interpret history. Lincoln had already been musing privately on the potentially harmful consequences before the Supreme Court announced their decision. After extensive research, Lincoln was amply prepared to attack Douglas's support of the Dred Scott decision when he rose to address his audience in the Capitol in Springfield on June 26, 1857.

Typical of Lincoln, he began his speech slowly, stating why he was there—namely, to attempt to rebut the arguments made by Stephen Douglas in favor of the Dred Scott decision two weeks prior. Lincoln announced his opposition to the Supreme Court decision and its claims made to justify it. Lincoln primarily appealed to the past to support his reasoning, stating that Democratic leaders were abusing history to satisfy their economic interests.

After explaining that it was possible to disagree with a Supreme Court decision without violently opposing it as Democrats claimed Republicans were doing, Lincoln stated that he believed that the decision was "erroneous," partly because it was "based on assumed historical facts which are not really true." One of these is that Chief Justice Taney argued "that negroes were no part of the people who made, or for whom was made, the Declaration of Independence, or the Constitution of the United States." Lincoln then cited Justice Benjamin Robbins Curtis's dissenting opinion that noted that free Blacks in five of the original thirteen states had participated in voting when the Constitution was being ratified. Thus, at the very least, they were part of the "We, the people of the United States" in the preamble of the Constitution.[2]

Next, Lincoln refuted Taney's assertion that the opinion of "civilized and enlightened portions of the world" on negroes had improved since the signing of the Declaration of Independence and the framing of the Constitution. Taney asserted that the words of the Declaration of

Independence "would seem to include the whole human family, and if they were used in a similar instrument at this day, would be so understood," but at that time were not. The implication that Taney made is that since the Founders and Framers denied the full humanity of Blacks, they must not affirm it in his present. Lincoln countered, "This assumption is a mistake [because] the change between then and now is decidedly the other way; and their ultimate destiny has never appeared so hopeless as in the last three or four years." Even though the number of states had more than doubled, not a single new state allowed Black suffrage, while two of the original five, New Jersey and North Carolina, rescinded it and New York severely curtailed it. Not only that, but states had also passed laws restricting the rights of owners to legally free their slaves and had written into their state constitutions forbidding state legislatures from declaring general emancipation. While they once restricted the spread of slavery, Congress now opened new territories to it, and the Supreme Court declared that Congress could no longer impede it. All once revered the Declaration of Independence, but by then some were openly assaulting it. Lincoln concluded this argument with a powerful statement about the direction in which the country's attitude towards Blacks was moving:

> All the powers of earth seem rapidly combining against him. Mammon is after him; ambition follows, and philosophy follows, and the Theology of the day is fast joining the cry. They have him in his prison house; they have searched his person, and left no prying instrument with him. One after another they have closed the heavy iron doors upon him, and now they have him, as it were, bolted in with a lock of a hundred keys, which can never be unlocked without the concurrence of every key; the keys in the hands of a hundred different men, and they scattered to a hundred different and distant places; and they stand musing as to what invention, in all the dominions of mind and matter, can be produced to make the impossibility of his escape more complete than it is.[3]

If the goal is to return to first principles, as Taney asserted, then it was Taney, Douglas, and the Democrats who are mistaken, not the Republicans.

While Lincoln was essentially correct in all these assertions, he was wrong when he argued that "in those days," meaning during the Revolution, the "Declaration of Independence was held sacred by all."[4] The act and the principles of the Declaration of Independence were cherished in the first two decades after 1776, but the text was little known. It was not until partisan contests at the end of the century that the text was celebrated, and its primary author became public knowledge. Only by the early nineteenth century did Americans generally consider the text itself sacred. As historian Pauline Maier, author of *American Scripture: Making the Declaration of Independence*, writes, "Considering how revered a position the Declaration of Independence later won in the hearts and minds of the American people, their disregard for it in the earliest years of the new nation verges on the incredible." Maier further says that it was treated as an "all-but-forgotten testament."[5] Lincoln's assertion was not technically true, but the principles of the Revolution, if not the text of the Declaration of Independence itself, were revered. Years before the text was cherished, many of the states began the process of gradual or immediate abolition, the Northwest Territory banned slavery, and the Framers kept the word *slave* out of the Constitution lest it be stained by what they considered a moral evil.

While Taney and Douglas argued that the Declaration of Independence did not mean to include Black Americans because they were neither free at the time nor did the Founders immediately move to free them, Lincoln countered that at that time not all Whites were equal (as there was no universal male suffrage), nor did the Founders immediately make them equal. However, until recently, no one ever questioned if the Declaration meant to include all White men. Anyone who started whittling down the phrase "all men are created equal" to something less than that was committing "obvious violence to the plain unmistakable language of the Declaration." Lincoln then moved into perhaps his most eloquent defense of the Declaration of the Independence:

> I think the authors of that notable instrument intended to include *all* men, but they did not intend to declare all men equal *in all respects*. They did not mean to say all were equal in color, size, intellect, moral developments, or social capacity. They defined with tolerable distinctness, in what respects they did consider all men created equal—equal in "certain inalienable rights, among which are life, liberty, and the pursuit of happiness." This they said, and this meant. They did not mean to assert the obvious untruth, that all were then actually enjoying that equality, nor yet, that they were about to confer it immediately upon them. In fact they had no power to confer such a boon. They meant simply to declare the *right*, so that the *enforcement* of it might follow as fast as circumstances should permit. They meant to set up a standard maxim for free society, which should be familiar to all, and revered by all; constantly looked to, constantly labored for, and even though never perfectly attained, constantly approximated, and thereby constantly spreading and deepening its influence, and augmenting the happiness and value of life to all people of all colors everywhere. The assertion that "all men are created equal" was of no practical use in effecting our separation from Great Britain; and it was placed in the Declaration, nor for that, but for

future use. Its authors meant it to be, thank God, it is now proving itself, a stumbling block to those who in after times might seek to turn a free people back into the hateful paths of despotism. They knew the proneness of prosperity to breed tyrants, and they meant when such should re-appear in this fair land and commence their vocation they should find left for them at least one hard nut to crack.[6]

Although Lincoln did not cite it, he almost certainly was referring to Jefferson's foresight in his *Notes on the State of Virginia*, which either he or his law partner Herndon owned and a portion of which Lincoln had cut and pasted into one of his scrapbooks of newspaper clippings.[7] In the part that Lincoln glued in, Jefferson, who was writing in the midst of the war, argued that his era was the time to secure the maximum amount of rights because the "spirit of the times" would not endure. Once the Revolution is over, Americans shall be "going down hill" and will "forget themselves," and the fight to secure rights will be subverted by the "sole faculty of making money." Jefferson, who was not writing about slavery in particular but rather tyranny in general, warned his readers, "The shackles, therefore, which shall not be knocked off at the conclusion of this war, will remain with us long, will be heavier and heavier, till our rights shall revive or expire in a convulsion."[8] Lincoln believed that the principles Jefferson expressed in the Declaration best represented the "spirit of the times" in elucidating goals that would forever be the "stumbling block" that would reproach those who would subvert the rights of man in the pursuit of his own self-interest.

In the present it is all too common to look at what the revolutionary generation was not able to accomplish rather than what it did. Despite all their contradictory notions, personal failings, and limited perspectives, to them goes the credit for leading the first of the great liberty movements in American history. They not only created a new nation and banished hereditary monarchy but they ended the establishment of state churches, spread religious freedom, worked towards universal White male suffrage, enacted the abolition of slavery in half of the states, banned slavery in territories north of the Ohio, and worked to suppress the international slave trade. What the South was doing during his time, according to Lincoln, was leading an *anti-liberty* movement. Not only were they working to spread, secure, and perpetuate slavery; they moved to restrict the rights of free people in their own states, denying their free speech by outlawing the criticism of slavery and banning the distribution of abolitionist tracts through the mail. Jefferson accurately prophesied this attitudinal shift in the country at large and, inadvertently, within himself. After the

United States secured the Northwest Territory in the Treaty of Paris, he was, in 1784, the leading proponent of the outlawing of slavery in those lands. However, when he secured the purchase of the Louisiana Territory as president nearly two decades later, in 1803, Jefferson did nothing to prevent the spread of slavery to those new lands, even though most of it was at the same latitude as that of the Northwest Territory. As constitutional scholar Akhil Reed Amar notes, this omission is emblematic of how both Jefferson and Madison were guilty of "betraying their own youthful anti-slavery ideals as they grew more powerful and successful."[9]

In his address Lincoln then contrasted his view of the Declaration of Independence with Douglas's. In a speech delivered around the same time that Lincoln was making these arguments, Douglas declared,

> No man can vindicate the character, motives and conduct of the signers of the Declaration of Independence except upon the hypothesis that they referred to the white race alone, and not to the African, when they declared all men to have been created equal—that they were speaking of British subjects on this continent being equal to British subjects born and residing in Great Britain—that they were entitled to the same inalienable rights, and among them were enumerated life, liberty and the pursuit of happiness.

Lincoln challenged his audience: "My good friends, read that carefully over some leisure hour, and ponder well upon it—see what a mere wreck—mangled ruin—it makes of our once glorious Declaration." He then reread those words to make sure the audience understood the full implications of Douglas's words and then elucidates the logical conclusion: "Why, according to this, not only negroes but white people outside of Great Britain and America are not spoken of in that instrument. The English, Irish and Scotch, along with white Americans, were included to be sure, but the French, Germans and other white people of the world are all gone to pot along with the Judge's inferior races." Again, Lincoln attacked Douglas's view of the Declaration: "I had thought the Declaration promised something better than the condition of British subjects; but no, it only meant that we should be *equal* to them in their own oppressed and *unequal* condition. According to that, it gave no promise that having kicked off the King and Lords of Great Britain, we should not at once be saddled with a King and Lords of our own." According to this formulation, the Declaration meant only a formal separation from Britain without a repudiation of the ancient principles that had, in some ways, still governed that nation. He then directly addressed his audience with biting irony:

> I understand you are preparing to celebrate the "Fourth," tomorrow week.
> What for? The doings of that day had no reference to the present; and
> quite half of you are not even descendants of those who were referred to
> at that day. But I suppose you will celebrate; and will even go so far as to
> read the Declaration. Suppose after you read it once in the old fashioned
> way, you read it once more with Judge Douglas' version. It will then run
> thus: "We hold these truths to be self-evident that all British subjects
> who were on this continent eighty-one years ago, were created equal to
> all British subjects born and *then* residing in Great Britain."[10]

Lincoln then challenged Douglas's fellow Democrats in the audience:
"And now I appeal to all—to Democrats as well as others,—are you really
willing that the Declaration shall be thus frittered away?—thus left no
more at most, than an interesting memorial of the dead past? thus shorn
of its vitality, and practical value; and left without the *germ* or even the
suggestion of the individual rights of man in it?" Lincoln believed that
politicians like Douglas were warring with history to justify their expedients of the present. According to Lincoln, the fight was clear—he and
other Republicans were fighting for a living and meaningful history over
the Democrats' version of a dead and irrelevant past.

Lincoln argued that there were two main reasons the Democrats
made war on the past, one explicit and the other largely implicit. The
explicit reason was because of racial prejudice. Lincoln noted that after
Douglas proposed his Kansas-Nebraska Act in 1854, "the country was
at once in a blaze," and many of Douglas's supporters suffered at the
polls. Douglas knew that he would be fighting for his political survival,
so Lincoln argued that Douglas would attempt to appropriate the nearly
universally held racial prejudice for his campaign.[11]

Lincoln, at this time, not only failed to denounce this racial prejudice
but professed that he readily agreed with it. He said, "Judge Douglas is
especially horrified at the thought of the mixing blood by the white and
black races: agreed for once—a thousand times agreed." To prevent this,
Douglas argued that slaves must not be freed, but Lincoln countered that
experience showed the opposite was true. According to Lincoln, it was
not the freedom for Blacks that was leading to the mixing of the races
but rather slavery, and he used statistics from the census to prove it. According to the 1850 Census, not only were there many more "mulattoes"
in slave states than in free states, but the proportion of free "mulattoes"
to free Blacks was much higher in slave states and those that severely
curtailed rights for free Blacks than in free states and in those that had
relatively liberal laws for free Blacks. All the figures he cited are correct.
Lincoln argued, "These statistics show that slavery is the greatest source

of amalgamation; and next to it, not the elevation, but the degeneration of the free blacks."[12] Moving from dry statistics to something more personal, Lincoln expressed his wish that Dred Scott and his family could have been declared free. Speaking of Dred Scott's two daughters, Lincoln continued:

> Could we have had our way, the chances of these black girls, ever mixing their blood with that of white people, would have been diminished at least to the extent that it could not have been without their consent. But Judge Douglas is delighted to have them decided to be slaves, and not human enough to have a hearing, even if they were free, and thus left subject to the forced concubinage of their masters, and liable to become the mothers of mulattoes in spite of themselves—the very state of case that produces nine tenths of all the mulattoes—all the mixing of blood in the nation.[13]

The historian Eric Foner noted that this was "one of the few times in his career that he referred even obliquely to the sexual abuse of slave women."[14] Lincoln used the argument to show why he believed colonization was the best course for all involved. He did not yet profess to believe in a multiracial United States of America where all enjoyed equal rights. Like his heroes Jefferson and Clay before him, Lincoln thought that by returning freed slaves to their ancestral homelands, they would be best able to enjoy the natural rights enumerated in the Declaration of Independence.[15]

Throughout much of his speech, Lincoln highlighted the hypocrisy of Douglas and many of the Democrats to show the second reason why they were making war on the past. For example, Lincoln expressed his agreement with Douglas that Utah needed to be made to respect the authority of the United States. However, Lincoln noted that, in this case, Douglas did not support his theory of popular sovereignty because he opposed the right of the people of Utah to be polygamous if they so chose. Furthermore, after the Dred Scott case Douglas argued that the decisions of the Supreme Court must be adhered to. Still, Lincoln pointed out that Douglas did not believe this was the case when the Democratic president Andrew Jackson disagreed with the Supreme Court. Lincoln provided a couple of quotes from President Jackson arguing that the Supreme Court was not the sole authority of the constitutionality of governance, an attitude Douglas had agreed with. Declaring him to be guilty of hypocrisy, Lincoln suggested that Douglas ought to be wary "and see how exactly his fierce philippics against us for resisting Supreme Court decisions, fall upon his own head." Lincoln's description of these acts is not simply a tu quoque fallacy, as he did directly address the issues involved in other parts of the speech. Lincoln brought out these examples to clarify to his audience the true principles of his opponents, which were not high-minded adherence to the precedents of the past but rather the pursuit of their own financial and political interests. According to Lincoln the avarice of Douglas and the Democrats had blinded them to their true history that was right there in front of them. Speaking of a coin, Lincoln quipped, "the plainest print cannot be read through a gold eagle."[16]

Over the coming years, Lincoln would repeatedly argue that his opponents were trying to erase the country's true history to readily pursue their profits. Lincoln fought so that their heritage would not simply be a "memorial of a dead past" but rather a "living history" that would guide their present.[17]

House Divided

Lincoln's 1857 Springfield address was the only one he delivered for more than a year, during which time he dedicated himself to his law career, but this lull was temporary. From June to November of 1858, Lincoln delivered more speeches than he ever would in a comparable timeframe. At the time this was seen as Lincoln's last chance at high office, as he would not run to unseat his fellow Republican Senator Trumbull in 1860, and he might not receive much support for a repeat campaign for the Senate in 1864 if he had already failed twice. He spent weeks crafting a new address to start his senatorial campaign, writing new ideas on scraps of paper as they came to him and carefully revising them until he felt satisfied. As Lincoln scholar Michael Burlingame has noted, Lincoln looked to his favorite speech for inspiration, Daniel Webster's famous 1830 reply to Robert Y. Hayne, penning an opening that closely parallels that of Webster.[18]

Since Stephen Douglas believed that the Lecompton Constitution that would have legalized slavery in Kansas did not honor his popular sovereignty policy, he broke with party ranks and openly opposed the admission as a state. In order to potentially woo a new and powerful ally, some East Coast Republicans urged their compatriots in Illinois to support Douglas's reelection bid. To forestall this movement, Lincoln's Republican supporters organized a nominating convention, only the second one in the country's history, to unify support behind him before the campaign began in earnest. On June 16, 1858, the convention met in the Springfield statehouse and officially nominated Lincoln for the Senate. That evening Lincoln delivered his acceptance speech, which in many ways was more radical than any other he would give during these years and that would live on in memory more than all but two of his public addresses.[19]

The opening lines of his address are the most famous:

> If we could first know *where* we are, and *whither* we are tending, we could then better judge *what* to do, and *how* to do it.
>
> We are now far into the *fifth* year, since a policy was initiated, with the *avowed* object, and *confident* promise, of putting an end to slavery agitation.
>
> Under the operation of that policy, that agitation has not only, *not ceased*, but has *constantly augmented*.
>
> In *my* opinion, it *will* not cease, until a *crisis* shall have been reached, and passed.
>
> "A house divided against itself cannot stand."
>
> I believe this government cannot endure, permanently half *slave* and half *free*.
>
> I do not expect the Union to be *dissolved*—I do not expect the house to *fall*—but I *do* expect it will cease to be divided.
>
> It will become *all* one thing, or *all* the other.
>
> Either the *opponents* of slavery, will arrest the further spread of it, and place it where the public mind shall rest in the belief that it is in course of ultimate extinction; or its *advocates* will push it forward, till it shall become alike lawful in *all* the States, *old* as well as *new*—*North* as well as *South*.[20]

As he had so often done before and would do later, Lincoln used wisdom from the Bible, specifically Matthew 12:25, to support his argument. This metaphor would burn into the memories of his listeners and would spread throughout the country. However, in order to prove his argument, he used the events of the past to gain wisdom about where the country was headed.

After his introduction Lincoln posed a question to his audience: "Have we no *tendency* to the latter condition?" namely the legalization of slavery throughout the nation. He detailed a series of events extending from Douglas's introduction of the Kansas-Nebraska Bill in January of 1854 to events of that year in 1858. Each of these would have been familiar to his audience, but it was essential to recount all of them because each action in and of itself may seem small. Still, the totality of the recent past showed the Slave Power moving irresistibly toward making slavery legal everywhere the American flag flew. He argued that the Democratic leaders in the past four years, Stephen Douglas, Franklin Pierce, Roger Taney, and James Buchanan, were constructing a building for this Slave Power, piece by piece, with each man fulfilling his role perfectly. To switch metaphors, Republicans had not suffered a decisive battle, but they were gradually losing a war of posts as the Slave Power slowly advanced forward. To clearly see where they were heading, they must not look solely to the present but rather the past in its entirety which would allow them to understand more subtle movements and changes in direction.

Since some Republicans supported Douglas because of his opposition to the Lecompton Constitution, Lincoln wished to draw a sharp distinction between Douglas and true Republicans. To do so he used another metaphor from scripture: "They remind us that *he* is a very *great man*, and that the largest of *us* are very small ones. Let this be granted. But 'a *living dog* is better than a *dead lion*.'" Lest his audience not comprehend his reference to the passage in Ecclesiastes, Lincoln elaborated: "Judge Douglas, if not a *dead* lion *for this work*, is at least a *caged* and *toothless* one. How can he oppose the advances of slavery? He don't *care* anything about it. His avowed *mission is impressing* the 'public heart' to *care* nothing about it."[21] To arrest the Slave Power, they must not elect someone who had helped build it up for the previous four years but rather someone who was their earnest and living opponent.

At the beginning of the speech, he argued that the Union would either become entirely slave or entirely free. If Democrats continued to be elected, the former course would become inevitable. What he left unsaid was, if he really believed that the Union could soon become entirely free, how that would come about, which left much to the imagination that his opponents could take advantage of. This speech, both its strengths and weaknesses, would set the tone for the rest of the campaign.[22]

Fragment on the Struggle against Slavery

Whenever Lincoln thought of an idea that he might use one day for a speech, he would quickly jot it down on whatever scrap of paper or back of an envelope he had available. Many of these notes that survive made it into his finished speeches. Others did not, but they still reveal Lincoln's thinking in his private moments.

One note that he wrote during this period that he did not use in the campaign shows him musing over the memory of the abolition movement in Great Britain. He saw their work to eradicate slavery in the British Empire as a direct analog to the struggle the Union was currently enduring. He wrote:

> I have not allowed myself to forget that the abolition of the Slave-trade by Great Brittain, was agitated a hundred years before it was a final success; that the measure had it's open fire-eating opponents; it's stealthy

"dont care" opponents; it's dollar and cent opponents; it's inferior race opponents; its negro equality opponents; and its religion and good order opponents; that all these opponents got offices, and their adversaries got none. But I have also remembered that though they blazed, like tallow-candles for a century, at last they flickered in the socket, died out . . . and were remembered no more. School-boys know that Wilbeforce, and Granville Sharpe, helped that cause forward; but who can now name a single man who labored to retard it? Remembering these things I can not but regard it as possible that the higher object of this contest may not be completely attained within the term of my natural life. But I can not doubt either that it will come in due time. Even in this view, I am proud, in my passing speck of time, to contribute an humble mite to that glorious consummation, which my own poor eyes may not last to see.[23]

The wisdom Lincoln gained from this memory of the past was that others had faced the same difficulties he and his contemporaries were then enduring, and after a struggle of generations, they too may be able to overcome the same forces arrayed against them, and the reward for their work would be to forever live on in memory.

1858 Chicago Speech

Although not an official debate, Lincoln delivered his July 10, 1858, address a day after Douglas gave his speech in that city. Throughout the campaign, Lincoln used all the rhetorical weapons he had been amassing over the course of his quarter century in politics and aimed them squarely at Stephen Douglas.

The first weapon he used against Douglas was humor. Near the beginning of the speech, Lincoln read a quote from Douglas accusing Republicans and Buchanan Democrats of forming an unholy alliance against him. Still, like the Russians at Sevastopol, Douglas did not care what array of allies was firing at him because he was going to take them all on at once. After reading this, Lincoln, with mock fear, replied, "Well now, gentlemen, is not that very alarming?" as the crowd laughed. He continued by alluding to Douglas's comments about him. (The audience's reaction is in brackets.): "Just to think of it! right at the outset of his canvass, I, a poor, kind, amiable, intelligent, [laughter] gentleman, [laughter and renewed cheers] I am to be slain in this way. Why, my friend, the Judge, is not only, as it turns out, not a dead lion, nor even a living one—he is the rugged Russian Bear! [Roars of laughter and loud applause.]" Lincoln continued that he did not think this was exactly the analogy Douglas meant to make because, after all, the allies defeated the

Russians at Sevastopol, to which the audience responded with "long and tremendous applause."[24] Lincoln frequently used humor to elicit a bit of wisdom, but he also used it to build a rapport with his audience when he had more serious arguments to make.

Like Blackstone and Greenleaf before him, Lincoln countered Douglas's arguments by defining words that were at the heart of contention. In this case, it was "alliance" and "popular sovereignty," and with the latter he used the wording of the Declaration of Independence as his guide.[25]

In his "House Divided" speech, Lincoln did not elucidate what Republicans would do if they gained power in Washington, and his opponent pounced on this and attempted to fill in the blanks for his constituents. Douglas professed that Lincoln meant that either the Republicans would lead an abolitionist war against the South or goad the South into making war on the North, either way with the same end in mind. Recognizing he had left an opening for his opponent, Lincoln acknowledged that he had only given a prediction and not a hope, but to clarify matters "so there need be no longer any difficulty," he expressed his hope that "slavery should be put in course of ultimate extincion." This hope was still a little too vague; so he gave a rather lengthy explanation. He acknowledged that the Union had survived more than eight decades with half of it free and half of it slave, saying, "I am tolerably well acquainted with the history of the country." He then argued that the Union had been maintained not because this was the natural state of equilibrium but because there was a general "belief that slavery was in course of ultimate extinction." According to Lincoln, "The adoption of the Constitution and its attendant history led the people" to believe this was so, and briefly illustrated the Founders' willingness to restrict the spread of slavery into new states and to allow the supply of new slaves to be cut off by the banning of the slave trade within twenty years. Lincoln told his audience frankly, "I have always hated slavery, I think as much as any Abolitionist . . . but I have always been quiet about it until this new era of the introduction of the Nebraska Bill began." He said this was because he believed that the attitude had shifted from a hope of a gradual extinction of what was generally agreed as a bad thing to the expansion and perpetuation of a something that many people were now arguing was a very good thing, or at the very least, something that was of no moral concern to those not directly involved. He then answered Douglas's charge by stating that he was not in favor of a general war to end slavery. Rather, he supported a return to the only policy that allowed there to be peace and unity for so long, which was to treat slavery as a bad thing and take measures to restrict its spread, putting it on the path of ultimate extinction.[26] For

Lincoln, a return to the policies of the past was the best way to secure union, peace, and liberty in the future.

After repeating essentially the same ideas about the Dred Scott decision that he expressed in his 1857 Springfield speech, Lincoln built up to one of the most powerful perorations of his career, an ardent statement against the dilution of the rights delineated in the Declaration. Moving into his closing slowly, Lincoln stated, "Now, it happens that we meet together once every year, sometime about the 4th of July, for some reason or other." What was this reason? Contrasting the levels of size, strength, and prosperity between the United States in 1776 and his own time, Lincoln continued his ruminations on the meaning of the memory of the revolutionary generation:

> We find a race of men living in that day whom we claim as our fathers and grandfathers; they were iron men, they fought for the principle that they were contending for. We hold this annual celebration to remind ourselves of all the good done in this process of time of how it was done and who did it, and how we are historically connected with it; and we go from these meetings in better humor with ourselves—we feel more attached the one to the other, and more firmly bound to the country we inhabit.

Many Americans in 1858 were directly connected by blood to this race of iron men who heroically fought for the principle that they were contending for. This naturally leads to the questions "What principle did they fight for?" and "What about the people not connected to this race of heroes by blood?" Lincoln continued:

> We have . . . among us perhaps half our people who are not descendants at all of these men, they are men who have come from Europe—German, Irish, French and Scandinavian—men that have come from Europe themselves, or whose ancestors have come hither and settled here, finding themselves our equals in all things. If they look back through this history to trace their connection with those days by blood, they find they have none, they cannot carry themselves back into that glorious epoch and make themselves feel that they are part of us, but when they look through that old Declaration of Independence they find that those old men say that "We hold these truths to be self-evident, that all men are created equal," and then they feel that that moral sentiment taught in that day evidences their relation to those men, that it is the father of all moral principle in them, and that they have a right to claim it as though they were blood of the blood, and flesh of the flesh of the men who wrote that Declaration, and so they are. That is the electric cord in that Declaration that links the hearts of patriotic and liberty-loving men together, that will link those patriotic hearts as long as the love of freedom exists in the minds of men throughout the world.[27]

For Lincoln, the Revolution was revolutionary; it was fought for the rights of all men for all coming time. To be a true American does not mean to be a member of a certain race or ethnicity but rather to be committed to the simple idea of the dignity of all men. Lincoln expressed his belief that the heritage of America could be treasured by all, no matter where they came from or who their ancestors were.

He then warned his audience that the inevitable outcome of diluting the message of the Declaration to mean that only the British subjects of 1776 were created equal would be to "rub out the sentiment of liberty in the country." According to Lincoln,

> They are the arguments that kings have made for enslaving the people in all ages of the world. You will find that all the arguments in favor of king-craft were of this class; they always bestrode the necks of the people, not that they wanted to do it, but because the people were better off for being ridden. That is their argument, and this argument of the Judge is the same old serpent that says you work and I eat, you toil and I will enjoy the fruits of it. Turn in whatever way you will—whether it come from the mouth of a King, an excuse for enslaving the people of his country, or from the mouth of men of one race as a reason for enslaving the men of another race, it is all the same old serpent, and I hold if that course of argumentation that is made for the purpose of convincing the public mind that we should not care about this, should be granted, it does not stop with the negro. I should like to know if taking this old Declaration of Independence, which declares that all men are equal upon principle and making exceptions to it where will it stop. If one man says it does not mean a negro, why not another say it does not mean some other man?[28]

Unlike Calhoun, Lincoln professed that the surest way Americans could guarantee their rights was not by perpetuating the enslavement of one class of men based on race but rather by cherishing the best of the values expressed in the Declaration.

Using the wisdom of the Bible, Lincoln quoted Matthew 5:48 and admonished his audience, "As your Father in Heaven is perfect, be ye also perfect." Lincoln acknowledged that no mortal could achieve perfection, but that was nevertheless the standard set up for Christians, and so should be the standard for Americans. For Lincoln, this meant, "In relation to the principle that all men are created equal, let it be as nearly reached as we can. If we cannot give freedom to every creature, let us do nothing that will impose slavery upon any other creature."[29]

Lincoln concluded not with his hope in the relatively modest goal that they would put slavery onto the course of ultimate extinction but rather with a bold vision of the total equality among the races. In a statement he would later walk back in subsequent speeches during the campaign, he proclaimed, "Let us discard all this quibbling about this man and the other man—this race and that race and the other race being inferior, and therefore they must be placed in an inferior position—discarding our standard that we have left us. Let us discard all these things, and unite as one people throughout this land, until we shall once more stand up declaring that all men are created equal."[30]

In this address to Chicago, Lincoln made very little use of the study of history, instead making emotional appeals to common heritage and a collective understanding of the past. This set a pattern for the rest of the campaign. He had researched history and had delivered almost scholarly dissertations on America's past for years. Now he was to make his most impassioned appeals to national memory in his career. Something else begins to become evident in his 1858 Chicago speech. When Lincoln concluded, the reporter noted that "Mr. Lincoln retired amid a perfect torrent of applause and cheers." Lincoln was building a passionate movement with every speech he made. Earlier in the address, Lincoln told his audience that he would attempt to quote a portion of this "House Divided" speech from memory. After he concluded his quotation, an audience member interjected, "That's the very language."[31] Not only was Lincoln making appeals to memory of the past; he was now beginning to shape the memory of the past.

July 17 Springfield Speech

"If you conscientiously believe that his principles are more in harmony with the feelings of the American people and the interests and honor of the Republic, elect him. If, on the contrary, you believe that my principles are more consistent with those great principles upon which our fathers framed this Government, then I shall ask you to so express your opinion at the polls."[32] Thus spoke Stephen Douglas to his audience in Springfield on the afternoon of July 17, 1858. Lincoln had been following Douglas throughout the state to take advantage of the crowds Douglas's fame naturally drew, and he delivered another speech that same evening. Douglas told his audience that they should support not the candidate with the most qualifications or best reputation but rather the one they believed had the most accurate interpretations of the past, a sentiment Lincoln did not challenge.

Much of what Lincoln argued that evening was a reiteration of what he had said earlier in the campaign: he defined key terms (when explaining the difference between a purpose and expectation, Lincoln said, "I have often expressed an expectation to die, but I have never expressed a *wish* to die") and quoted President Jackson when he argued that the Supreme Court's rulings should not be blindly accepted. He added a couple of new wrinkles to this address. Lincoln told his audience, "In public speaking it is tedious reading from documents." Yet he nevertheless proceeded not only to do so but also to cite his source, stating that the letter by Thomas Jefferson he was quoting from was "found in the seventh volume of his correspondence, at page 177." In this letter Jefferson wrote that to "consider the judges as the ultimate arbiters of all constitutional questions" was "a very dangerous doctrine" that "would place us under the despotism of an oligarchy." Jefferson, however, promoted the idea that all the branches should be "co-equal and co-sovereign." After citing another Supreme Court decision, the one that declared the National Bank to be constitutional, and showing how Douglas had worked against it for two decades, Lincoln argued that the real principle that Douglas stood on was not reverence for the Supreme Court. Rather, Lincoln said, "He is for the Dred Scott decision because it tends to nationalize slavery."[33]

Lincoln then noted that Preston Brooks, the South Carolina congressman who had caned Charles Sumner on the floor of the Senate, stated that the Framers did not believe slavery would last to their time and had worked towards its extinction, but because of the invention of the cotton gin, slavery had now become necessary.[34] Brooks delivered the address Lincoln referred to in 1854 on the floor of the House of Representatives during the debate over Douglas's Kansas-Nebraska Bill, a debate Lincoln had carefully followed in Illinois. In this speech Brooks admitted that many of the Founders, "men high in fame for wisdom and patriotism," spoke out against slavery, with some expressing their belief that the institution would not last. Brooks said that it was not surprising that men who had fought a destructive war for their own liberty would be guilty of "extravagances of opinion and of act" that were "dangerous." Victory brought the "intoxications of liberty," and it was only natural that wise men should form unwise opinions, believing "that the light of liberty . . . should have been reflected from the white to the black man." Not only did the Revolution make them delusional but they also did not have the advantage of the experience of the intervening years that men of 1854 then had. In this speech Brooks proclaimed, "It is worse than absurd to quote the individual opinions of any man against the institution of slavery which were expressed before those great staples which are now grown so abundantly in the South," had become so financially fruitful. The main reason why many of the Founding Fathers spoke out against slavery was because, at that time, the destruction of the war had "rendered property in slaves not only valueless, but an absolute incumbrance." The Founders could not have foreseen how an invention like the cotton gin, along with new circumstances, would make slavery so profitable. According to Brooks, "The times were propitious both to schemes of emancipation and to the entertainment of sentiments of pseudo-philanthropy." The Founders' statements against slavery, Brooks felt, should not be adhered to because they made them not out of an enduring principle but from a temporary interest. During the Revolution the perpetuation of slavery was not in the Founders' financial interest, so they opposed it, but now that slavery had become so lucrative, it was both necessary and right. [35] Lincoln would allude to this speech repeatedly over the next two years to show that Southerners were abandoning the original ideas of the Founders in pursuit of no higher principle than their own financial interests—or as he later put it, they do not "stand upon the basis upon which our fathers placed" slavery, which was the course of ultimate extinction, but rather they have "put it upon the cotton gin basis," thus perpetuating it as long as men possessed a financial interest in it.[36] Lincoln alluded to Brooks's speech many times because, as he learned in his readings of Greenleaf, a witness that testifies against one's perceived interests can be considered more credible than one that does not; the admission by the most ardent of the fire-eaters, the cane-wielding Preston Brooks of South Carolina, that proponents of the Slave Power were in disagreement with a majority of the universally revered Founding Fathers would meet this criterion.

Crisscrossing the Prairie State

While Lincoln tailed Douglas throughout the state, attempting to speak to the same crowds, Republican newspapers needled Douglas, implying cowardice on Douglas's part for not agreeing to debate Lincoln formally. Even though he had much to lose and little to gain, Douglas eventually relented. In addition to seven formal debates, they would crisscross the state, each man delivering several dozen speeches between July and November. Douglas traveled the new railroads in a private car (possibly provided free of charge by the vice president of the Illinois Central Railroad, George McClellan) stocked with liquor and a booming cannon to announce his arrival in town. Lincoln, conversely, traveled in regular cars with ordinary passengers.[37]

Carl Schurz, a leader of the failed 1848 revolution in Germany and an immigrant living in Wisconsin, vividly recounted first meeting Lincoln

on one of these train cars and the general atmosphere these debates produced. Schurz became a leader of the German American community,
an important demographic group as thousands migrated after the failed
uprising. The Republican State Committee invited Schurz to campaign
on Lincoln's behalf. Schurz recalled:

> All at once, after the train had left a way station, I observed a great com-
> motion among my fellow-passengers, many of whom jumped from their
> seats and pressed eagerly around a tall man who had just entered the
> car. They addressed him in the most familiar style: "Hello, Abe! How
> are you?" and so on. And he responded in the same manner: "Good-
> evening, Ben! How are you, Joe? Glad to see you, Dick!" and there was
> much laughter at some things he said.

After a lengthy description of Lincoln's appearance, Schurz wrote that he
had never seen someone who looked "so uncouth, not to say grotesque."
After several minutes of shaking hands in the crowded car, Lincoln was
introduced to Schurz and sat down next to him. Schurz recalled, "He
received me with an off-hand cordiality, like an old acquaintance. In a
somewhat high-pitched but pleasant voice he began to talk to me, telling me much about the points he and Douglas had made in the debates
at different places, and about those he intended to make." Schurz felt
flattered by the attention and remembered:

> When, in a tone of perfect ingenuousness, he asked me—a young begin-
> ner in politics—what I thought about this and that, I should have felt
> myself very much honored by his confidence, had he permitted me to
> regard him as a great man. But he talked in so simple and familiar a
> strain, and his manner and homely phrase were so absolutely free from
> any semblance of self-consciousness or pretension to superiority, that I
> soon felt as if I had known him all my life and we had long been close
> friends. He interspersed our conversation with all sorts of quaint stories,
> each of which had a witty point applicable to the subject in hand, and
> not seldom concluding an argument in such a manner that nothing more
> was to be said. He seemed to enjoy his own jests in a childlike way, for
> his unusually sad-looking eyes would kindle with a merry twinkle, and
> he himself led in the laughter; and his laugh was so genuine, hearty, and
> contagious that nobody could fail to join in it.

They arrived the night before a debate, and Schurz recalled the tumult
they witnessed when they exited the train: "The blare of brass bands and
the shouts of enthusiastic, and not in all cases quite sober, Democrats
and Republicans, cheering and hurrahing for their respective champions,
did not cease until the small hours." The next morning there was an almost carnival-like atmosphere:

The country people began to stream into town for the great meeting, some singly, on foot or on horseback, or small parties of men and women, and even children, in buggies or farm wagons; while others were marshaled in solemn procession from outlying towns or districts with banners and drums, many of them headed by maidens in white with tricolored scarfs, who represented the Goddess of Liberty and the different States of the Union, and whose beauty was duly admired by everyone, including themselves.

Even though it was a heated campaign about the most serious issues, "the crowds remained very good-natured, and the occasional jibes flung from one side to the other were uniformly received with a laugh." Schurz, who fled autocratic Prussia, reveled in this newfound democratic atmosphere.[38]

The Lincoln-Douglas debates have lived on in memory as the most famous debates in American history, and justly so. The excitement of the crowds and the thrust and parry of the competitors brought a sense of urgency and excitement, while the issues they discussed cut to the core of the American experiment. In each of the seven formal debates and the dozens of speeches interspersed throughout the campaign, Lincoln repeated many of the same arguments about the past that he had been making since his Springfield speech in 1854 that do not bear repeating. However, in each of these debates there was a flicker of something new, sometimes based on prior research. Mostly we see him crafting and recrafting his emotional appeals to the past.

Ottawa

Lincoln and Douglas held their first joint debate on August 21 in Ottawa, a newly settled town in north-central Illinois at the confluence of the Fox and Illinois rivers. Lincoln had tramped through there in what had been wilderness more than a quarter century earlier when he was part of the Illinois militia during the Black Hawk War. One of the dignitaries on stage with Lincoln and Douglas was Chief Shabbona, a warrior of the Ottawa Tribe who had warned White settlers of impending attacks during the war and was one of the few Native Americans to remain in northern Illinois in the 1850s. Also on stage was Lincoln's friend and political ally Owen Lovejoy of Princeton, who now represented Ottawa's congressional district.

In his speech Douglas attacked Lincoln's "house divided" metaphor. Lincoln quipped that if Douglas disagreed with him, then the point of contention was not between the two of them "but between the Judge and an authority of a somewhat higher character." Lincoln acknowledged that

Douglas might not disagree with the maxim but rather how Lincoln applied it, arguing that the house really was not divided. Lincoln agreed that there were many differences between the states that frequently helped unite the country, as some states could produce goods that other states were lacking. Lincoln then asked, "But can this question of slavery be considered as among *these* varieties in the institutions of the country?" Alluding to the ancient Greek myth of Eris and the golden apple that caused a disagreement that eventually led to the Trojan War, Lincoln argued that slavery had always been an "apple of discord" that threatened the Union. He then asked rhetorically if slavery would continue to bring division after their generation passed away and asserted that it always would so long as it existed, thus proving his application of the metaphor correct. Lincoln argued, as he did in earlier speeches, that the Union survived thus far not because the division of free and slave states provided a stable equilibrium but rather because they treated slavery as a bad thing that they supposedly put on the course of its ultimate extinction. Lincoln argued, "Now, I believe if we could arrest the spread, and place it where Washington, and Jefferson, and Madison placed it, it *would be* in the course of ultimate extinction, and the public mind *would*, as for eighty years past, believe that it was in the course of ultimate extinction."[39] Here Lincoln used wisdom derived both from the Bible and the past to promote a course for the future.

After making the same arguments that he had made in earlier speeches about how Presidents Jefferson and Jackson did not believe the Supreme Court was the sole authority on what was constitutional, Lincoln introduced a new argument to show that Douglas did not also treat judicial decisions to be sacred. Lincoln noted that they could find this story in *A History of Illinois*, one of the few history books he ever cited. It was written by a former governor of Illinois, Thomas Ford, and much of what he wrote was based on his personal experience. Lincoln accurately recounted how more than a decade earlier, Democrats in Illinois disagreed with a decision of the state supreme court; so they packed it with Democrats like Douglas so that they could overturn it, and that happened to be how Stephen Douglas earned the title "judge."[40] Douglas claimed, according to Lincoln, that if Republicans now supported the nomination of justices who would overturn the Dred Scott decision, the Republicans would politicize the court and make it "prostituted." Lincoln quipped, "You know best, Judge; you have been through the mill."[41]

The crowd loved this type of humor, and they erupted in laughter after a heckler interrupted Lincoln to demand that he talk about someone other than Dred Scott: "Yes; no doubt you want to hear something that don't hurt."[42]

More seriously, Lincoln explained why he believed Douglas's words were more dangerous than his legislation. Lincoln argued, "In this and like communities, public sentiment is everything. With public sentiment, nothing can fail; without it nothing can succeed. Consequently he who moulds public sentiment, goes deeper than he who enacts statutes or pronounces decisions. He makes statutes and decisions possible or impossible to be executed."[43] Lincoln believed Douglas was the more dangerous form of politician because he tried to dilute their heritage and make slavery palatable and thus perpetual.

Lincoln scorned Douglas's attempt to portray himself as the true successor to Henry Clay, Lincoln's "beau ideal of a statesman." As he had done in earlier speeches, he quoted from memory his favorite lines from Clay about those who would dilute the statement of rights in the Declaration of Independence. Douglas, according to Lincoln, was not only not a statesman in the mold of Henry Clay but rather the type of demagogue Clay warned people about:

> To my thinking, Judge Douglas is, by his example and vast influence, doing that very thing in this community, when he says that the negro has nothing in the Declaration of Independence. Clay plainly understood the contrary. Judge Douglas is going back to the era of our Revolution, and to the extent of his ability, muzzling the cannon which thunders its annual joyous return. When he invites any people willing to have slavery, to establish it, he is blowing out the moral lights around us. When he says he "cares not whether slavery is voted down or voted up,"—that it is a sacred right of self government—he is in my judgment penetrating the human soul and eradicating the light of reason and the love of liberty in this American people.[44]

For Lincoln, Americans must draw wisdom and inspiration from the past if they want to protect everything they hold dear in their heritage.

Freeport

The second debate was on August 27 in the extreme northern edge of the state in Freeport. This debate is mainly remembered for the fact that Lincoln got Douglas to say in front of reporters what he had said before— namely, that territories had the lawful right to exclude slavery if they chose (a policy that contradicted Chief Justice Taney's opinion in the Dred Scott decision, an opinion Douglas also publicly supported). This was significant because his words would then travel throughout the country because of the national interest in the debates and because the debate between popular sovereignty versus the absolute right to own property in men was an issue that threatened to divide the Democratic Party.

This debate is important for understanding how Lincoln used the past because of how Lincoln reacted to a historical error Douglas made in the first debate. In Ottawa Douglas read a series of radical (for that time) resolutions from a document and accused Lincoln of drafting them at a meeting in Springfield in 1854. Lincoln denied the accusation because he was not at that meeting and was unfamiliar with the resolutions. It was true that a group of Republicans met in Springfield in 1854 and passed a series of resolutions, but the ones Douglas read in Ottawa were not the same ones. In the six days after the debate, the press discovered and reported that those resolutions had not been passed in Springfield but rather at an obscure meeting in Aurora, more than 150 miles away.[45] After pointing out the specifics of the error, Lincoln proclaimed that it was "most extraordinary" that someone of Douglas's station and fame would "venture upon the assertion of that which the slightest investigation would have shown him to be wholly false." What made this even "more extraordinary," Lincoln said, is that Douglas was "in the habit, in almost all the speeches he makes, of charging falsehood upon his adversaries."[46] Lincoln, no doubt, made mistakes about the past, but he always fought against the idea that power matters more than truth when discussing history.

Edwardsville: Liberty is the Heritage of All Men

Lincoln crisscrossed the center of the state between his second and third debates, delivering several addresses, some preserved by traveling stenographers. The best of these was his September 11 speech in Edwardsville, thirteen miles southeast of Alton above the broad Mississippi flood plain. Before the coming of the railroads, Edwardsville was connected to Springfield by the Edwards Trace, one of the old paths that wound through forests and prairies linking distant communities throughout the state. Even though it was relatively old by Illinois standards, Edwardsville was still a small, agrarian community.

At the beginning of the speech, Lincoln told his audience that a man in their town had asked him to explain the difference between Republicans and Democrats. Lincoln professed that he believed the question to be a good one and, always a stickler for clarity, explained his views: "The difference between the Republican and the Democratic parties on the leading issue of this contest, as I understand it, is, that the former consider slavery a moral, social and political wrong, while the latter *do not* consider it either a moral, social or political wrong." All the dis-agreements and strife boiled down to one issue: Republicans thought slavery wrong and treated it as such, while Democrats did not and acted accordingly. They may have disagreed amongst themselves about tactics, but Republicans sought to restore the "policy of the fathers" and would "oppose, in all its length and breadth, the modern Democratic idea that slavery is as good as freedom."[47]

Some have claimed that Lincoln never used racial slurs in his public addresses, which is not true. When he did so after 1854, he almost always did so by paraphrasing or mocking the racial attitudes of his opponents, which can be seen in his Edwardsville address. He defined the term *popular sovereignty*, as he did in many of his earlier speeches, showing how he believed his definition was more faithful to the Founders' original intent than Douglas's definition. Lincoln then mocked Douglas, claiming that Douglas "discovered that the right of the white man to breed and flog niggers in Nebraska was POPULAR SOVEREIGNTY!"[48]

The point of this part of his address was not to denigrate but rather to affirm the humanity of African Americans, which Lincoln believed Douglas was attacking. Lincoln rebuked the ideas put forth by Justice Taney and Douglas that Blacks have no more rights than cattle:

> Now, when by all these means you have succeeded in dehumanizing the negro; when you have put him down, and made it forever impossible for him to be but as the beasts of the field; when you have extinguished his soul, and placed him where the ray of hope is blown out in darkness like that which broods over the spirits of the damned; are you quite sure the demon which you have roused *will not turn and rend you*?

In many ways, Lincoln had asserted that the arguments of masters to own slaves were of the same nature and principle of monarchs to rule men, and here was one of the few times Lincoln alluded to the fact that, just as men can rise up and overthrow monarchs, so too can men rise up and overthrow masters. Lincoln argued that it was in the slave owner's long-term interest to recognize and respect their common humanity. Lincoln closed:

> What constitutes the bulwark of our own liberty and independence? It is not our frowning battlements, our bristling sea coasts, the guns of our war steamers, or the strength of our gallant and disciplined army. These are not our reliance against a resumption of tyranny in our fair land. All of them may be turned against our liberties, without making us stronger or weaker for the struggle. Our reliance is in the *love of liberty* which God has planted in our bosoms. Our defense is in the preservation of the

spirit which prizes liberty as the heritage of all men, in all lands, every where. Destroy this spirit, and you have planted the seeds of despotism around your own doors. Familiarize yourselves with the chains of bondage, and you are preparing your own limbs to wear them. Accustomed to trample on the rights of those around you, you have lost the genius of your own independence, and become the fit subjects of the first cunning tyrant who rises. And let me tell you, all these things are prepared for you with the logic of history.

Seldom did Lincoln wax so eloquently in defense of universal liberty. It was the "love of liberty," not military strength, that was the principal guarantee of their freedom. With the ancient Roman and more recent French republics in mind, Lincoln argued that the "logic of history" shows how republican societies can be overthrown and ruled by a Caesar or Napoleon when too many citizens make a virtue of trampling on the rights of others. According to Lincoln, only by heeding the wisdom of history would Americans be able to preserve their liberty. [49]

Jonesboro

For their third debate, Lincoln and Douglas journeyed south to Jonesboro, which lay at a more southerly latitude than Richmond, Virginia. The extreme southern tip of Illinois was solidly Democratic. Douglas claimed in an earlier speech that when he mentioned that he was going to "trot" Lincoln down to Jonesboro, Lincoln trembled in his knees, needed to be carried off the stage, and was laid up for seven days. After Lincoln read Douglas's words to his Jonesboro audience, Lincoln quipped, "Now that statement altogether furnishes a subject for philosophical contemplation." After pausing for the laughter to subside, Lincoln continued, "I have been treating it in that way, and I have really come to the conclusion that I can explain it in no other way than by believing the Judge is crazy." He challenged Douglas to see if he could "set my knees trembling again, if he can." In another part of the speech, Lincoln claimed that Douglas had been repeatedly lying about another matter. Lincoln professed, "I have no way of making an argument up into the consistency of a corncob and stopping his mouth with it" aside from demanding evidence for the charge or that he should drop it altogether. [50]

Lincoln demanded proof and evidence for far more serious matters in this debate. For example, he reiterated an argument he had been making that the most significant cause of discord in America's past had always been slavery and that it always would be so long as it threatened to grow and spread. Lincoln professed to his audience, "Like causes produce like effects."[51] This idea was not new to Lincoln, and consciously or unconsciously, Lincoln was quoting from David Hume, whom Lincoln likely read.[52] Hume, an eighteenth-century British historian and philosopher, wrote in his 1739 *A Treatise on Human Nature*:

> The same cause always produces the same effect, and the same effect never arises but from the same cause. This principle we derive from experience, and is the source of most of our philosophical reasonings.[53]

While Lincoln did not quote Hume in his 1839 Sub-Treasury speech, Lincoln expressed nearly the same ideas when he argued that "what has once happened, will invariably happen again, when the same circumstances which combined to produce it, shall again combine in the same way," such as when "blast of wind extinguishes the flame of a candle."[54] In the 1858 Jonesboro debate, Lincoln cataloged the manifold ways the spread of slavery had been a source of discord in the country's past and predicted that it always would be in the future. Lincoln also echoed the title of Hume's *A Treatise on Human Nature* when asked rhetorically, "Do you think that the nature of man will be changed—that the same causes that produced agitation at one time will not have the same effect at another?"[55] Even though Lincoln knew that most of the people in his Jonesboro audience did not care about slavery, he believed that they cared passionately about the Union. Lincoln argued that the wisdom of history showed that the best way to preserve the Union was to stop the spread of the one thing that threatened to destroy it.

Charleston

On September 18 Lincoln and Douglas traveled to Charleston for their fourth debate. Located near the border with Indiana, this community was familiar to Lincoln, as he occasionally visited his family south of town. Even though Lincoln argued for the common humanity of Blacks and the protection of their natural rights, he gave his clearest and lengthiest statement on his belief in the social and political inferiority of Blacks in his Charleston address, which has consequently lived in infamy. He made his statement to ward off the attacks made by Douglas that a vote for Lincoln would mean voting, service on juries, and racial intermarriage for Blacks, ideas that were politically suicidal in the context of pursuit of statewide offices in Illinois in 1858. Douglas understood, perhaps even earlier than Lincoln did, that in concrete terms, protecting one's natural rights would necessarily entail voting and jury service to secure them and, for those who wished, intermarriage to enjoy them.

One theme Lincoln returned to repeatedly throughout his campaign and which became most evident in his Charleston address was that when Douglas talked about the past, he did everything he could to avoid the real issues by obfuscating and resorting to outright lies. For example, Douglas charged Lincoln and the Republican U.S. senator from Illinois, Lyman Trumbull, with conspiring to "sell out" the Whig and Democratic parties, but Lincoln demanded Douglas supply proof. When he did not, Lincoln taunted him, saying, "He didn't bring the record" to support his claims "because there was no record for him to bring." Douglas also accused Trumbull of forging "his evidence from beginning to end, and by falsifying the record he endeavors to bolster up his false charge" against Douglas. Lincoln demanded that Douglas specify exactly what evidence Trumbull forged. When Douglas failed to do so during his part of the debate, Lincoln asked his audience a series of questions:

> You all heard me call upon him to say *which of these pieces of evidence was a forgery*? Does he say that what I present here as a copy of the original Toombs bill is a forgery? ["No," "no."] Does he say that what I present as a copy of the bill reported by himself is a forgery? ["No," "no," "no."] Or what is presented as a transcript from the *Globe*, of the quotations from Bigler's speech is a forgery? [No, no, no.] Does he say the quotations from his own speech are forgeries? ["No," "no," "no."] Does he say this transcript from Trumbull's speech is a forgery? [Loud cries of "no, no." "He didn't deny one of them."] *I would then like to know how it comes about, that when each piece of a story is true, the whole story turns out false?* [Great cheers and laughter.]

Time and time again, Lincoln ruthlessly attacked Douglas's distortions of the past, and Lincoln told his audience he knew what Douglas was really doing:

> I take it these people have some sense; they see plainly that Judge Douglas is playing cuttlefish, [Laughter] a small species of fish that has no mode of defending itself when pursued except by throwing out a black fluid, which makes the water so dark the enemy cannot see it and thus it escapes. [Roars of laughter.] Ain't the Judge playing the cuttlefish? ["Yes, yes," and cheers.][56]

Here Lincoln the statesman exposes the true talent of demagogues and tyrants of all times and places: the ability to confuse others and hide who they really are and what they are doing. Lincoln always believed that clarity of expression and truthfulness of argument were the best ways to defeat demagogues and their lies about the past.

Galesburg

"WHITE MEN OR NONE" was the message embroidered on the dresses of a group of young women attending the fifth debate in Galesburg on the campus of Knox College. Located about ninety miles northwest of Springfield, Galesburg was Lincoln country, as antislavery New Englanders had settled the community two decades prior. Galesburg was also a stop on the Underground Railroad. Nevertheless, as the group of women attested, there were still plenty of Douglas supporters there.[57]

Lincoln used humor at Galesburg frequently to illustrate his points. Lincoln accused Douglas of recycling a "fraud" from 1854 used to get a Democrat, Thomas L. Harris, elected to Congress in his 1858 campaign. Lincoln told a story to describe what Douglas was doing: "As the fisherman's wife, whose drowned husband was brought home with his body full of eels, said when she was asked, 'What was to be done with him?' *'Take the eels out and set him again.'*[great laughter]" To those who failed to understand the parable, Lincoln elaborated: "Harris and Douglas have shown a disposition to take the eels out of that stale fraud by which they gained Harris' election, and set the fraud again more than once. [Tremendous cheering and laughter.]" Lincoln then urged his audience to check the Congressional records to see that his assertions were true.[58] Lincoln used the earthiest humor to bring clarity when a bare statement of facts alone would not do.

In the Galesburg debate, Lincoln opened a new line of attack on the Dred Scott decision and, as Lincoln saw it, Chief Justice Taney's misrepresentation of the past. Lincoln argued that the "essence" of the decision was to be found in the following assertion by Taney: "The right of property in a slave is distinctly and expressly affirmed in the Constitution." After repeating it to make sure his audience fully understood, Lincoln set about to define key terms by asserting that "'*affirmed*' in the Constitution" means "Made firm in the Constitution—so made that it cannot be separated from the Constitution without breaking the Constitution—durable as the Constitution, and part of the Constitution." Lincoln argued that if one accepts Taney's premises, that the Constitution explicitly guaranteed slavery, then nothing can be legally done by the federal government or state governments to restrict, curtail, or abolish that right. However, this argument is not logical because "the right of property in a slave *is not* distinctly and expressly affirmed in the Constitution." As Lincoln would argue in other speeches, quite the opposite was true, and the Framers deliberately and purposefully avoided using the word *slave* in the Constitution.[59] Lincoln had previously said that the Dred Scott decision was based on a false history, and he used the tools of the historian to clarify matters and give them wisdom for the present.

Lincoln continued to quote Jefferson and Jackson on the Supreme Court and Henry Clay on the Declaration of Independence, as he did in his earlier addresses. For the first time, he also added a new quote by Jefferson that he would return to in the future. After reminding his audience that Jefferson was a slave owner, he quoted him, stating that he "trembled for his country when he remembered that God was just."[60] Lincoln spoke from memory and got some of the wording but not the meaning wrong. In his 1785 *Notes on the State of Virginia*, Jefferson wrote, "Indeed I tremble for my country when I reflect that God is just: that his justice cannot sleep for ever."[61] Again, Lincoln challenged his audience not to be deluded by Douglas and used examples from the past to help illustrate his belief that slavery was wrong and must be treated accordingly.

Quincy

Lincoln and Douglas held their sixth debate on October 13 in Quincy, a burgeoning port city on the Mississippi. The crowd gathered to cheer on their champions in Washington Park, which was just three blocks uphill from the river and railroad station.

In Douglas's portion of the debate, he summarized his understanding of America's past, and he envisioned its future. Douglas proclaimed:

> If we will stand by that principle, then Mr. Lincoln will find that this republic can exist forever divided into free and slave States, as our fathers made it and the people of each State have decided. Stand by that great principle and we can go on as we have done, increasing in wealth, in population, in power, and in all the elements of greatness, until we shall be the admiration and terror of the world.

For Douglas slavery was never the real issue; he was an ultranationalist who saw nothing at all wrong with America one day becoming the world's "terror."[62]

Lincoln thanked Douglas for stating succinctly what he had been arguing Douglas really meant all along: "I wish to return Judge Douglas my profound thanks for his public annunciation here to-day, to be put on record, that his system of policy in regard to the institution of slavery *contemplates that it shall last forever*. [Great cheers, and cries of 'Hit him again.']" Since Douglas got the past wrong, he drew the wrong conclusion about the future:

> Judge Douglas asks you "why cannot the institution of slavery, or rather, why cannot the nation, part slave and part free, continue as our fathers made it *forever?*" In the first place, I insist that our fathers *did not* make this nation half slave and half free, or part slave and part free. [Applause, and "That's so."] I insist that they found the institution of slavery existing here. They did not make it so, but they left it so because they knew of no way to get rid of it at that time. ["Good," "Good," "That's true."]

Slavery had existed in the thirteen colonies for more than 150 years before the Declaration of Independence had been signed and in the world from time immemorial. The Founders did not decide to create a country that was half-slave and half-free as if that were the optimal condition, but rather, as Lincoln asserted, they limited what they considered a bad thing as much as they could without tearing the country apart. Lincoln proclaimed:

> When Judge Douglas undertakes to say that as a matter of choice the fathers of the government made this nation part slave and part free, *he assumes what is historically a falsehood.* [Long continued applause.] More than that; when the fathers of the government cut off the source of slavery by the abolition of the slave trade, and adopted a system of restricting it from the new Territories where it had not existed, I maintain that they placed it where they understood, and all sensible men understood, it was in the course of ultimate extinction ["that's so"]; and when Judge Douglas asks me why it cannot continue as our fathers made it, I ask him why he and his friends could not let it remain as our fathers made it? [Tremendous cheering.][63]

Lincoln, who had researched the issue for years, decried Douglas's vision of the future because it was based on a mistaken view of the past. Lincoln and Douglas were battling over how the revolutionary generation should live on in memory because it spoke to their identity in their present and thus the type of future they hoped to inhabit. Judging from the reactions Lincoln was getting from the crowds, he was not altogether unsuccessful in this attempt.

Alton

The day after the Quincy debate, both Lincoln and Douglas took the same steamboat downriver and arrived in Alton at five in the morning on October 15. They would speak in front of the new city hall, which was just a few blocks east of the warehouse and printing press Elijah Lovejoy died defending two decades prior. The strain of the campaign was wearing down Douglas, who struggled with his voice to make himself understood.

Gustave Koerner, a prominent Republican from nearby Belleville who had not seen Douglas in two years, was shocked by his appearance. Koerner recalled that Douglas's face looked "bloated" and "his looks were haggard, and his voice almost extinct." According to Koerner, Douglas delivered a good speech, but it could only be heard by "a very small circle immediately near him." While Douglas was breaking down, as most men weary under the brunt of heavy labor, Lincoln was growing stronger, as a few men only really start pitching into it once the going gets tough. According to Koerner, Lincoln was just "as cool and collected as ever," and Lincoln grew more eloquent in this final debate than any of the preceding six.[64]

Lincoln started by remarking how much he enjoyed watching Douglas attack his fellow Democrat President Buchanan and hoped Buchanan would reciprocate. Lincoln said that reminded him of the story of a woman whose no-good husband was attacked by a bear. Instead of shooting the bear or getting help, she yelled out, "Go it, husband!—Go it, bear!"[65]

Much of this final speech was fought over the meaning of Henry Clay's legacy. Lincoln had quoted him in the Galesburg debate arguing that Clay believed Blacks were included in the Declaration of Independence, but in the intervening days, someone had written in a Chicago paper that the opposite was true. Lincoln quoted Clay's speech at greater length, explaining that it was delivered on the occasion when Clay was traveling through Indiana when he was petitioned to free all his slaves. Even though he said that he would not and that there would be many practical problems if there was a general abolition immediately declared, Clay stated that on principle, "there is no doubt of the truth of that declaration" that "all men are created equal" and "it is desirable *in the original construction of society, and in organized societies,* to keep it in view as a great fundamental principle." Lincoln quoted Clay's profession to be against slavery itself:

> I look upon it as a great evil; and deeply lament that we have derived it from the parental government; and from our ancestors. But here they are and the question is, how can they be best dealt with? If a state of nature existed and we were about to lay the foundations of society, *no man would be more strongly opposed than I should be, to incorporating the institution of slavery among its elements.*

Lincoln never attempted to prove that Clay was an abolitionist or that his actions in private always matched those in public, but instead that Clay believed both that slavery was wrong in principle and that Blacks were included in the Declaration of Independence. Furthermore, he added that, by Clay's standard, slavery should not be introduced into new societies. Under Lincoln's (questionable) interpretation, they could now apply this principle to new territories in the West. Lincoln proclaimed, "I insist that we have *his warrant*—his license for insisting upon the exclusion of that element, which he declared in such strong and emphatic language *was most hateful to him.*"[66]

Quite often, Lincoln used authorities from the past to bolster his argument, but he just as frequently used a unique mixture of both reason and passion to move his audience, such as when he displayed his thoughts on his opponent's idea that rights delineated in the Declaration of Independence were not meant for Blacks:

> And when this new principle . . . is brought forward, *I combat it* as having an evil tendency, if not an evil design; I combat it as having a tendency to dehumanize the negro—to take away from him the right of ever striving to be a man. I combat it as being one of the thousand things constantly done in these days to prepare the public mind to make property, and nothing but property of the *negro in all the States of this Union.* [Tremendous applause. "Hurrah for Lincoln."][67]

Lincoln then moved into a lengthy discussion on the Founders and Framers' attitudes to slavery. As he had done many times before, he argued that they limited the spread of slavery and banned the importation of new enslaved people for a reason. He asked rhetorically, "Why stop its spread in one direction and cut off its source in another, if they did not look to its being placed in the course of ultimate extinction?" He then detailed what the Constitution said about slavery and that it was no accident that the Framers excluded the word "slave" within it. Lincoln argued:

> I understand the contemporaneous history of those times to be that covert language was used with a purpose, and that purpose was that in our Constitution, which it was hoped and is still hoped will endure forever—when it should be read by intelligent and patriotic men, after the institution of slavery had passed from among us—there should be nothing on the face of the great charter of liberty suggesting that such a thing as negro slavery had ever existed among us.

The revolutionary generation, according to Lincoln, not only did not justify slavery but rather "left this institution with many clear marks of disapprobation upon it." Speaking of the wisdom that can be gained from the past, Lincoln proclaimed that "experience does . . . speak in thunder tones, telling us that the policy which has given peace to the country heretofore, being returned to, gives the greatest promise of peace again."[68]

Lincoln argued that slavery was not just threatening to divide the country politically but that it was a poisonous miasma, overspreading and rending social society. Lincoln asked, "Is it not this same mighty, deep seated power that somehow operates on the minds of men, exciting and stirring them up in every avenue of society—in politics, in religion, in literature, in morals, in all the manifold relations of life?" This was not the work of politicians agitating their constituents in order to get votes. This was the fundamental issue dividing the country, and they must address it.[69]

Lincoln then challenged Douglas, saying no statesman would seek to avoid the only issue that for decades had threatened to tear the country apart politically and socially. Douglas had claimed that he did not care one way or another if slavery spread into new territories and tried to convince Northerners to think likewise:

> This is the policy here in the North that Douglas is advocating—that we are to care nothing about it! I ask you if it is not a false philosophy? Is it not a false statesmanship that undertakes to build up a system of policy upon the basis of caring nothing about *the very thing that every body does care the most about!* ["Yes, yes," and applause]—a thing which all experience has shown we care a very great deal about? [Laughter and applause.]

A statesman, according to Lincoln, does not disregard experience but learns from it to lead the people. Lincoln knew that these would be his final words to the people of Illinois in the campaign, and he wanted to make sure they understood this difference:

> That is the real issue. That is the issue that will continue in this country when these poor tongues of Judge Douglas and myself shall be silent. It is the eternal struggle between these two principles—right and wrong—throughout the world. They are the two principles that have stood face to face from the beginning of time; and will ever continue to struggle. The one is the common right of humanity and the other the divine right of kings. It is the same principle in whatever shape it develops itself. It is the same spirit that says, "You work and toil and earn bread, and I'll eat it." [Loud applause.] No matter in what shape it comes, whether from the mouth of a king who seeks to bestride the people of his own nation and live by the fruit of their labor, or from one race of men as an apology for enslaving another race, it is the same tyrannical principle.[70]

Seldom did Lincoln reach the heights of eloquence that he did near the end of the Alton debate.

Conclusion

Once again, Lincoln lost. At that time, state legislatures elected senators and not the people by popular vote. Illinois elected more Democrats than Republicans to the legislature, and thus Douglas won fifty-four to forty-six. However, this vote did not accurately reflect how the people voted. Since the districts had not been reapportioned to adequately represent the influx of new settlers to the predominantly Republican voting northern half of the state, Democrats in the southern half possessed disproportionate power in the legislature. According to historian Allen C. Guelzo, even though Democrats won a majority of seats, Democratic candidates only received 176,325 of the votes in the state compared to 190,468 for Republicans. Although not a direct analog, this provides the closest measurement of the people's views on the two candidates because they understood these state representatives would be electing the next senator. As Guelzo dryly notes, "Oddly, it was the candidate whose gospel was popular sovereignty who would be reelected to the Senate on the basis of a popular vote he had, technically, lost."[71]

Lincoln was disappointed but not disheartened. He counseled friends not to grow despondent and that there would be more fights before long. He wrote to one friend about his campaign, "I hope and believe seed has been sown that will yet produce fruit."[72] From the audiences' reactions at the debates and speeches, it was clear that he was building a movement in his state that was by no means spent.

While Lincoln's 1857 Springfield speech shows extensive historical research, Lincoln predominantly used emotional appeals to the past in the largely extemporaneous speeches of his 1858 campaign. Even then, Lincoln's historical research is still discernible as he cited collections of public speeches and private correspondence, official records from Congress, newspaper articles, and even a history of Illinois. Lincoln made perhaps his most eloquent emotional appeals to the past in this raucous campaign, but in the following two years, he would return to the cool and dispassionate analysis of the past, delivering his strongest address using the study of history to a much different audience.

Chapter 6

Right Makes Might

LINCOLN'S ADDRESS AT COOPER UNION (1859–60)

Preserving Personal History

"I tell you that you are like Byron, who woke up one morning and found himself famous." These words were written by Charles H. Ray, editor of the *Chicago Tribune*, to his good friend Abraham Lincoln during the senate campaign of 1858. Ray was not reporting on the acclaim Lincoln was earning in Chicago but rather on how Lincoln's fame was spreading across the North, which Ray witnessed everywhere he visited on his way to upstate New York. Ray told Lincoln, "In my journey here from Chicago, and even here—one of the most out-of-the-way, rural districts in the State, among a slow-going and conservative people, who are further from railroads than any man can be in Illinois—I have found hundreds of anxious enquirers burning to know all about the newly raised-up opponent of Douglas." Ray wrote this letter to cheer Lincoln on in his campaign and to remind him of his earlier request that Lincoln write an autobiography to supply the desire of the people to know more about the man who had risen up to challenge the Little Giant.[1] While Lincoln would not write an autobiography during the campaign, his friends kept urging him to do so, even after he lost the election. Jesse Fell of Bloomington, owner of the *Pantagraph*, had a similar experience to Ray everywhere he went throughout the Midwest and Northeast. While he could answer their queries about his political career, he couldn't answer basic questions about Lincoln's personal life. Fell urged him to write a "private history," because he felt that if people knew more about Lincoln, he could be a viable candidate for the Republican nomination for the presidency in 1860. Initially, Lincoln rejected the idea, feeling it a useless endeavor. However, in the coming months, Lincoln began to believe that his friends were on to something, and he set his sights squarely on the presidency.[2]

Until 1859 almost all of Lincoln's writings about the past were about American history. However, there was now a demand for Lincoln's own history. He supplied this in two spare autobiographies and a collection of his and Douglas's speeches in 1858. These works of personal history in the years 1859–60 introduced Lincoln to a wider audience, and it was a speech he delivered in New York in 1860 about American history that made him a viable candidate for the presidency.

The two autobiographies he produced were especially short for someone hoping to reach the highest office in the land. Lincoln stressed to Fell that any biographies made from the first one must be "modest" and must not "go beyond the materials." In his first autobiography, he failed to mention his wife and children. In the second and lengthier one, he dedicated forty-one words to them and twenty-five to his mother, but 122 to a story from his youth about the tying of hogs' eyes shut in order to drive them onto a river boat. Lincoln, curator of his own history, included only the aspects of his past he felt would help his chances for the presidency, namely his boyhood on the frontier, his self-education, his becoming a self-made man, and his opposition to slavery. Likewise, Lincoln carefully preserved his 1858 debates with Douglas to be published in a book, stressing that Douglas's words must be fairly and accurately reported. Lincoln realized that his personal and political history, like his autobiographies, were beginning to matter nationally, and he took active steps to preserve and shape his history to advance his political career.[3]

The Dividing Line between Federal and Local Authority: Popular Sovereignty in the Territories

As the country was beginning to split apart, Douglas took the middle ground to attempt to hold it together. On one political side, he had Republicans who argued that the federal government had the absolute constitutional authority to forbid slavery from spreading into new territories, and on the other, he had members of his own party in the South who argued that neither Congress nor local territorial governments had any right to restrict their right to their "property." With his eye toward the presidential election next year, Douglas began planning an article he felt would justify his middle position of popular sovereignty. This article, published in the September 1859 issue of *Harper's New Monthly Magazine*, would be Douglas's lengthiest and most serious work of history. As historian Robert W. Johannsen noted, "Like so many others, both in his own day and in ours, Douglas was convinced that his position would be unassailable if he could trace it back to the Founding Fathers." And that is what he set out to do.[4]

When he had time to spare from his work in the Senate, Douglas diligently studied works of history in the Library of Congress, including Blackstone's *Commentaries* and George Bancroft's *History of the United States*. Douglas also wrote for additional help to Bancroft, who as a Democrat and Douglas supporter, was more than willing to do so. Bancroft replied that he could trace the principle of popular sovereignty back to the colonial era and argued that matters of emancipation "were always decided as the colonies pleased." He supplied additional documents for Douglas to use. Douglas also received help from his private secretary, the prominent Springfield resident Ninian W. Edwards, who happened to be Abraham Lincoln's brother-in-law.[5] While almost none of Lincoln's historical research has survived, the Stephen A. Douglas Papers at the University of Chicago preserve Douglas's notes and drafts, as well as historical reports and memos in several different hand writings (such as transcribed documents from the *Niles Register* and the *Documentary History of the American Revolution* by R. W. Gibbes; notes on Blackstone's *Commentaries*, Bancroft's *History*, and Jonathan Elliot's *Journal and Debates of the Federal Constitution*; a lengthy chart detailing changes in voting rights state by state; and various newspaper clippings), showing that this was indeed a team effort.[6] Douglas argued that popular sovereignty was the guiding principle of the Revolution and that slavery was always meant to be regulated at the state level. Reviews for "The Dividing Line Between Federal and Local Authority: Popular Sovereignty in the Territories," were mixed, but the *New York Times*, no friend of Douglas, praised Douglas's work of history, stating admiringly that he did "not leave the work of manufacturing a public sentiment in favor of his position to ingenious friends and elaborate advocates."[7] After publication, Douglas took his message on the road, arguing that his popular sovereignty was the true policy of the Founders.

Lincoln carefully read Douglas's article and the transcripts of Douglas's autumn speeches. He immediately began taking notes privately in preparation for speeches he planned to give in the coming months.[8] Even though Lincoln and Douglas would not be competing for a Senate seat, Lincoln had every reason to believe that Douglas would be a strong candidate to be the Democrat's nominee for president the following year. Lincoln knew that he had at least an outside chance at the Republican nomination; so Lincoln would not let Douglas's article and speeches go unchallenged. Douglas's essay was a deeply researched work of history, and Lincoln knew that in order to effectively challenge Douglas, he too must use the tools of the historian. In the final months of 1859 and the first two months of 1860 Lincoln gradually honed his historical arguments from speeches he had delivered in 1859 to carefully craft his greatest historical effort in his Cooper Union Address on February 27, 1860. According to historian Harold Holzer, Douglas's article and Lincoln's subsequent speeches over the coming months deserve, "to be recognized as the final round of the Lincoln-Douglas debates: Harper's vs. Cooper Union."[9] Lincoln, Douglas, and their contemporaries engaged in what later generations would call "History Wars," using the past to argue over what was the true meaning of the American project.

The Speeches of 1859

Lincoln challenged Douglas's *Harper's* article almost immediately, starting with an address in Columbus, Ohio, nine days after Douglas had spoken in the same city. Lincoln mocked Douglas's most recent statements on popular sovereignty: "His explanations explanatory of explanations explained are interminable." Lincoln then called his audience's attention to Douglas's *Harper's* article, noting that Douglas wrote that the first recorded instance of discord in America over the issue of slavery was in 1699. In the past, Douglas had tried to downplay the slavery controversy, but Lincoln, who had many times prior stated that history shows that slavery was the only true threat to the Union, remarked, "Now it would seem to me that it might have occurred to Judge Douglas, or anybody who had turned his attention to these facts, that there was something in the nature of that thing, Slavery, somewhat durable for mischief and discord."

Lincoln felt the most important problem with the article was that, while Douglas attempted to show that the Founders believed in his conception of popular sovereignty, he never addressed how they applied this principle to the spread of slavery into new territories. Lincoln reused several of the same arguments about the revolutionary generation consistently working to restrict slavery as much as possible that he had made about in earlier speeches.

He also brought a new argument, stating that while Indiana was still a territory, it petitioned Congress to remove the article in the Ordinance of

1787 that banned slavery, which Congress rejected. Although somewhat vague in this claim, Lincoln did note that "Mr. Randolph," a slaveholder from Virginia, rejected this petition because it violated the Ordinance of 1787. [10] Lincoln was correct in this assertion, because in 1803 Congressman John Randolph of Virginia chaired the committee in charge of responding to the petition, which they rejected, noting that they "deem it highly dangerous and inexpedient to impair a provision wisely calculated to promote the happiness and prosperity of the Northwestern country."[11] Lincoln could have added that the residents of St. Clair and Randolph counties, home to the original French settlements in southwestern Illinois and the locus of early American migration during the territorial stage, repeatedly petitioned Congress to remove Article 6 of the Northwest Ordinance banning slavery in the territory. This was in spite of the federal government's lack of enforcement thus far, and the petitioners complaining that many slave owners had crossed the Mississippi to Missouri where there was no prohibition. Their complaint was to no avail.[12] Had Douglas's popular sovereignty policy been allowed in Indiana and Illinois, they almost certainly would have come in as slave states, thus proving the value of the Ordinance of 1787.

As he had done before, Lincoln chastised Douglas for getting his history wrong: "Is it not a most extraordinary spectacle that a man should stand up and ask for any confidence in his statements, who sets out as he does with portions of history calling upon the people to believe that it is a true and fair representation, when the leading part, and controlling feature of the whole history, is carefully suppressed." Lincoln theorized "There are two ways of establishing a proposition. One is by trying to demonstrate it upon reason; and the other is, to show that great men in former times have thought so and so, and thus to pass it by the weight of pure authority."[13] He argued that Douglas neither proved his position by reason nor precedent.

The next day Lincoln delivered a speech in Cincinnati with many of the same ideas expressed the day before in Columbus, with the noted exception that he addressed specifically any Kentuckians who might have crossed the river to hear him speak. Fears in the South had been growing about what would happen if a Republican were to be elected president. Lincoln sought to allay their concerns by appealing to history, noting that they would be treated the same way they had been by Washington, Jefferson, and Madison. Lincoln followed up this promise of peace with a not-so-veiled threat that if the South attempted to secede and start a war, they would not be successful. He said that there was no doubt that Southerners were both "gallant" and "brave," but not more so than Northern men, and since there were more men in the North than the South, the South would fail in their attempt at "whipping" Northern men.[14]

In December, Lincoln traveled to the territory of Kansas and gave a more specific threat to those who would rend the Union. Speaking of John Brown's execution for treason after his failed slave revolt, Lincoln warned, should Southerners "destroy the Union" in the event that the Republicans were successful in the presidential election, "It will be our duty to deal with you as old John Brown has been dealt with."[15]

Invitation and Research

Lincoln's law partner William Herndon later remembered that, shortly after returning from one of his trips, Lincoln "came rushing into the office one morning, with the letter from New York City, inviting him to deliver a lecture there."[16] Lincoln had received a telegram inviting him to speak in the Brooklyn church of Henry Ward Beecher, the famous abolitionist preacher and brother of the author of *Uncle Tom's Cabin*, Harriet Beecher Stowe. He would be paid $200 for his services, and he would have the opportunity to address influential New Yorkers for the first time. Sensing a perfect opportunity to introduce himself to an East Coast audience just months before the Republican convention, Lincoln readily accepted and began preparing almost immediately for the speech he would deliver in February.[17] As he did in his Ohio speeches, Lincoln would focus on Douglas's claim that the Founders had supported his interpretation of his popular sovereignty policy. Lincoln would, however, thoroughly research the topic, which he did not do when preparing his Ohio speeches. He replaced vague and sometimes rambling and loose claims with specificity and tightness to his assertions. There was nothing new to what Lincoln was doing; rather, Lincoln's speech at Cooper Union in 1860 was the culmination of more than two decades of historical work, representing his mastery of the process.

From October 1859 to February 1860 Lincoln spent untold hours researching for his New York address. He was not without distraction, as it was during the same period that he traveled to Kansas to give a series of speeches, he was working to get his 1858 speeches published, and he was engaged in a busy and ever more profitable legal career. Unlike Douglas, he performed all the labor himself, spending every moment he could spare in the effort.

Although it is impossible to trace Lincoln's process and methods with any certainty, there is more testimony that survives about his research for this speech than any other one he delivered. Herndon recalled, "No former effort in the line of speech-making had cost Lincoln so much time and thought as this one." According to Herndon, "He was painstaking and thorough in the study of his subject" as he "searched through the dusty volumes of congressional proceedings in the State library, and dug deeply into political history." The source Lincoln consulted the most, according to Herndon, was Jonathan Elliot's *Journal and Debates of the Federal Constitution* (either Lincoln or Herndon owned at least the first two volumes), which included a large compilation of documents from the proceedings, the ratification process, and the aftermath.[18] According to Robert Todd Lincoln many years later, he had in his possession his father's copy of John Sanderson's *Biography of the Signers to the Declaration of Independence*, which he believed his father used in preparation for this speech.[19] When asked about his research after delivering his speech, Lincoln confessed that he did not preserve his notes. However, he wrote that he used an article in the *New York Weekly Tribune* that copied a particular piece of evidence from the "Journal of the Confederation Congress for the session at which was passed the Ordinance of 1787" that he could not find locally.[20] This source, an open letter by Horace Greeley, was likely both a source of information and inspiration, as parts of Lincoln's Cooper Union Address parallel Greeley's. At the same time, the opposite may also be true, as Greeley made some of the exact same arguments Lincoln made a month earlier in his speeches in Ohio.[21] According to the historian Harold Holzer, some of the other works Lincoln likely consulted were James Kent's *Commentaries on The Constitution*, Charles Lanman's *Dictionary of the United States Congress*, the *Autobiography of Thomas Jefferson*, *The Papers of James Madison*, Madison's *Debates in the Federal Convention of 1787*, the *Annals of Congress*, the *Congressional Globe*, old newspaper clippings, and Douglas's article in *Harper's*.[22]

After four months of work, Lincoln was finally ready to deliver his speech on February 27, 1860. Lincoln never labored over any other speech as much as he did this one. As Holzer writes, "With no researchers to assist him, no professional scholars to feed him documents, no secretary to take dictation, Lincoln sought his own 'access to history,' and, amidst the pressures of law and politics, the 'leisure to study it.' And now, armed with history, he was ready to answer Stephen A. Douglas one last time."[23]

Cooper Union

When Lincoln checked into the Astor House in New York City, he found out for the first time, by reading it in the *New York Tribune*, that he would not be delivering his speech at Rev. Beecher's church but rather at the Great Hall of Cooper Union in Manhattan. Lincoln had prepared his address for a church audience, and he now spent a day revising it to match his new circumstances.[24]

The morning that he was scheduled to deliver his speech, he fortuitously met George Bancroft in the studio of the preeminent American photographer, Matthew Brady. One witness to their meeting later recalled, "The contrast in the appearance of the men was most striking—the one courtly and precise in his every word and gesture, with the air of a trans-Atlantic statesman; the other bluff and awkward, his every utterance an apology for his ignorance of metropolitan manners and customs."[25] It is a remarkable coincidence that on the day that Lincoln delivered his greatest speech on history, he met the first great historian in American history. We can only wonder what ran through Lincoln's mind while he talked with Bancroft, but he may have wondered how his history would compare to Bancroft's.

William Cullen Bryant, the famous poet and older brother of John Bryant of Princeton, chaired the event. Many dignitaries were on the stage with Lincoln and Bryant, including Horace Greeley, founder and editor of the *New York Tribune* and perhaps the nation's most famous member of the press. Witnesses reported that Lincoln seemed nervous before the speech, and Lincoln later confessed to Herndon that he felt embarrassed about his ill-fitting and wrinkled suit. Lincoln began slowly and softly, too quiet to reach people in the back of the hall. His nerves eased as he warmed up, and his voice grew stronger. One eyewitness recalled, "pretty soon, he began to get into his subject: he straightened up, made regular and graceful gestures; his face lighted as with an inward fire; the whole man was transfigured. I forgot his clothes, his personal appearance, and his individual peculiarities."[26]

His speech can be divided into three parts, with the first one being an extended lesson in history. He started slowly, remarking that much of what he was going to discuss was not new, except perhaps his "mode of presenting the facts, and the inferences and observations," drawn from those facts. Lincoln introduced a statement Douglas made in a speech delivered in Columbus in 1859 that Lincoln would use to frame his own lecture: "*Our fathers, when they framed the Government under which we live, understood this question just as well, and even better, than we do now.*" Lincoln accepted Douglas's premise but disagreed with its implications. Lincoln turned this statement into his analytical question for the whole speech: "*What was the understanding those fathers had of the question mentioned?*"[27]

After clearly stating his question, Lincoln then followed the lessons of Blackstone by defining the key terms involved in his research. The "frame of Government under which we live" was the Constitution and the amendments subsequently added to it. "Our fathers that framed the Constitution" were the thirty-nine men who created and signed the Constitution, also known as the Framers. For Lincoln the question Douglas referred to as being understood by the Framers better than by those of his own generation was this: "Does the proper division of local from federal authority, or anything in the Constitution, forbid *our Federal Government* to control as to slavery in *our Federal Territories?*"[28] Thus, in order to answer his question, he must investigate what the Framers of the Constitution believed about the federal government's ability to regulate slavery in the new territories.

Lincoln argued that the best way to understand if the Framers believed that the federal government could rightfully regulate and restrict slavery in the new territories was to see how these Framers acted when they had the chance to vote on this issue. As Lincoln explained, "actions speak louder than words, so actions, under such responsibility, speak still louder." Lincoln listed a series of votes, stretching from 1784 to 1820, that regarded the national government's ability to control slavery in the territories, and he detailed how each one of the Framers voted on each specific issue.[29]

The first relevant test was the results of a vote in 1784 by the Confederation Congress, three years before the Constitution was signed, concerning slavery in the new territories. The bill before them would ban slavery in the territories then owned by the national government, which at that time were the lands north of the Ohio River. Three of the men who would three years later sign the Constitution, Roger Sherman, Thomas Mifflin, and Hugh Williamson, voted in favor of the ban. One, James McHenry, did not, but he did not leave a record explaining his vote, never stating whether he voted against it because he did not believe that the national government had the power to regulate slavery in the territories or for some other reason.[30]

The second test, in 1787, involved the same issue: whether or not slavery should be allowed in the territories north of the Ohio. Two members of the Confederation Congress who were concurrently serving in the Constitutional Convention, William Blount and William Few, voted to prohibit slavery in the territories.[31]

Neither the final document of the Constitution nor the records of the debates at the convention directly address the issue, and so the third test regarded the bill before the first Congress under the Constitution in 1789, concerning the enforcement of the Ordinance of 1787, which prohibited slavery in the territories north of the Ohio. The bill passed unanimously and without opposition, thus showing that the sixteen Framers who served in the First Congress, (John Langdon, Nicholas Gilman, William S. Johnson, Roger Sherman, Robert Morris, Thomas Fitzsimmons, William Few, Abraham Baldwin, Rufus King, William Paterson, George Clymer, Richard Bassett, George Read, Pierce Butler, Daniel Carroll, and James Madison) approved of the federal government's ban on slavery in those territories. This bill became law when one of the Framers, President Washington, signed it.[32]

Shortly thereafter, the states of North Carolina and Georgia ceded to the federal government the lands that would become the states of Alabama, Mississippi, and Tennessee. They did this on the stipulation that Congress would not abolish the slavery that already existed in these territories. However, Congress still believed it had the power to regulate slavery in these territories, and when they did, they did so with an eye towards further restriction.[33]

The fourth test came in 1798 when Congress organized the Mississippi Territory and banned the foreign importation of slaves into the new territory ten years before it was constitutionally allowed to do so in the states. It was unanimously approved with the Framers John Langdon and Abraham Baldwin then serving in Congress.[34]

The fifth test came in 1804 when Congress organized the newly acquired Louisiana Territory. In the part that would become Louisiana, slavery had already grown pervasive under French and Spanish control. Congress did not abolish slavery but strictly regulated it by not only banning the foreign importation of slaves into the territory but also setting severe limits on the ability to move slaves from other parts of America into it. The bill passed unanimously, with two Framers, Abraham Baldwin and Jonathan Dayton, then serving in Congress.[35]

The sixth test came in 1819 and 1820 over the controversy of allowing Missouri as a slave state. One of the Framers, Rufus King, consistently voted for the abolition of slavery in Missouri, while another, Charles Pinckney, voted against those proposals.[36]

After each piece of evidence Lincoln detailed, he provided a warrant to show that the Framers, in that case, believed the federal government had a right to regulate slavery in the territories. For example, after showing that George Washington signed a law that prohibited slavery in the Northwest Territories, Lincoln argued that Washington was "thus showing that, in his understanding, no line dividing local from federal authority, nor anything in the Constitution, forbade the Federal Government, to control as to slavery in federal territory."[37]

Lincoln then stated that these six cases were the only ones where any of the Framers had the opportunity to vote on the issue of the national government's power to regulate slavery in the territories that he had "been able to discover," thus providing a hedge to note uncertainty and the need for further research.[38] Tabulating the results, Lincoln showed that of the twenty-three who had the opportunity to vote on the issue, twenty-one voted in favor of the national government's power to regulate slavery in the territories. Lincoln noted that he had limited his research to the Framers who voted on that issue and argued that many of those sixteen who never had the opportunity to do so were some of the "most noted anti-slavery men of those times," like Benjamin Franklin, Alexander Hamilton, and Gouverneur Morris, and they almost without a doubt would have voted in favor of the federal government regulating slavery in the territories, while only John Rutledge of South Carolina may have voted against it. Through inductive reasoning, Lincoln had built up to his thesis for his section on history:

> The sum of the whole is, that of our thirty-nine fathers who framed the original Constitution, twenty-one—a clear majority of the whole—certainly understood that no proper division of local from federal authority, nor any part of the Constitution, forbade the Federal Government to control slavery in the federal territories; while all the rest probably had the same understanding. Such, unquestionably, was the understanding of our fathers who framed the original Constitution; and the text affirms that they understood the question "better than we."[39]

Lincoln had made this general argument in the past, but he had never supported it as thoroughly as he did with the research evident in this lecture.

Lincoln then proceeded to address contrary viewpoints. Some argued that the Fifth Amendment, which protects a person's right to property, shows that the federal government could not regulate slavery in the territories, while others argue that Tenth Amendment, which explains that all rights not given to the federal government belong to the state governments or the people. To counter these assertions, Lincoln applied the lesson he learned in his reading of Blackstone—namely, that if there was any confusion or controversy over the law, it was necessary to look at the original intentions of the legislators.[40] According to Lincoln, those amendments must not be interpreted to mean that Congress had no right to regulate slavery in the territories, because the legislators who voted for those amendments were the very same legislators who voted to enforce the Ordinance of 1787 that prohibited slavery in the territories north of the Ohio River. Lincoln asked his audience, "Is it not a little presumptuous in any one at this day to affirm that the two things which that Congress deliberately framed, and carried to maturity at the same time, are absolutely inconsistent with each other?" Hammering home his point with irony, Lincoln asked, "And does not such affirmation become impudently absurd when coupled with the other affirmation from the same mouth, that those who did the two things, alleged to be inconsistent, understood whether they really were inconsistent better than we—better than he who affirms that they are inconsistent?"[41] Lincoln used both logic and irony to prove that those two amendments were not meant to ban the federal government from interfering with slavery in the territories.

Lincoln ended this first section of his speech by discussing the importance of getting history right and the limitations of the lessons of the past. After spending so much time establishing the genuine opinions of the Framers, Lincoln declared, "I do not mean to say we are bound to follow implicitly in whatever our fathers did. To do so, would be to discard all the lights of current experience—to reject all progress—all improvement." Lincoln here was limiting his argument, stating that his generation must not blindly follow the precedents of the past. Lincoln continued: "What I do say is, that if we would supplant the opinions and policy of our fathers in any case, we should do so upon evidence so conclusive, and argument so clear, that even their great authority, fairly considered and weighed, cannot stand; and most surely not in a case whereof we ourselves declare they understood the question better than we."[42] This statement echoes Blackstone's *Commentaries*, which says that the people of the present must "abide by former precedents" because "we owe such a deference to former times as not to suppose that they acted wholly without consideration," only overturning their precedents when they were "most evidently contrary to reason" or "clearly contrary to the divine law."[43]

Lincoln would always be inspired by the lessons of the past but never imprisoned by its precedents. Lincoln then argued that any man had the right to claim he now understood the matter better than the Framers and supported their assertion with evidence but had no right to abuse the past to claim the Founders supported his position when a preponderance of the evidence was to the contrary. Lincoln argued that people have "no right to mislead others, who have less access to history, and less leisure to study it, into the false belief" that the Framers believed the federal government had no right to regulate slavery in the territories. When they do so, they are guilty of "substituting falsehood and deception for truthful evidence and fair argument." As he had done so many times in his political career, Lincoln here reserved his harshest attacks for those who manipulated the past to justify their political positions in the present.[44]

Lincoln then moved into his second part of the speech, and even though his primary focus was no longer the past, he continued to use the lessons of history to support his arguments. Like he had done several times since 1854, he used the rhetorical device of addressing Southerners, even though there were not likely many in his audience that night. Lincoln first criticized them, stating that people were not allowed to voice their opinions in the South on slavery unless they agreed with those of the majority who supported the Slave Power. He addressed the criticism Southerners had of the Republican Party—that it was a sectional party—by arguing that they had not changed in their primary view that the precedents of the Framers should be upheld, but it was the sectional Southerners who proposed to abandon this view. While some Southerners criticized Republicans because Washington warned about sectional parties, Lincoln noted that not only did Washington sign legislation limiting the spread of slavery but he also wrote in a letter to General Lafayette expressing his support of this limitation and his hope that one day all the states would be free. Lincoln claimed that Republicans were the true conservatives, and he invited Southerners to once again adhere to the spirit of the Founders which would cease their discord.[45]

He then addressed the claim of Southerners that Republicans promoted slave uprisings. Again, touching on the matter of free speech, Lincoln argued that even if the claim were true, slaves would never know of it because slave owners control what they hear. Southerners blamed Republicans for the raid on Harpers Ferry the year before, which Lincoln denied as none of the assailants were technically Republican Party members. Republicans, according to Lincoln, were not responsible for slave uprisings, and Lincoln alluded to the memory of the deadliest slave uprising in U.S. history, the Nat Turner rebellion, which preceded the formation of the Republican Party by more than two decades. It was not any agitation on the part of any party looking for votes that led to rebellions but the very fact that human nature finds the institution repellent. Lincoln quoted Jefferson's thoughts on the matter: "It is still in our power to direct the process of emancipation, and deportation, peaceably, and in such slow degrees, as that the evil will wear off insensibly; and their places be, *pari passu*, filled up by free white laborers. If, on the contrary, it is left to force itself on, human nature must shudder at the prospect held up." Lincoln argued that Southerners could defeat and break up the Republican Party but could never erase human nature. He proclaimed,

"Human action can be modified to some extent, but human nature cannot be changed. There is a judgment and a feeling against slavery in this
nation, which cast at least a million and a half of votes. You cannot destroy that judgment and feeling—that sentiment—by breaking up the
political organization which rallies around it." Lincoln, with what may
have been a veiled threat, argued that the party must not be broken up,
because then human nature would likely seek less peaceful methods to
express itself.[46]

Lincoln then moved to the Dred Scott decision, asserting that it did
not permanently settle the issue of slavery in the territories. Lincoln argued that there was a difference between a "decision and dictum," meaning that the Supreme Court decided that Dred Scott was still a slave but
could not restrict slavery from being forbidden in the territories based on
the opinion of only one of the justices in a divided court.[47] He then reused
many of the same arguments he made in his 1857 Springfield speech, only
they were now tighter and more precise. As he had done earlier, Lincoln
argued that Taney's opinion in the Dred Scott decision was "based upon a
mistaken statement of fact—the statement in the opinion that 'the right
of property in a slave is distinctly and expressly affirmed in the Constitution.'" Taney, according to Lincoln, did not argue that the Constitution
implied a right to enslave people but "distinctly and expressly" affirmed
this right. Following the lessons of Blackstone, Lincoln defined *distinctly*
as meaning "not mingled with anything else" and expressly as "words
meaning just that, without the aid of any inference, and susceptible of
no other meaning." According to these definitions, the Constitution did
no such thing as distinctly and expressly affirm the right to own slaves.
Instead, the Framers deliberately employed circumlocutions to avoid
using the word *slavery*. According to "contemporaneous history," the
Framers avoided using the term "to exclude from the Constitution the
idea that there could be property in man."[48] Although he did not mention
him by name, Lincoln was quoting the notes James Madison kept during
the Constitutional Convention in which he explained that he believed
that the Constitution shouldn't admit and validate "the idea that there
could be property in men."[49] Lincoln reiterated that the Framers, by their
actions, showed that they agreed with the position the Republicans now
held regarding slavery in the territories.[50]

Lincoln then concluded that by all appearances, the South was not
motivated by reverence to the Constitution and the precedents set by
the Framers because they were threatening to break up the Union and
defy the Constitution if they lost power in 1860. The South, according
to Lincoln, was not committed to any higher principle than power.[51]

In the third and final section of his speech, Lincoln detailed what Northerners must and must not do. Lincoln argued that they must not compromise on the extension of slavery into the territories. Some, he said, argue that if Northerners were to give in and allow slavery there, then the controversy would end, but this would not work because Southerners were demanding what Northerners did not have the power to give: the end of slave insurrections in the South. According to Lincoln, there was only one thing that would satisfy Southerners: "Cease to call slavery *wrong*, and join them in calling it *right*. And this must be done thoroughly—done in *acts* as well as in *words*. Silence will not be tolerated—we must place ourselves avowedly with them." Northerners must abandon free speech, snuff out any word of disapprobation of slavery, return all fugitive slaves, remove prohibitions against slavery in their state constitutions, and join Southerners in expressing their belief in the moral good, for both the slave and slave master, of the no-longer-peculiar institution.[52] Lincoln understood that the very nature of the Slave Power was tyranny and that tyrants will always see free speech as a threat to their power. Lincoln intuitively understood that authoritarians cannot be happy with anyone acquiescing to their authority while also expressing disagreement because that implies a legitimate source of morality outside of themselves. They cannot accept anyone remaining silent because silence, in their minds, implies dissent. Tyrants demand not acquiescence but affirmative approval and submission in both word and deed. Lincoln had a deep understanding of human nature, believing that anyone who demands not acquiescence or silence but rather cheerful obedience is not sowing the seeds of liberty but something else entirely.

As Lincoln had argued in the past, the biggest difference between Republicans and Democrats was that Republicans believed slavery was wrong while Democrats did not. Republicans could give in to all the demands of the Democrats if they thought slavery was right, but since they did not, they must not.[53] By appealing to morality, religion, common sense, and history, Lincoln made an emotional appeal to his audience to hold fast to their beliefs.

In Lincoln's peroration, he admonished his audience to take heed and act with courage because there was strength inherent in their values. Lincoln closed: "Neither let us be slandered from our duty by false accusations against us, nor frightened from it by menaces of destruction to the Government nor of dungeons to ourselves. LET US HAVE FAITH THAT RIGHT MAKES MIGHT, AND IN THAT FAITH, LET US, TO THE END, DARE TO DO OUR DUTY AS WE UNDERSTAND IT."[54]

According to one witness, when Lincoln finished, the audience "broke out in wild and prolonged enthusiasm," and the "cheering was tumultuous." Another witness recalled, "When I came out of the hall, my face glowing with an excitement and my frame all aquiver." Mason Brayman, another witness who knew Lincoln in Springfield, described the speech as "MASTERLY," a "triumph," and the reaction Lincoln received from his audience, he said, "might justly awaken the pride of any living statesman." Brayman, who had heard Lincoln's speeches at home in Illinois, marveled at Lincoln's transformation:

> It was . . . somewhat funny, to see a man who at home, talks along in so familiar a way, walking up and down, swaying about, swinging his arms, bobbing forward, telling droll stories and laughing at them himself, here in New-York, standing up stiff and straight, with his hands quiet, pronouncing sentence after sentence, in good telling english, with elaborate directness, though well condensed, and casting at each finished period, a timid, sidelong glance at the formidable array of Reporters who surrounded the table close at his elbow, as if conscious, that after all the world was his audience, on whose ear his words would fall from the thousand multiplying tongues of the Press.

The newspapers reprinted Lincoln's speech in full the next day, and he received laudatory compliments from them. Lincoln's address had an immediate effect on Republicans and non-Republicans alike. One editor remembered "that he made an army of friends at once," and that even proslavery men who hated abolitionists were telling him, "I like that man, if I don't agree with him . . . He doesn't make you mad as Garrison and Phillips do."[55] In his Cooper Union Address, a clear and crisp lecture, Lincoln was able to illuminate the lessons of history to both inspire and guide the public and help shape their understanding of the past.

Two men who had helped organize the event, Charles C. Nott and Cephas Brainard, decided to publish Lincoln's Cooper Union Address in a small book form. Not only did they send a copy to Lincoln with proposed stylistic changes but they also asked Lincoln if he had preserved his research in order to annotate it. Lincoln, pleased with the idea, wrote that he had not done so and that he did not have the time to redo his research, and he rejected most of the proposed changes. Nott and Brainard then set about to recreate his research and added copious footnotes to Lincoln's speech to provide further historical background on his assertions. They spent three weeks deep in research in the New York libraries and interviewing experts, including George Bancroft, to evaluate and delineate Lincoln's historical work. Among the manifold assertions

Lincoln made about history, the editors found two small errors: in one quotation Lincoln used the word "granted" when it should have been "delegated," and Lincoln asserted that Abraham Baldwin had voted for the Ordinance of 1787 when he had not been present in Congress at the time, and so the total number of Baldwin's votes in favor of the national government to regulate slavery was changed from four times to three.[56] Another likely error wasn't spotted until many years later when the historian Richard Brookhiser discovered that George Read was not in Congress in 1798 and that Lincoln probably confused him with another Read who was then serving, thus changing the number of times he voted to restrict slavery from two times to once.[57] However, none of these errors changes the total number of Framers who at some point voted for the national government's right to restrict slavery.

Nott found another potential error, but it was not until after the annotated speech had been published and Lincoln elected president that Nott notified him. Nott wrote that some had recently questioned the authenticity of a quote that Lincoln paraphrased in his speech—namely a letter from Washington to Lafayette, which Lincoln said was written "about one year after he penned" his "Farewell Address" in which he expressed his hope that all the states would become free states.[58] Nott and Brainard, in one of their footnotes to Lincoln's speech, gave the full quotation of Washington's letter to Lafayette along with another letter Washington wrote, this one to Robert Morris in 1786 in which he stated that he hoped for the abolition of slavery through legislative authority, which he would always vote for when given a chance. Neither Lincoln nor Nott and Brainard provided citations for these letters, but today Washington's letter to Morris can be found in the Washington Papers collection on the Founders Online website of the National Archives. The collection has no record of the supposed letter to Lafayette. Lincoln almost certainly first encountered this quotation in a newspaper, as it appeared in his local *Daily Illinois State Journal* and other papers throughout the North as early as 1855.[59] The Library of Congress owns one of Lincoln's scrapbooks from this time period, and in it there is what appears to be a newspaper clipping showing George Washington's quote, but neither its source nor its date is recorded.[60] Lincoln did not challenge the common understanding that the quote was authentic, but there was no fully accurate collection of Washington's papers then available nor did Lincoln have a team of researchers at the Washington Papers to contact to verify the quotation as researchers today do. Lincoln, in practicing history, was working within the limitations of his own historical context. Even though

the letter to Lafayette almost certainly was not legitimate, it would disprove neither the argument Lincoln was making here nor his overall argument because Washington expressed himself in similar terms in other
bona fide documents, like his letter to Morris. In a lecture of more than
seven thousand words, Lincoln made three historical errors and likely
a fourth, but none were as serious as the population error in his Peoria
speech of 1854, and none detract, disprove, or weaken in any significant
way his overall argument that a solid majority of the Framers believed
the federal government had a right to interfere with slavery in the territories. Despite its flaws, Lincoln's Cooper Union Address exemplifies
perhaps the best historical work possible in his time and place.

Nott and Brainard, in their introduction to Lincoln's annotated Cooper Union Address, praise Lincoln's work as a historian. They write the
lengthiest defense of Lincoln as a historian thus far:

> No one who has not actually attempted to verify its details can under-
> stand the patient research and historical labor which it embodies. The
> history of our earlier politics is scattered through numerous journals,
> statutes, pamphlets, and letters; and these are defective in completeness
> and accuracy of statement, and in indices and tables of contents. Neither
> can any one who has not travelled over this precise ground, appreciate
> the accuracy of every trivial detail, or the self-denying impartiality with
> which Mr. Lincoln has turned from the testimony of "the fathers," on
> the general question of Slavery, to present the single question which
> he discusses . . . A single, easy, simple sentence of plain Anglo-Saxon
> words contains a chapter of history, that, in some instances, has taken
> days of labor to verify, and which must have cost the author months of
> investigation to acquire. And, though the public should justly estimate
> the labor bestowed on the facts which are stated, they cannot estimate
> the greater labor involved on those which are omitted—how many pages
> have been read—how many works examined—what numerous statutes,
> resolutions, speeches, letters, and biographies have been looked through.

Many historians today may scoff at the idea that Lincoln performed anything close to the work of the historian, but Nott and Brainard, the two
who spent weeks attempting to replicate his research, did not. They pro-
nounced it a "historical work" that was "profound, impartial, truthful—
which will survive the time and the occasion that called it forth, and be
esteemed hereafter."[61]

What is striking is that even though he received no formal training
as a historian, he included in his Cooper Union Address many of the
elements that any professional historian would recognize and utilize
today. These include such aspects as defining key terms ("I suppose the

'thirty-nine' who signed the original instrument may be fairly called our fathers who framed that part of the present Government"), posing an analytical question (i.e., What did the fathers who framed our government think about the federal government's ability to control slavery in the territories?), answering that question with a thesis (a clear majority believed the federal government had the power to "control slavery in the federal territories"), supporting the thesis with evidence (twenty-one of the thirty-nine signers of the Constitution voted at least once as members of the federal government to regulate slavery in the territories, while many of those who did not leave a voting record on that topic likely would have since they were the "most noted anti-slavery men of those times"), addressing opposing viewpoints (some of his opponents believed that the Fifth and Tenth Amendments should be interpreted as limiting the federal government's right to restrict slavery), and providing hedges for his arguments (saying that his facts were based on the best information that he was "able to discover").[62] The Cooper Union Address was not an anomaly but rather a culmination of more than two decades of creating works of history to provide wisdom for the present.

Equally if not more important than process in the pursuit of history is product. The production of new knowledge about the past is ultimately what a historian is judged for, and the ability to enlighten the broader public with this new knowledge of value is how the historian best serves society. Abraham Lincoln utilized the tools of the historian not on some arcane or obscure matter but rather on the greatest question of that era: whether or not Congress had a constitutional right to restrict slavery in the territories. Better than any contemporary, Lincoln used the process of historical inquiry to craft the best reasoned, most conclusive, and most eminently influential argument on one of the most consequential political issues to ever test the American experiment. In spite of his limited background and all his prior failings, it was his effort at Cooper Union that, more than anything, made Lincoln a true statesman historian.

Effects and Aftermath

Harold Holzer, who has written the definitive book on Lincoln's Cooper Union Address, argues convincingly that this speech was essential to Lincoln winning the Republican nomination and then the presidential election later that year, in 1860.[63] Lincoln's 1854 speeches in Springfield and Peoria brought him prominence in the state of Illinois, his 1858 debates with Stephen Douglas brought him national renown, and his 1860 Cooper Union Address propelled him to the Republican nomination and ultimately the White House. In each one of these speeches, Lincoln made his arguments primarily about history. Unlike other men who have become president, Lincoln was not a general, senator, vice president, ambassador, cabinet member, or businessman; nor did he hold any powerful position that placed him in the public eye on the national stage. He won the office not by any of the traditional ladders to the presidency but almost entirely based on the speeches he made, and all the important ones were lectures on history. Perhaps at no other time would America's sense of its past matter more than during the ongoing conflict over slavery, as it was fundamentally centered on identifying the true principles on which the American experiment was founded. People of every political stripe looked to the past for wisdom, and it is only fitting that at that moment, they elevated to the highest office in the land the preeminent statesman historian of the era, Abraham Lincoln.

Conclusion

Many historians tend to think that the goal of historical study is solely to create as accurate an account as possible and usually abjure any political motivation. Many tend to believe that any attempt to use the past for political purposes or to attain power, either explicitly or implicitly, will inevitably corrupt history, and experience demonstrates ample evidence of people and communities manipulating the events of the past to support their own interests in the present. Throughout his political career, including at his Cooper Union Address, Lincoln scorned and combatted those who he felt were misusing the past in this way. He did this not by manipulating the past in a different way but by going straight to the original sources whenever possible, performing countless hours of research, and constructing accurate narratives for his audiences in his speeches spanning more than two decades. Lincoln spent so much time researching and creating accurate arguments about the past because there is wisdom to be found there that can only be accessed through truthful reconstructions and not willful manipulations. For Lincoln, there was an unrelenting, inescapable, and irrepressible power found in the pursuit of the truth about the past that can only be discovered through the process of history. As Lincoln eloquently puts it, "Let us have faith that right makes might."[64]

Chapter 7

The Mystic Chords of Memory (1861–62)

Principles of Southern Secession

Speaking on the floor of the House of Representatives on April 4, 1860, Lincoln's friend Owen Lovejoy began to say, "I cannot go into a Slave State and open my lips in regard to the question of Slavery" before being interrupted by Elbert S. Martin of Virginia: "No: we would hang you higher than Haman." When Lovejoy continued, William Barksdale of Mississippi interrupted him again: "The meanest slave in the South is your superior." What prompted these remarks was Lovejoy's fiery denunciation of slavery:

> Slaveholding has been justly designated as the sum of all villainy. Put every crime perpetrated among men into a moral crucible, and dissolve and combine them all, and the resultant amalgam is slaveholding . . . It has the violence of robbery, the blood and cruelty of piracy; it has the offensive and brutal lusts of polygamy, all combined and concentrated in itself, with aggravations that neither one of these crimes ever knew or dream of.

One congressman interjected that he must surely be joking, while the threats and accusations caused chaos on the floor of the House. Lovejoy did not back down, stating that Southerners could try and kill all the abolitionists they could, just as they "shed the blood of [his] brother on the banks of the Mississippi twenty years ago," but it would do them no good. "I am here to-day, thank God," he concluded, "to vindicate the principles baptized in his blood." Southerners might kill one abolitionist, but that would only inspire even more men to rise up in righteous indignation.[1]

Southern congressmen interrupted Lovejoy throughout his address, calling him "crazy," a "black-hearted scoundrel," a "despicable wretch," an "infamous, perjured villain," a "negro-thief," and a "nigger-stealing thief." At one point the reverend paused his speech and addressed them directly: "Now, gentlemen, I know you are in a mood to take a little advice. [Laughter.] I tell you I love you all. [Renewed Laughter.]" Congressman John McQueen replied, "I utterly repudiate your love." When Lovejoy finished his speech, Congressman Martin warned him "if you come among us we will do with you as we did with JOHN BROWN—hang you up as high as Haman. I say that as a Virginian." Lovejoy replied, "I have no doubt of it."[2] These congressmen were not content to disagree with Lovejoy or settle for name-calling; they went so far as to threaten the reverend on the floor of the House with a lynching.

Such was the mood of Southern congressmen before the election of 1860. Many promised that if a Republican were to be elected president, they would break up the Union, and after the election of Abraham Lincoln, that is what they set out to do. Most Southern men who served in Congress would renounce their vows to the United States and join the Confederacy, including Elbert S. Martin, William Barksdale, and John McQueen. After South Carolina declared its independence from the Union, its congressman John McQueen wrote that it was unconscionable to remain in a union with a people who "have chosen their leader upon the single idea that the African is equal to the Anglo-Saxon, and with the purpose of placing our slaves on equality with ourselves and our friends of every condition!" According to McQueen, Southerners must hold "sacred" the "memory of a common ancestry" so that "white men shall rule our destinies, and from which we may transmit to our posterity the rights, privileges and honor left us by our ancestors."[3]

South Carolina detailed its official reasons for separation when it issued the Declaration of the Immediate Causes Which Induce and Justify the Secession of South Carolina from the Federal Union on December 24, 1860. It cited the precedent of the Declaration of Independence, which states that a people can separate and form a new country when the old one no longer is living up to its obligations. It went into a lengthy discussion of the Northern states and their lack of enforcement of the fugitive slave laws. It complained that a man "whose opinions and purposes are hostile to slavery" had been elected president. Likewise, it bitterly denounced Northern states for "elevating to citizenship, persons who, by the supreme law of the land, are incapable of becoming citizens"; that is, Blacks.[4] Therefore, South Carolina felt justified in leaving the Union.

Not all the other states that seceded before Lincoln became president officially detailed their justifications for leaving the Union, but those that did listed similar complaints. The second state to secede, Mississippi, announced, "Our position is thoroughly identified with the institution of slavery—the greatest material interest of the world." Further, it justified secession because the North "denies the right of property in slaves," "advocates negro equality," and elected a man that "destroyed the last expectation of living together in friendship and brotherhood." Mississippi declared, "For far less cause than this, our fathers separated from the Crown of England," and now they will "follow their footsteps."[5] When Georgia seceded, it gave a lengthy history of wrongs committed by antislavery Northerners, including their refusal to return fugitive slaves and their fight to keep them from bringing their slaves to the new territories. Georgia argued, "[The] avowed purpose [of the Republican Party] is to subvert our society and subject us not only to the loss of our property but the destruction of ourselves, our wives, and our children, and the desolation of our homes, our altars, and our firesides." Therefore they must "seek new safeguards for . . . liberty, equality, security, and tranquillity."[6] Texas justified its separation by blaming Northern states for not enforcing the fugitive slave laws, for the restrictions placed on them from taking their slaves in the territories, and for electing as president a man who would bring about the "ruin of the slave-holding States." It criticized Republicans for "proclaiming the debasing doctrine of equality of all men, irrespective of race or color—a doctrine at war with nature, in opposition to the experience of mankind, and in violation of the plainest revelations of Divine Law." The society of Texas was to be based on the principle that "all white men are and of right ought to be entitled to equal civil and political rights." The Texans professed that slavery was "mutually beneficial to both bond and free," which "should exist in all future time."[7] These Southern states believed they were following the precedent of their fathers by separating from an unjust union led by a man they felt threatened to deny them the protection of their natural right to property.

For nearly a year, from May of 1860 when he was nominated for president until he took the oath of office in March of 1861, Lincoln largely remained silent. Lincoln did not publicly campaign for the presidency, holding to the precedent that candidates should *stand* and not *run* for office. After he was elected and the secession crisis deepened, he largely remained silent because any words he spoke would do no good, at least until he was invested in the power to properly back them up.

When he finally spoke, he had a challenging course ahead of him. At first glance, the secessionists seemed to have the advantage of precedent, because they believed they were doing nothing different than what the Founding Fathers, who were universally revered, had done. In his inaugural address, delivered two weeks before Lincoln would give his, Jefferson Davis argued that the Confederates were the ones who truly understood and were enacting the precedents of the revolutionary generation. "Doubly justified by the absence of wrong on our part," according to Davis, "[God knows the] sincerity with which we labored to preserve the Government of our fathers in its spirit" in drafting the new Constitution, with minor changes, because they "have a light which reveals" the "true meaning" of the original intent of the Framers of the Constitution. Likewise, Jefferson Davis argued that the successionists were merely adhering to the sentiments of his namesake in the Declaration of Independence: "Our present condition, achieved in a manner unprecedented in the history of nations, illustrates the American idea that governments rest upon the consent of the governed, and that it is the right of the people to alter or abolish governments whenever they become destructive of the ends for which they were established."[8] Complicating the task was the fact that Lincoln himself had, on the floor of the House of Representatives in 1848, expressed the same sentiments that Jefferson Davis did in 1861, stating, "Any people anywhere, being inclined and having the power, have the *right* to rise up, and shake off the existing government, and form a new one that suits them better." This principle, according to Lincoln then, was "a most sacred right—a right, which we hope and believe, is to liberate the world."[9] However, Lincoln saw nothing sacred or liberating in this new revolution. The reaction to Reverend Lovejoy's speech in 1860 in Congress showed that his opponents were not the great freedom fighters they had professed to be. Lincoln would now make the case that revolutions are not always just; there are some contexts when they are justified, while in others they are not. He would attempt to argue that this was not one of those times, that the Confederates were leading a great antiliberty movement, and that he would use the lessons of history to delegitimize the Confederacy.

Farewell

On the gloomy, cold, and rainy morning of February 11, 1861, one of the most unusual political gatherings in American history took place in Springfield. Lincoln was scheduled to depart from the Great Western

Railway depot at eight o'clock to begin his meandering journey to Washington. In contrast to the festive atmosphere that had seemed to accompany Lincoln wherever he had gone in Illinois during the preceding few years, this day's mood was somber, reinforced by a cold February rain. As hundreds gathered outside, dozens of friends and well-wishers lined up to shake Lincoln's hand as he waited inside the brick depot. Lincoln largely remained silent and downcast, and the journalist Henry Villard reported, "His face was pale, and quivered with emotion so deep as to render him almost unable to utter a single word."[10] The *Illinois Daily State Journal* reported: "A subdued and respectful demeanor characterized the vast assemblage. All seemed to feel that they were about to witness an event which, in its relations to the future, was of no ordinary interest."[11]

When it was time to leave, Lincoln slowly walked to the platform on the back of the train, shaking hands along the way. Lincoln removed his hat, and despite the rain, many in the crowd did so as well. According to the *Journal*, Lincoln "paused for several seconds, till he could control his emotions" and then proceeded to speak "slowly, impressively, and with profound emotion."[12] This short farewell address was the most poignant of his career:

> My friends—No one, not in my situation, can appreciate my feeling of sadness at this parting. To this place, and the kindness of these people, I owe every thing. Here I have lived a quarter of a century, and have passed from a young to an old man. Here my children have been born, and one is buried. I now leave, not knowing when, or whether ever, I may return, with a task before me greater than that which rested upon Washington. Without the assistance of that Divine Being, who ever attended him, I cannot succeed. With that assistance I cannot fail. Trusting in Him, who can go with me, and remain with you and be every where for good, let us confidently hope that all will yet be well. To His care commending you, as I hope in your prayers you will commend me, I bid you an affectionate farewell[13]

According to Villard, during his speech both Lincoln and his audience "were moved to tears."[14] The *Journal* wrote, "We have known Mr. Lincoln for many years; we have heard him speak upon a hundred different occasions; but we never saw him so profoundly affected."[15] After the train pulled off, Lincoln recorded his short speech and then sat alone, brooding silently.[16]

Lincoln had rarely appealed to his personal memory before in his political career. When the twenty-eight-year-old Lincoln had arrived in Springfield in 1837, he was nearly penniless, but upon arrival he was given a place to stay and befriended by Joshua Speed. Twenty-four years later, he was departing Springfield as the president-elect. Rarely did Lincoln acknowledge the aid of others, fashioning himself as the archetypal self-made man. However, here at his farewell he professed that he owed everything to "the kindness of these people."[17] Lincoln's attachment was not just to the people but to the place itself, and recognizing that he was leaving a part of himself behind, he emphasized that Springfield was not only where his sons had been born but was the place where one son was buried. Lincoln, who since his twenties had publicly questioned how much longer he would live, acknowledged that he might never return.

Lincoln briefly appealed to America's history, noting that his challenge was greater than any president's before him, including Washington. Few would have doubted him. Lincoln always looked to the past to light the path ahead. However, Lincoln was starting to realize that he was in a truly unprecedented situation and that he would need to rely more on the light of his own reasoning to guide him.

This speech is also unique because it begins to show Lincoln making more explicit remarks about God and faith. Regardless of the nature of his belief at this stage, Lincoln was beginning to acknowledge he needed aid because there were much greater forces at work.

The historian Ronald C. White has noted the contrast between Lincoln's first speech in Springfield, his 1838 Lyceum Address, and his last one, his 1861 Farewell Address. According to White, in 1838 "Lincoln had spoken of the lesser role of his own generation in relation to the giants of the revolutionary generation, of whom George Washington stood in the lead." As a young man Lincoln had feared that the revolutionary generation had already harvested the richest fruits of glory and that the most his could hope for was to maintain and transmit what had been gloriously achieved earlier. However, according to White, "By some unsearchable fate or providence he was being summoned to *a task . . . greater than . . . Washington*."[18] Lincoln understood that his future was fraught with peril. Still, he was beginning to recognize that he had the opportunity to live on in memory unlike any other American before him, including the greatest of the Founding Fathers.

The Almost Chosen People

Lincoln stopped at every city and many of the small towns along the way to Washington, delivering short speeches of a few minutes and some that could not have lasted more than a few seconds. Lincoln's difficult task was both to speak and to say nothing too specific about his plans. While these addresses were delivered mostly extemporaneously and are largely forgettable, a few do offer some insights into how he was interpreting his past as he was preparing to take office.

The same day he bid farewell to Springfield, he addressed a large crowd in Indianapolis. After quoting Ecclesiastes 3 ("there is a time to keep silence"), Lincoln, intentionally or not, broke his silence on the secessionists. After a short definition of terms and a critique of the secessionists' views, Lincoln returned to the humor of his stump speeches. Speaking of secessionists, Lincoln quipped, "In their view, the Union, as a family relation, would not be anything like a regular marriage at all, but only as a sort of free-love arrangement,—[laughter,]—to be maintained on what that sect calls passionate attraction. [Continued laughter.]" Then he questioned what gave a state—and not a county or any other like-minded community—a right to secede. He did not then elaborate on the principle, but he would explore it further in his inauguration.[19]

Lincoln delivered perhaps his best short address of this trip to the New Jersey Senate in Trenton, the site of a famous battle of the Revolutionary War. Lincoln recalled being a young boy reading Parson Weems's "Life of Washington." He said, "[Of all the events detailed in it], none fixed themselves upon my imagination so deeply as the struggle here at Trenton, New-Jersey. The crossing of the river; the contest with the Hessians; the great hardships endured at that time, all fixed themselves on my memory more than any single revolutionary event." He remarked that they all knew "how these early impressions last longer than any others." For Lincoln, it was not simply a good story, but there was wisdom to be gained from this memory. He continued:

> I recollect thinking then, boy even though I was, that there must have been something more than common that those men struggled for. I am exceedingly anxious that that thing which they struggled for; that something even more than National Independence; that something that held out a great promise to all the people of the world to all time to come; I am exceedingly anxious that this Union, the Constitution, and the liberties of the people shall be perpetuated in accordance with the original idea for which that struggle was made, and I shall be most happy indeed if I shall be an humble instrument in the hands of the Almighty, and of this, his almost chosen people, for perpetuating the object of that great struggle.

As Lincoln had been arguing for years, he believed that the War of Independence was more than just that but one for a higher principle—that it was truly revolutionary. These ideas truly existed outside of time; they were true for all people in all ages. Like the Israelites of old, Americans have a sacred mission, and they must not relent or lose heart and give in to their fears or short-sighted self-interest because they possessed the heritage of the *almost chosen people*. Later that day, he expressed his hope that this inheritance would be preserved peacefully, but he noted, "It may be necessary to put the foot down firmly." According to the reporter who witnessed the speech, "Here the audience broke out into cheers so loud and long that for some moments it was impossible to hear Mr. L.'s voice."[20]

Lincoln had another opportunity to explore the memory of the American Revolution when he spoke at Independence Hall in Philadelphia on February 22. Lincoln opened his remarks by stating, "I am filled with deep emotion at finding myself standing here in the place where were collected together the wisdom, the patriotism, the devotion to principle, from which sprang the institutions under which we live." He then expressed what the Declaration had meant to him: "I have never had a feeling politically that did not spring from the sentiments embodied in the Declaration of Independence. [Great cheering.]" Lincoln took comfort from the memory of all the dangers and tribulations the founding generation had endured and the fact that they were able to create something revolutionary:

> I have often pondered over the dangers which were incurred by the men who assembled here and adopted that Declaration of Independence—I have pondered over the toils that were endured by the officers and soldiers of the army, who achieved that Independence. [Applause.] I have often inquired of myself, what great principle or idea it was that kept this Confederacy so long together. It was not the mere matter of the separation of the colonies from the mother land; but something in that Declaration giving liberty, not alone to the people of this country, but hope to the world for all future time. [Great applause.] It was that which gave promise that in due time the weights should be lifted from the shoulders of all men, and that *all* should have an equal chance. [Cheers.] This is the sentiment embodied in that Declaration of Independence.

Lincoln was never moved by just the words of the Declaration of Independence; it was the principles behind those words, which embodied the revolutionary generation who had sacrificed so much for liberty, that he cherished. Lincoln closed: "I have said nothing but what I am willing to live by, and, in the pleasure of Almighty God, die by."[21]

In all these short speeches, Lincoln appealed to America's national memory, arguing that the country's heritage was so precious that its citizens must be willing to endure terrible sacrifices, including sacrificing life itself, to preserve it.

The Mystic Chords of Memory: Lincoln's First Inaugural

There was an element of uncertainty in Lincoln's first inauguration unlike any other in history. Seven states in the Deep South had already seceded, and the slave states in the Upper South were threatening to follow
suit. Since the government was unable to provide adequate security as
the president-elect crossed through the slave state of Maryland, Lincoln
did not arrive in the capital in triumph as planned but had to sneak in
under the cover of darkness. Secessionists and their sympathizers still
filled the city, and one could never be too sure about the loyalties of government workers. The city was filled with rumors of war, treason, and
assassination. Even some of those who remained loyal were dubious allies, like the man who would administer Lincoln's oath of office, Justice
Roger Taney. There were also many abolitionists who wanted to let the
Confederate states go so that they would no longer have to compromise
with them, and they could then live under a pure government free from
the stain of slavery.

Lincoln's first inaugural address marks a turning point of sorts for
Lincoln's use of the past, as it would be the last time that he would have
weeks to dedicate to research into a historical topic for an address, and
even then it was harried as thousands traveled to Springfield to talk with
the president-elect. When hostilities broke out, people would no longer
attempt to settle the disagreements between the North and South by appeals to history but rather by a call to arms, and Lincoln began researching methods of war and war tactics. However, he would never completely
abandon the process of the study of history, and he continued to investigate the past for guidance. In his presidential addresses, Lincoln showed
that he was inspired by multiple sources of wisdom, including history,
logic, analogies, and wisdom literature. His first inaugural address was
a perfect example of this.

Lincoln's law partner, William Herndon, recalled Lincoln consulting
Jackson's Nullification Proclamation of 1832, Henry Clay's great speech
on the Compromise of 1850, Webster's 1830 Reply to Hayne, and the Constitution in preparation for his first inaugural address.[22] While we have
numerous accounts of Lincoln spending countless hours of research in
the Illinois State Library, we only have one record indicating that he ever
checked out a book from there for his personal use: he borrowed the first
two volumes of the *Statesman's Manual* on November 13, 1860, just a
few days after being elected president.[23] These two volumes contained a
collection of historical documents that Lincoln certainly consulted, such
as the Articles of Confederation and Perpetual Union, the Constitution,

and Jackson's Nullification Proclamation. They also contain Washington's Farewell Address, which I believe was a source of inspiration for Lincoln's "First Inaugural" due to similarities in theme and language.[24]

His overall thesis is that the Union must be preserved, and one way he chose to support this assertion was with legal arguments informed by history. Lincoln asserted that "in legal contemplation, the Union is perpetual, confirmed by the history of the Union itself." This is true is because the "Union is much older than the Constitution." He first cited the 1774 Articles of Association, a document written by the first Continental Congress to bind the colonies together to get the British government to respect their natural rights. This Union, according to Lincoln, "was matured and continued by the Declaration of Independence in 1776."[25] He then cited the Articles of Confederation, a document that, when finally ratified in 1781, called for a "perpetual union" three times and stated the "union shall be perpetual" twice. In fact, the official title of the document is not the "Articles of Confederation," as commonly known, but rather the "Articles of Confederation and *Perpetual Union*" (emphasis added).[26] Then he cited the Constitution itself, one of the purposes of which was, according to its preamble, "to form a more perfect union." Then Lincoln argued that secession inherently makes the Union "less perfect" and no longer perpetual, and thus unconstitutional. Since he was taking an oath to uphold the Constitution, he argued that it was his duty to maintain and perpetuate the Union.[27] The historian Garry Wills, in his Pulitzer Prize–winning *Lincoln at Gettysburg*, notes that Lincoln was not the first person to make this type of argument. Supreme Court justices James Wilson and Joseph Story, along with the renowned lawyer and senator Daniel Webster, also argued that the people and not the states created the Union and that this Union preceded the Constitution.[28] Even though he critiques Lincoln's views of the nature of the Union before the Constitution was written and argues that Lincoln missed the most important point in his favor—that all understood in 1787–88 that a state could not unilaterally secede from the Union once it ratified the Constitution—legal scholar Akhil Reed Amar argues that Lincoln more accurately interpreted the Constitution than Jefferson Davis "by a wide margin."[29]

Lincoln also used logic and reason to argue that the Union must be preserved. Some Southerners believed the United States was not a true nation but rather a group of states bound together by a contract. Lincoln argued that if this really were true, then, like a contract, it could not be lawfully absolved without an agreement by all parties. Lincoln argued that there was a correct time and place for revolution—namely, when people are deprived of a "vital" constitutional right.[30] He argued that not only had Southerners not been deprived of any constitutional rights but his party had also pledged repeatedly to uphold them. Although he does not cite it here, he is referring to the same principle expressed in the Declaration of Independence: that people should rebel when the government violates their natural rights. Short of that, the Declaration states, "Prudence, indeed, will dictate that Governments long established should not be changed for light and transient causes." The natural rights of Southerners had not been violated but rather they lost an election, and Lincoln thought that was the very definition of a "light and transient cause."[31] If a minority can secede because it loses an election, it will set a dangerous precedent. If a state could secede because it did not like the results of a national election, what was to stop a county from seceding from a state if it did not like the results of a state election? This process of breaking up into even smaller political units could go on ad infinitum. Lincoln argued, "Plainly, the central idea of secession, is the essence of anarchy."[32] This principle, that a minority may secede whenever it loses an election, was not only a threat to the Union but to democracy itself.

Just as he had done in his speeches since 1854, Lincoln used the rhetorical device of addressing the South when his real audience was men like Stephen Douglas, his political foe of more than a quarter century who sat behind him during his address. As Lincoln rose to deliver his speech, he fumbled awkwardly looking for somewhere to place his hat. Douglas rose and said, "Permit me, sir," and held his hat during the entire address—an address that Douglas had worked so hard to deliver himself.[33] Lincoln promised to maintain the Union in his speech, but he would not assail the South. He vowed to protect their rights, including their right to own slaves, just as Southerners always had. Lincoln vowed there would be no war unless the Southerners were the aggressors.[34] "Good," "That's so," and "Good again," were Douglas's responses to Lincoln's promises throughout.[35] Using the same strategy that he had employed when he was a lawyer, Lincoln did not press every issue of contention but rather gave up all of them except the one that had the potential to garner the broadest amount of support: that the Union must be maintained. Even though Douglas would be in his grave in three short months, he spent his last few weeks on Earth drumming up support for the administration and its policies. Although Lincoln would always face virulent opposition from Democrats over the next four years, a majority of Democrats were prepared to endure terrible sacrifices to preserve the one principle Lincoln held fast to in this address. By limiting his objectives and practicing strategic patience, Lincoln was able to maintain the unity in the North necessary to successfully confront the secessionists in the South.

After his logical arguments using history and reason, Lincoln concluded by making an emotional appeal to the memories that united them. Although his primary audience may have been those in the North, his final appeal to Southerners to recall their truly common history was sincere:

> I am loth to close. We are not enemies, but friends. We must not be enemies. Though passion may have strained, it must not break our bonds of affection. The mystic chords of memory, streching from every battlefield, and patriot grave, to every living heart and hearthstone, all over this broad land, will yet swell the chorus of the Union, when again touched, as surely they will be, by the better angels of our nature.[36]

Despite all that had been said and done, Lincoln still expressed his hope that their common heritage would one day reunite the country. Here he was looking both to a past memory and a hoped-for future memory that would unite the country.

His words would not be heeded. More than anything, a single shot helped unite the North in a way that it had never been before. At 4:30 on the morning of April 12, the first shot rattled windows, echoed through the streets of Charleston, and reverberated throughout the country. This shot, fired by Confederates in South Carolina who were determined to deny provisions to the Union fort in the Charleston Harbor, was fired in a state that declared that its independence was dedicated to the idea that Blacks were "incapable of becoming citizens."[37] For decades the American people had fought a war of words over the meaning of the past. Now this conflict would be made up of something more than words.

Baltimore

More than two months prior, while still en route to the capital, the railroad detective Alan Pinkerton provided Lincoln with information that there were credible threats on his life when he was to pass through Baltimore on his way to Washington. While Maryland had not seceded, it was still a slave state and was rife with secessionists. Not only were men planning to form mobs in Baltimore to attack him but rumors spread that the authorities had also ordered the police to stand down, or at least do no more than look like they were doing their duty, should a mob attack the president-elect. Pinkerton proposed to Lincoln that rather than sticking to his published schedule, he should secretly board a night train so that he could pass through Baltimore unobserved. After listening to Pinkerton deliver his report, Lincoln sat in silence for a few minutes in contemplation before agreeing to the plan. After Lincoln delivered a speech to the Pennsylvania General Assembly, he, Pinkerton, and his friend and bodyguard Ward Lamon covertly boarded a night train to Baltimore in the early evening. They arrived there about 3:30 in the morning and secretly switched to a train bound for Washington. As they lay silently waiting for their train to depart, they were amused to listen to a night watchman bang on the side of a wooden building with his club for twenty minutes trying to wake up the ticket agent. Perhaps to alleviate the atmosphere of fear, Lincoln told several jokes about this in a hushed voice. The train pulled off at 4:15, and they arrived in DC at 6:00. When they stepped off the car, a man approached Lincoln and said, "Abe you can't play that on me." Thinking their ruse had been discovered, Pinkerton punched the man and would have done more had Lincoln not stopped him, explaining that this was his friend from Illinois, Congressman Elihu B. Washburne.[38]

Things did not improve in Baltimore after hostilities began. After Lincoln called for seventy-five thousand volunteers to put down the rebellion, Virginia, Arkansas, North Carolina, and Tennessee seceded. Before the troops arrived, the capital lay virtually defenseless, surrounded on three sides by the restive Maryland and by Confederate Virginia on the fourth. To reach Washington the troops faced the same problem as Lincoln, the only rail link to that city from the North was through Baltimore. The Sixth Massachusetts Volunteer Infantry arrived on April 19 and had to switch trains just as Lincoln had done. When word spread that there were Yankees in the city, an angry mob gathered and began throwing stones and bricks at the Massachusetts men. The city authorities were either unwilling or unable to restrain them. The fully armed volunteers opened fire, and twelve civilians and four soldiers died in the melee.[39]

In the immediate aftermath, Baltimore mobs with police escorts spread out into the countryside to destroy bridges to deny "foreign troops" the use of the railroad so that they would not "pollute the soil of the State of Maryland" and "slaughter . . . Southern citizens, who only ask[ed] to be let alone and allowed to govern themselves." On the day of the riot, the mayor of Baltimore, George William Brown, wrote a letter and sent a committee to dispatch it to the president, along with a separate concurring message from Governor Thomas H. Hicks. Brown wrote to Lincoln to demand that he no longer bring troops through the city, and said that if he continued to do so, "the responsibility for the bloodshed [would] not rest upon [him]."[40]

The committee delivered their letter to the president, and another committee, the Young Men's Christian Associations of Baltimore, arrived on April 22 to demand likewise that he send no more troops through the city. In indignation, Lincoln replied by letter that very day. He first decried the hypocrisy of these Baltimore men: "You, gentlemen, come here to me and ask for peace on any terms, and yet have no word of condemnation for those who are making war on us. You express great horror of bloodshed, and yet would not lay a straw in the way of those who are organizing in Virginia and elsewhere to capture this city."[41] Others may give in to rebellion and mob violence, but not Lincoln: "The rebels attack Fort Sumter, and your citizens attack troops sent to the defense of the Government, and the lives and property in Washington, and yet you would have me break my oath and surrender the Government without a blow. There is no Washington in that—no Jackson in that—no manhood nor honor in that."[42]

Because of geographic necessity, the troops had to pass through Maryland to defend the capital. Using vivid figurative language, Lincoln argued, "Our men are not moles, and can't dig under the earth; they are not birds, and can't fly through the air. There is no way but to march across, and that they must do."[43] The Union troops would continue to cross Maryland, but there was no need for any violence as long as the Baltimore mobs left them alone. However, Lincoln warned darkly, "If they do attack us, we will return it, and that severely." Some mistook Lincoln for soft, as he freely gave away all that he felt he could not convince others the truth of, but he always held fast to the single most important point of contention, and he would do so ruthlessly. On April 27, in order to prevent railroads from being destroyed and telegraph wires from being cut, Lincoln ordered the suspension of habeas corpus in Maryland.

This letter shows Lincoln attempting to make sense of these unsettled early days of the war by looking to the past for precedent. It was Washington who had raised and ridden at the head of an army to put down the Whiskey Rebellion in 1794. It was Jackson who had threatened to use the full force of the military if South Carolina rebelled in the Nullification Crisis of 1832–33. Even though his crisis was much greater than the ones his predecessors had experienced, Lincoln drew wisdom from their responses, and he would not break their precedents.

Furthermore, Lincoln would not allow rebellion and mob violence to deter him from doing what he felt was right. By taking the stand that he did, Lincoln was walking down the path that would eventually lead to an assassin's bullet. Considering the costs, in terms of both blood and treasure, giving in to it might have been the path of least resistance and, in many ways, would have been expedient, but according to Lincoln, there was *no manhood nor honor in that.*[44]

Message to Congress in Special Session

Lincoln called for a special session of Congress to meet starting July 4, 1861. There had been minor skirmishes both east and west, but the first major battle of the war, the First Battle of Bull Run, was still a few weeks away. Like many wartime leaders before and since, Lincoln exaggerated how well the Union was doing. For example, he argued that a majority of the people in the South remained loyal to the Union.[45] This may have been true in Appalachia, but the rebellion was incredibly popular for the vast majority of the South in 1861. However, the main part of his argument claimed that the war was not just about whether the Union would survive in particular but whether or not democracy could endure in principle and practice. In his Independence Day message, he used both history and logic to argue the necessity of preserving the Union.

Lincoln was careful to frame this war as a struggle to determine whether the government they cherished was fatally flawed. Lincoln asked, "Must a government, of necessity, be too *strong* for the liberties of its own people, or too *weak* to maintain its own existence?"[46] The war was a test to see if the people really could govern themselves.

Lincoln addressed the obvious question of how this could be a war to maintain freedom if he had taken on unprecedented power. To protect the vital rail link through Baltimore, he had suspended the writ of habeas corpus in Maryland before Congress had convened. Lincoln argued that he had taken an oath to uphold the Constitution, and in order to do so, it was necessary that the laws be enforced in all the states and that the Union be maintained. To those who would argue that the suspension of habeas corpus was unconstitutional, Lincoln asked, "To state the question more directly, are all the laws, *but one*, to go unexecuted, and the government itself go to pieces, lest that one be violated?" While Lincoln was always ready to concede an argument he deemed unnecessary to hold his position, he did not concede that what he did was illegal. He noted that the federal government does have the lawful right to suspend habeas corpus, since the Constitution states, "The privilege of the writ of habeas corpus, shall not be suspended unless when, in cases of rebellion or invasion, the public safety may require it." The current rebellion clearly necessitated it. There were questions as to whether the president had the authority to unilaterally suspend habeas corpus. As

Lincoln noted, the Constitution does not clearly and explicitly say how to do so and who may do so. However, it may be implied that the power rested solely with Congress because it was mentioned in Article I of the Constitution, which is dedicated to the legislative branch. Lincoln was probably unaware that an original draft of that clause did state that it was the Legislature who could suspend habeas corpus, but that detail was removed in the final draft. Thus, as Lincoln scholar Michael Burlingame notes, "The Framers implicitly rejected the notion that Congress alone was authorized to suspend the privilege."[47] Congress would later end the controversy by explicitly granting Lincoln that authority. Nevertheless, Lincoln argued that "it cannot be believed the framers of the instrument intended, that in every case, the danger should run its course, until Congress could be called together; the very assembling of which might be prevented, as was intended in this case, by the rebellion."[48]

Lincoln also used history to elaborate on his arguments during his first inaugural address. As he had done previously, Lincoln argued that the Union not only preceded the Constitution but that it also preceded independence. When the "United Colonies" declared their independence, they did not "declare their independence of one another, or of the Union" but rather their independence as a united country. Paraphrasing the conclusion to the Declaration of Independence, Lincoln argued that the colonies had been united in a "mutual pledge" through their "mutual action." Lincoln then addressed the idea of state sovereignty in the same way he had addressed issues for years: by defining the term of contention and showing how this definition clarified the point. "What is a 'sovereignty,' in the political sense of the term? Would it be far wrong to define it 'A political community, without a political superior'? Tested by this, no one of our States, except Texas, ever was a sovereignty." Even Texas, which was once an independent republic, had agreed to submit to the full authority of the Constitution and was no longer independent. Therefore, "the States have their *status* IN the Union, and they have no other *legal status*." Should the states declare their independence from the Union, "they [could] only do so against law." Lincoln argued that experience showed it was only through the Union, and not individual states, that Americans had achieved their liberty: "The Union, and not themselves separately, procured their independence, and their liberty. By conquest, or purchase, the Union gave each of them, whatever of independence, and liberty, it has."[49] Lincoln here touches upon a universal principle—namely, that only in a people's union can liberty flourish. No matter how many Swamp Foxes or

Gamecocks prowled the Palmetto State, South Carolina by itself could never have faced down the full might of the British Empire and won its freedom alone. Lincoln did hold something of a mystical attachment to the Union, but this mysticism did not trump his judgement that the Union was necessary to perpetuate human liberty. Divided states, rather than a United States, would be open to intrigue and domination by avaricious European powers pursuing their interests, interests that would not likely correspond to the rights and liberties of Americans. There can be no freedom without some kind of union of people to protect it. Union is essential—the prerequisite—to human liberty.

Lincoln argued that the secessionists were rebelling, both in fact and in principle, against the American Revolution. Lincoln read the several declarations of independence by the seceding states and noted a curious omission: "Unlike the good old one, penned by Jefferson, they omit the words 'all men are created equal.' Why?" They explicitly state the opposite. Lincoln had also read the Constitution for the Provisional Government of the Confederate States of America, and while most of it is the same as the American Constitution, Lincoln noticed another curious difference: "They have adopted a temporary national constitution, in the preamble of which, unlike our good old one, signed by Washington, they omit 'We, the People,' and substitute 'We, the deputies of the sovereign and independent States.'" Lincoln then asked rhetorically, "Why this deliberate pressing out of view, the rights of men, and the authority of the people?" For Lincoln, the seceders were radicals and revolutionaries, but rather than fighting for the rights of men, they were fighting to suppress them. According to Lincoln, "This is essentially a People's contest. On the side of the Union, it is a struggle for maintaining in the world, that form, and substance of government, whose leading object is, to elevate the condition of men—to lift artificial weights from all shoulders—to clear the paths of laudable pursuit for all—to afford all, an unfettered start, and a fair chance, in the race of life."[50] The American Revolution expressed the essential dignity of mankind, that the people are capable of governing themselves and that they can break the shackles that bind them. For Lincoln, this war was a fight to protect that dream.

The American project was an experiment, and while it had already passed two tests, it had to pass a third to show that it was successful: "Our popular government has often been called an experiment. Two points in it, our people have already settled—the successful *establishing*, and the successful *administering* of it. One still remains—its successful *maintenance* against a formidable attempt to overthrow it." America's political antecedents had provided precedents to guide them, but now the people had to set their own precedents:

> It is now for them to demonstrate to the world, that those who can fairly carry an election, can also suppress a rebellion—that ballots are the rightful, and peaceful, successors of bullets; and that when ballots have fairly, and constitutionally, decided, there can be no successful appeal, back to bullets; that there can be no successful appeal, except to ballots themselves, at succeeding elections. Such will be a great lesson of peace; teaching men that what they cannot take by an election, neither can they take it by a war—teaching all, the folly of being the beginners of a war.[51]

No government of the people can survive if the results of an election are not respected—if any minority may rise up and violently rebel any time they lose a constitutionally sanctioned contest. As Lincoln argued, this principle will lead to anarchy. Instead, they must prove the lesson that an appeal to ballots and not bullets is the only proper action in a democracy. Lincoln looked to the past throughout his life to provide wisdom for his present. Now, at this early stage in the war, he was becoming increasingly aware that his present would provide precedents for the future. He was determined that his actions would provide wisdom for future generations.

A Vast Future

Both in public and in private during the early months of the war, Lincoln increasingly expressed his understanding of how his actions would be interpreted in the future. On November 15, 1861, the historian George Bancroft wrote to him that his administration would "be remembered as long as human events find a record," and "posterity will not be satisfied with the result" unless slavery is rooted out. Bancroft, a prominent Democrat, argued that this was the "hope of men of all parties." Lincoln already knew that regardless of success or failure, he would live on in memory, but he also knew the desire for abolition was far from unanimous. Lincoln wrote back to Bancroft, stating that he was grateful to receive a letter from him and that he was already contemplating his suggestion but not ready to act on it, as he must proceed with "all due caution" following his "best judgment." These two men, for whom history was so important, understood intuitively at this early date the significance of the present for the future and were motivated by how they would live on in posterity. As Lincoln would state later that year, "The struggle of today, is not altogether for today—it is for a vast future also."[52]

On May 9, 1862, Lincoln revoked General David Hunter's unilateral order to emancipate slaves in the states of Florida, Georgia, and South Carolina, arguing that the power to do so rests solely with the commander in chief and that he only has the power to do so if it is a military necessity. However, he did not stop with a simple revocation. Under his urging, Congress had already passed a resolution to support states who would voluntarily enact gradual emancipation schemes. He appealed to states to take advantage of the plan, using language reminiscent of Matthew 16:3: "You can not if you would, be blind to the signs of the times."

In the coming weeks, Lincoln addressed the fears of those who worried about the consequences of a potential emancipation. On August 14, Lincoln invited a group of Black leaders to promote the act recently passed to colonize free Blacks in Africa, the Caribbean, or Latin America. Lincoln used many of the same arguments he had been using for years, yet he was never as eloquent in his support as Henry Clay was, and he certainly was not eloquent in this case. He told them, "Your race are suffering, in my judgment, the greatest wrong inflicted on any people." Even if slavery were to end, he felt Whites were too prejudiced to allow anything like equality; so he argued that the best way to end that suffering was for them to separate and go to a land to rule themselves. He acknowledged that many would be unwilling to do so, noting that this would incur great sacrifice for some. Lincoln then used the memory of Washington to argue his point, stating that Washington could have lived more comfortably under British rule but that he challenged it, enduring terrible sacrifices for the hope of a better future.[53] Lincoln did not repudiate his frequent statements of his hope that all men could be free because, still at this time, he claimed that different races could best enjoy this freedom separately and not collectively.

Eight days later Lincoln responded to an open letter to him by Horace Greeley, published in the *New York Tribune*, criticizing his policy towards slavery. Lincoln took the opportunity to make it abundantly clear what his war aims were:

> If there be those who would not save the Union, unless they could at the same time *save* slavery, I do not agree with them. If there be those who would not save the Union unless they could at the same time *destroy* slavery, I do not agree with them. My paramount object in this struggle *is* to save the Union, and is *not* either to save or to destroy slavery. If I could save the Union without freeing *any* slave I would do it, and if I could save it by freeing *all* the slaves I would do it; and if I could save it by freeing some and leaving others alone I would also do that. What I do about slavery, and the colored race, I do because I believe it helps

to save the Union; and what I forbear, I forbear because I do *not* believe it would help to save the Union. I shall do *less* whenever I shall believe what I am doing hurts the cause, and I shall do *more* whenever I shall believe doing more will help the cause. I shall try to correct errors when shown to be errors; and I shall adopt new views so fast as they shall appear to be true views.

Lincoln acknowledged that his duties as president did not always allow him to act on his personal views: "I have here stated my purpose according to my view of *official* duty; and I intend no modification of my oft-expressed *personal* wish that all men every where could be free."[54] For Lincoln, preserving the Union was the paramount issue. As he had been arguing since taking office, the conflict was about more than the immediate issues at hand. This conflict was to show whether people were capable of governing themselves. If secession along the principles promoted by the Confederates were left to stand, it would lead to tyranny or anarchy, a situation in which nobody's natural rights would be protected.

In his address to prominent Black leaders at the White House and his letter to Greeley, Lincoln was burnishing his conservative credentials and preparing the nation to understand that his primary goal was to save the Union. He did not want them to forget this after he publicly issued the paper that was then lying inside his desk in the White House, a document that would prove to be the most radical paper in American history.

Conclusion

Because of the press of events, Lincoln rarely researched the past to make new historical arguments during his presidency, but he never completely abandoned it. Like he had all his political career, he continued to follow the lessons of history as he interpreted them. However, since Lincoln had a deep appreciation of the past, he understood that he must not be solely guided by it but rather act with the understanding that future generations would look back to learn lessons from his life. Furthermore, in order to "preserve" and "vindicate" the precedents of the past, he came to understand that he would have to establish new precedents for the future, including precedents on slavery.

Chapter 8

We Cannot Escape History (1862–63)

Antietam: Infernal Work

Just outside Sharpsburg, Maryland, on the night of September 16, 1862, some Union soldiers bedded down in a cornfield a short distance from Robert E. Lee's army, each man taking up a spot between the rows of corn. Light rain fell, and the evening was quiet, save the occasional picket shots. Miles C. Huyette, a private from the 125th Pennsylvania Infantry, remembered, "The air was perfumed with a mixture of crushed green corn stalks, ragweed, and clover." Knowing that the morning would bring a battle, many soldiers lay sleepless in the field. Even though the day before they had enjoyed filling their haversacks with ripe apples as they marched through orchards, one soldier, Rufus Dawes, recalled that he spent much of this "dismal" night in the drizzle awake and ruing the coming morning: "Nothing can be more solemn than a period of silent waiting for the summons to battle, known to be impending." Before dawn, the officers roused their men, who wiped away the dew and gathered up their bundles. A late-summer fog hovered over Antietam Creek, and a breeze out of the south blew low-hanging clouds over the hills. Soldiers hurriedly ate their breakfast of johnnycakes and "fixins" in the twilight, many of these young men enjoying the last small pleasure of their earthly existence before entering into the maelstrom.[1]

The attack began at 5:30, when stars still hung in the sky, with a duel of Union and Confederate artillery and the swell of rifle fire. Federal artillerist Albert Monroe remembered the opposite Confederate hill lined with cannons that "seemed suddenly to have become an active volcano, belching forth flame and smoke." Confederates tore apart an oak grove and a farmhouse, knocking over beehives and sending angry swarms to attack Yankees and Rebels alike. The immediate Union objective was the small, whitewashed Dunker Church that housed a small congregation that stressed pacifism and modesty. It was located ahead on a low rise past the cornfield, and the two sides fought fiercely throughout the morning, with neither side gaining the advantage. General Hooker, who had command of the Union right wing at the cornfield, later recalled, "In the time that I am writing, every stalk of corn in the northern and greater part of the field was cut as closely as could have been done with a knife, and the slain lay in rows precisely as they had stood in their ranks a few moments before."[2]

As the morning progressed, the most intense fighting moved south to the center of their lines near the Sunken Road, which provided a natural breastwork for the rebel defenders. At 9:30 the Union attacked, and for the next three and a half hours they fought valiantly in the open field in front of the well-defended Rebels. Charles Carleton Coffin, a war correspondent and eyewitness, described the scene: "There are flashes, jets of smoke, iron bolts in the air above, also tearing up the ground or cutting through the ranks; they feel the breath of the shot, the puff of air in their faces, and hear the terrifying shriek. A comrade leaps into the air, spins around, or falls like a log to the ground. They behold a torn and mangled body." At about 1:00 the Union forces gained the top of the ridge over the Sunken Road, slaughtering the Rebels who could not escape. Coffin wrote that the Rebel line was "consumed like a straw in a candle's flame. It melt[ed] like lead in a crucible. Officers and men [went] down, falling in heaps." The Union troops "plunge[d] into the road, trampling down the dying and dead," scattering the surviving rebels. The Union men, however, had suffered too many casualties to pursue their opponents effectively.[3]

While the battle raged to his left and center in the morning, Lee weakened his right to reinforce his threatened points, leaving a scant force to defend a low hill overlooking a stone bridge spanning the Antietam Creek. Beginning at 9:30 Union forces wedged onto the bridge, trying to advance to the ridge beyond. Coffin described the advance: "Up to the bridge, upon it, dash the men in blue, their eyes glaring, their muscles iron, their nerves steel. The front rank goes down. Men pitch headlong from the parapet into the water. Stones fly from the arches. Shells, shrapnel, canister, tear the ranks asunder."[4] The first two charges failed, but the third proved successful, scattering the Rebels beyond.

The Union troops reformed after gaining the hill, creating a line that stretched for a mile, and prepared to attack. The Rebels regrouped as well with additional reinforcements, and when the Union line advanced, they put up the stiffest fight yet. The Union moved into a storm of fire and iron. Lt. Matthew J. Graham of the 9th New York Volunteers recalled: "I was lying on my back, supported on my elbows, watching the shells explode overhead and speculating as to how long I could hold up my finger before it would be shot off, for the very air seemed full of bullets." Then he was given the order to attack. Pvt. David L. Thompson remembered, "When bullets are whacking against tree trunks and solid shot are cracking skulls like eggshells, the consuming passion in the breast of the average man is to get out of the way." However, they kept advancing and were about to push the Rebels back into Sharpsburg when Confederate reinforcements arrived, blunting the Union attack. Fighting continued as long as there was daylight, but neither side gained the advantage. Clara Barton, who nursed men on the field, recalled bringing a cup of water to a soldier's lips, "When I felt a sudden twitch of the loose sleeve of my dress—the poor fellow sprang from my hands and fell back quivering in the agonies of death—a ball had passed between my body—and the right arm which supported him—cutting through the sleeve, and passing through his chest from shoulder to shoulder." The correspondent Coffin wrote, "I recall a soldier with the cartridge between his thumb and finger, the end of the cartridge bitten off, and the paper between his teeth when the bullet had pierced his heart, and the machinery of life—all the muscles and nerves—had come to a standstill." As the fighting ebbed, Pvt. Thompson, too frightened to attack and too scared to run away, was left lying in the dust as bullets struck a locust tree above. He lay there until dusk, speculating "on the impatience with which men clamor, in dull times, to be led into fight."[5]

When night fell, it was not all dark. The burning buildings and thousands of fires lit by soldiers created a lurid glow so that both armies could carry the wounded from the field. The next day, the two foes stood face to face daring the other to attack, but by the third day, the Rebels had vanished, fleeing in the night. The Battle of Antietam was the bloodiest single day of the Civil War, as more than three thousand Union and Confederate soldiers were killed and thousands more were wounded. Major William Child, a surgeon with the 5th Regiment New Hampshire Volunteers, recalled the scene in a letter to his wife Carrie: "The days after the battle are a thousand times worse than the day of the battle—and the physical pain is not the greatest pain suffered. How awful it is. The dead appear sickening but they suffer no pain. But the poor wounded mutilated soldiers that yet have life and sensation make a most horrid picture." Contemplating the scene, Child wrote, "I pray God may stop such infernal work—though perhaps he has sent it upon us for our sins. Great indeed must have been our sins if such is our punishment."[6]

Great Sins

We see the thief preaching against theft, and the adulterer against adultery. We have men sold to build churches, women sold to support the gospel, and babes sold to purchase Bibles for the *poor heathen! all for the glory of God and the good of souls!* The slave auctioneer's bell and the church-going bell chime in with each other, and the bitter cries of the heart-broken slave are drowned in the religious shouts of his pious master.[7]

Whereas the Union surgeon at Antietam wondered abstractly about the great sins of the nation, thirty years earlier and ninety miles away, near Saint Michaels, Maryland, a teenaged Frederick Douglass lived a life that gave him a much more concrete understanding of the evils of the land. Born in 1818, Douglass could read by the time he was a teenager, and unlike most enslaved people, he had mainly avoided heavy fieldwork.

That changed in 1833 when his master hired him out to Edward Covey in order to break him. Douglass was unused to fieldwork and was initially bad at it and was punished severely for any mistake. When he lost control of the oxen he was driving and they wrecked a gate, Covey demanded that Douglass take off his shirt so that he could switch him. When Douglass refused, Covey came at him "with the fierceness of a tiger," tore off his clothes, and lashed him until all his switches broke. The lashing left gaping wounds in his "flesh as large as [his] little finger." In those first few months at Covey's, Douglass noted sadly that Covey had succeeded in breaking him, and at times he felt he had no option but to take his own life. He wrote: "My natural elasticity was crushed, my intellect languished, the disposition to read departed, the cheerful spark that lingered about my eyed died; the dark night of slavery closed in upon me; and behold a man transformed into a brute!"[8]

That August, he collapsed from heat and exhaustion while carrying wheat to be fanned. When Covey found him lying on the ground, he kicked him in his side and told him to get up. Douglass attempted to do so but fell again. Covey kicked him again, got a slat of hickory wood, and beat him in the head until blood gushed out onto the ground. When Douglass recovered enough to stand again, he did not go back to work but instead fled and staggered seven miles to his master's house to plead with him to send him somewhere else. By the time he got there, Douglass reported, "My hair was all clotted with dust and blood; my shirt was stiff with blood. My legs and feet were torn in sundry places with briers and thorns, and were also covered with blood." Although not unaffected by the sight, his master sent him back because he would lose all the money for hiring him out if he did not fulfill the contract. Douglass returned and hid in the woods until Sunday morning. Covey, who was deeply religious, treated him that day as though nothing had happened. The next morning while Douglass was feeding the horses, Covey took a rope and tried to tie him up by the legs, but Douglass grabbed him by the throat. When Covey yelled for another man to help him, Douglass kicked and felled him, leaving Covey alone to confront him. They, according to Douglass, fought for two hours until Covey left, claiming that he would not have whipped him so hard if he had not resisted. Covey had not whipped him but instead was trying to maintain the reputation of a slave breaker, which was so key to his livelihood. Although he continued to threaten Douglass, he never whipped him again. Douglass reported with satisfaction, "This battle with Mr. Covey was the turning-point in my career as a slave. It rekindled the few expiring embers of freedom, and revived within me a sense of my own manhood. It recalled the departed self-confidence, and inspired me again with a determination to be free."[9] Douglass had a very concrete understanding of the meaning of tyranny because of experiences like this from his youth. He also learned the wisdom that, no matter how hopeless the situation may seem, tyranny could be successfully resisted, by force if necessary.

Douglass successfully escaped from slavery four years later and became a famous abolitionist, author, and lecturer. Even though Lincoln was a Republican, Douglass was deeply critical of him during his first two years in office and pushed public sentiment to demand immediate abolition. Douglass criticized Lincoln's first inaugural address, arguing that Lincoln was "announcing his complete loyalty to slavery in the slave States" and that this showed Lincoln to be "weak."[10] In September 1862, Douglass called emancipation a "national necessity" and said that the "wisest and best statesmen in the national councils [we]re lifting up their voices in favor of employing the sable arm of the nation for the salvation of the country."[11] Douglass contrasted the work of the *best statesmen* with Lincoln, eviscerating him for his short speech to Black leaders on colonization: "The President of the United States seems to possess an ever increasing passion for making himself appear silly and ridiculous." Further, Douglass said Lincoln had "been unusually garrulous, characteristically foggy, remarkably illogical and untimely in his utterances."[12] Douglass argued, "Mr. Lincoln is quite a genuine representative of American prejudice and Negro hatred and far more concerned for the preservation of slavery." Further, he said, "[The speech] leaves us less ground to hope for anti-slavery action at his hands than any of his previous utterances."[13] By September 1862, Frederick Douglass had almost abandoned hope that Lincoln would address what he believed to be the true cause of the war.

My Fondest Hopes

The president, according to Attorney General Edward Bates, "seemed wrung by the bitterest anguish—said he felt almost ready to hang himself."[14] Bates wrote these words following a September 2, 1862, cabinet meeting after the disastrous Second Battle of Bull Run, which marked the low point for the Union during the war. The North had won a series of victories in the west, but they had suffered nothing but defeat in the east. In January Lincoln had told one of his generals that "the bottom was out of the tub," and that was before the Union endured embarrassing defeats during Stonewall Jackson's Valley Campaign, the Seven Days Battle, and the Second Battle of Bull Run.[15] There were also the personal tragedies Lincoln suffered during the first year of the war: the deaths of Col. Elmer Ellsworth (who studied in his law office), Col. Edward Baker (who was his close friend for nearly three decades), and his boy Willie.

Lincoln presented a draft of the Emancipation Proclamation to his cabinet in July and requested their comments. Secretary of State Seward recommended that Lincoln wait until the North won a major victory so that he could appear to issue it from a position of strength rather than desperation. Five days after the Union victory at Antietam, Lincoln called his cabinet together and announced that he was ready to issue it publicly and sought their advice on its language. Even though Lincoln seldom talked about his personal faith, Secretary of the Treasury Salmon Chase recorded a revealing exchange in his diary. Lincoln told his cabinet, "I made the promise to myself, and [hesitating a little] to my Maker." That promise was that he would issue the Emancipation Proclamation if the Rebel army was driven from Maryland. This account was confirmed by Secretary of the Navy Gideon Welles, who wrote in his diary about Lincoln's professed "covenant" with God.[16] On September 22, Lincoln issued his Preliminary Emancipation Proclamation, declaring that all slaves in territories still under rebellion on January 1, 1863, would be free.

When the new year arrived and the Rebels had yet to put down their arms, Lincoln delivered the official Emancipation Proclamation, declaring that "all persons held as slaves" within the rebellious territories "shall be then, thenceforward, and forever free," and he made provision for Black men to join the army and navy.[17]

Lincoln did not ground the Emancipation Proclamation in abstract morality or eternal truths but rather on military necessity, a necessity made constitutional in his mind as commander in chief that in ordinary times would not be. By freeing slaves and arming those who wished to enlist, Lincoln subtracted power from the South and added it to the North. The slaves in the Border States were not freed because he could not justify that as a military necessity, as those slave states had remained loyal.

The Emancipation Proclamation was a military document issued by the commander in chief in time of war as a military necessity, but unlike Lincoln's other military proclamations, like those on the blockade of the South, this one was revolutionary. For the rest of his life, Lincoln would be committed not just to restoring the Union but also to freeing slaves. Lincoln had come to understand that if he wanted to vindicate the principles of the Revolution that he had cherished, he must lead the nation to live them out more fully. While many in that generation hoped for an eventual abolition of slavery, Lincoln believed that to preserve the Constitution and the principles of the Declaration of Independence, the time had come to make that long-hoped-for future a reality in the present.

Lincoln's former roommate and perhaps closest friend, Joshua Speed of Kentucky, visited Lincoln several times in the White House. Two decades earlier, Lincoln was so depressed that Speed had taken away his knives and razors in fear that he might kill himself. One time when Speed traveled to the White House, Speed, a slave owner, told Lincoln he felt the Emancipation Proclamation was a mistake. Lincoln defended it and then reminded Speed of a conversation they had had more than two decades prior, when Speed feared Lincoln might take his life. As Speed remembered it, "At the time of his deep depression—He said to me that he had done nothing to make any human being remember that he had lived" and he desired to live so that he could achieve something so that he could live on in memory, a sentiment that his law partner William Herndon recalled him expressing to him as well. According to Speed, "He reminded me of the conversation—and said with earnest emphasis—I believe that in this measure (meaning his proclamation) my fondest hopes will be realized."[18] While his personal memory of the past brought him to the brink of self-destruction, his desire to live on in collective memory drove him to the greatest feats of human achievement. Without this will to live on in memory, there would have been no *Lincoln*.

1862 Message to Congress

After issuing the Preliminary Emancipation Proclamation, Lincoln's first significant communication with the public was his Annual Message to Congress on December 1, 1862. In it Lincoln cataloged a range of issues for Congress to consider, including colonization, which he now insisted must be voluntary. For the first time, Lincoln also made the argument that, should Blacks remain in America as free people, it would do no harm to Whites, as they would be no greater competition for labor as free people than as slaves. Lincoln dedicated the lengthiest portion of this message to a new scheme for the gradual emancipation of slaves. Unlike earlier plans, this would be mandatory for all states, and it would provide that all slaves, including those in the loyal states, would be freed by the end of the century. He argued that while expensive, if it were stretched out over the course of decades, it would not be onerous on the taxpayer. He used facts from the past, namely census records, to predict the future— namely, that if the population of the United States continued to increase at the same rate that it had been increasing at in previous decades, then the ever-increasing tax base over the coming decades would find it ever more affordable to continue to pay for this gradual emancipation. Despite this plan, he did not revoke his Preliminary Emancipation Proclamation, and by the end of the month, he declared all slaves held within Rebel territory to be free immediately. Lincoln believed his plan for emancipation "would end the struggle . . . and save the Union forever."[19]

Lincoln understood that there was a broad spectrum of opinion among Unionists about slavery. It ranged from those who were against all forms of emancipation to those who demanded immediate and uncompensated emancipation among loyal and disloyal states alike. This issue threatened to irrecoverably divide the Unionists and make it impossible to win the war, so Lincoln knew he must tread carefully. Lincoln argued that emancipation would shorten the war and lessen the expenses committed. Understanding that a likely majority of Unionists thought him either too radical or not radical enough, Lincoln asked, "It is not 'can *any* of us *imagine* better?' but 'can we *all* do better?'" Due to the nature of the war, Lincoln had already abandoned his long-standing belief that slavery should not be interfered with in the states it was already legal in. He urged people to understand that the struggle they were undergoing demanded radical new thinking: "The dogmas of the quiet past, are inadequate to the stormy present. The occasion is piled high with difficulty, and we must rise with the occasion. As our case is new, so we must think anew, and act anew. We must disenthrall our selves, and then we shall save our country."[20]

Lincoln's generation, he explained, who grew up listening to and cherishing the memories of the past, must come to understand that, like the Founders, they, too, for better or worse, would live on in memory:

> Fellow-citizens, *we* cannot escape history. We of this Congress and this administration, will be remembered in spite of ourselves. No personal significance, or insignificance, can spare one or another of us. The fiery trial through which we pass, will light us down, in honor or dishonor, to the latest generation. We *say* we are for the Union. The world will not forget that we say this. We know how to save the Union. The world knows we do know how to save it. We . . . hold the power, and bear the responsibility. In *giving* freedom to the *slave*, we *assure* freedom to the *free*—honorable alike in what we give, and what we preserve. We shall nobly save, or meanly lose, the last best, hope of earth. Other means may succeed; this could not fail. The way is plain, peaceful, generous, just—a way which, if followed, the world will forever applaud, and God must forever bless.[21]

Lincoln's conclusion in his message to Congress is perhaps his most remarkable statement on the past. In his three decades in politics, the wisdom of the past along with his personal logic had guided him more than anything else. In this message, Lincoln is still inspired by the past and used it to inform his current decisions, including what appears to be some significant research that he conducted to predict future population growth based on past figures. However, Lincoln here believed that while the past can serve as a guide, it must not be a limit to actions in the present. Americans should be inspired by history but not imprisoned by it. By making new precedents, they will live on in future history "to the latest generation."

Correspondence

Lincoln mostly remained silent, publicly, in the coming months as the press of events forced him to focus on the war effort. However, his correspondence during this time offers valuable insights into his evolving thoughts about the past.

In December 1862 Lincoln received word that Lieutenant Colonel William McCullough, the clerk at the court in Bloomington, had died in a battle in Mississippi. Lincoln wrote to his daughter Fanny McCullough to console her. In this letter, he was guided by the personal memory of the tragedies he had suffered in the past. Perhaps thinking of his mother, who died when he was eight, Lincoln wrote, "In this sad world of ours, sorrow comes to all; and, to the young, it comes with bitterest agony, because it takes them unawares. The older have learned to ever expect it."[22]

Lincoln wrote that he wished he could alleviate her suffering, but only time could do so, which he knew from experience. Lincoln concluded with his thoughts on the nature of memory: "The memory of your dear Father, instead of an agony, will yet be a sad sweet feeling in your heart, of a purer, and holier sort than you have known before."[23] Just as was evident from the hymns he liked by Isaac Watts and the poetry he read and wrote, Lincoln always believed there was something sacred about memory that can bring comfort and guidance to the present.

While in office, job seekers constantly pressed the president for sinecure, and even his wife was not immune to such requests. In February 1863 she received a letter from Edgar Harriott asking if she could influence her husband to gain him an appointment. He claimed to be a "a direct decendent of John Randolph of Roanoke," a man Lincoln had spoken of in earlier speeches. Mary showed the letter to her husband, and Lincoln, knowing Randolph had been childless and was thought to be impotent, inscribed on the note without returning it, "A direct descendant of one who never was a father."[24] This shows Lincoln in the darkest times being able to find, even in obscure details, the humor in history.

In June Lincoln responded to resolutions passed by a group of New York Democrats led by Congressman Erasmus Corning. They criticized Lincoln's suspension of the writ of habeas corpus, among other things, and Lincoln responded by using lessons of the past to justify his seemingly unprecedented actions. The New Yorkers cited the Constitution as protecting against military arrests of civilians. They went back further into history to the rights won after the English Civil War: "They were secured substantially to the English people, after years of protracted civil war, and were adopted into our constitution at the close of the revolution." Lincoln's response did not challenge the facts but questioned the appropriateness of their application: "Would not the demonstration have been better, if it could have been truly said that these safe-guards had been adopted, and applied *during* the civil wars and *during* our revolution, instead of *after* the one, and at the *close* of the other." He wrote that he, too, was for protecting these rights, except during times of rebellion or invasion when necessitated to secure public safety, as the Constitution had prescribed. Lincoln argued that the reason that provision was included in the Constitution was because of "the understanding of those who made the constitution that ordinary courts of justice are inadequate to 'cases of Rebellion,'" and thus people could be arrested and imprisoned who, under normal circumstance, would remain free. For Lincoln, context was everything. Lincoln argued that had the government acted sooner and arrested known sympathizers of secession, it could have prevented many of the best generals, like Robert E. Lee and Joseph E. Johnston, from joining the Rebels. To those who argued that those who induced Union soldiers to break the law and desert should not be arrested, Lincoln argued, "Long experience has shown that armies can not be maintained unless desertion shall be punished by the severe penalty of death." Then he asked rhetorically, "Must I shoot a simple-minded soldier boy who deserts, while I must not touch a hair of a wiley agitator who induces him to desert?" Lincoln used an analogy to argue that the extreme measures undertaken during rebellion are easily discarded when peace is returned: he said that just as a drug is necessary when one is sick but is not taken when one is well, measures taken during times of rebellion are not taken during times of peace. The analogy would have worked better when less was known about the addictive nature of certain medications.[25]

Lincoln then argued that his actions were not without precedent. Most people then criticizing Lincoln's actions, like Congressman Corning, were Democrats, the party founded by Andrew Jackson, a man Democrats almost universally admired. Lincoln, the history teacher, provided a lesson on how Jackson acted during a time of invasion:

> After the battle of New-Orleans, and while the fact that the treaty of peace had been concluded, was well known in the city, but before official knowledge of it had arrived, Gen. Jackson still maintained martial, or military law. Now, that it could be said the war was over, the clamor against martial law, which had existed from the first, grew more furious. Among other things a Mr. Louiallier published a denunciatory newspaper article. Gen. Jackson arrested him. A lawyer by the name of Morel procured the U.S. Judge Hall to order a writ of Habeas Corpus to release Mr. Louiallier. Gen. Jackson arrested both the lawyer and the judge. A Mr. Hollander ventured to say of some part of the matter that "it was a dirty trick." Gen. Jackson arrested him. When the officer undertook to serve the writ of Habeas Corpus, Gen. Jackson took it from him, and sent him away with a copy. Holding the judge in custody a few days, the general sent him beyond the limits of his encampment, and set him at liberty, with an order to remain till the ratification of peace should be regularly announced, or until the British should have left the Southern coast. A day or two more elapsed, the ratification of the treaty of peace was regularly announced, and the judge and others were fully liberated. A few days more, and the judge called Gen. Jackson into court and fined him a thousand dollars for having arrested him and the others named. The general paid the fine, and there the matter rested for nearly thirty years, when congress refunded principal and interest.[26]

Lincoln almost certainly remembered reading about this incident in the *Congressional Globe* when Congress debated refunding Jackson. Since he essentially recounted the story accurately, provided a direct quote, and correctly spelled all the names of the people involved (including the ten-letter French name Louiallier), Lincoln must have researched the records to make this accurate historical argument. To Lincoln, the lesson was that extraordinary powers in times of rebellion and invasion (regardless of varying opinions of their constitutionality) were exactly that, *extra ordinary*. History shows how ordinary civil authority resumed its normal course once the constitutionally defined threat was removed, and it would do so again once this current rebellion was suppressed. In this letter, Lincoln believed that history showed that his policies were not just constitutional but also supported by historical precedent.

Although the end of the war was not in sight, Union victories at Gettysburg and Vicksburg in July had considerably brightened their prospects. On August 26, Lincoln wrote a letter to James C. Conkling to be read aloud at a public rally in September in Springfield. Near the close of the letter, Lincoln argued that Americans were creating historical lessons for the future by proving the principle that an aggrieved coalition cannot take by violence what they were unable to take through Constitutional elections, and that Black men were a part of that history:

> Peace does not appear so distant as it did. I hope it will come soon, and come to stay; and so come as to be worth the keeping in all future time. It will then have been proved that, among free men, there can be no successful appeal from the ballot to the bullet; and that they who take such appeal are sure to lose their case, and pay the cost. And then, there will be some black men who can remember that, with silent tongue, and clenched teeth, and steady eye, and well-poised bayonet, they have helped mankind on to this great consummation; while, I fear, there will be some white ones, unable to forget that, with malignant heart, and deceitful speech, they have strove to hinder it.

As he had previously expressed, Lincoln hoped Americans were setting precedents that would last in America for "all future time," and he was now beginning to envision Black men living on in that history. "In more colors than one," Lincoln wrote, "the history" of this great conflict was being "jotted down in black and white."[27] According to Lincoln, by winning a history in America, they were winning a future in America, one free of slavery.

Gettysburg Address

In the early morning light on November 19, Abraham Lincoln toured the Gettysburg battlefield with Secretary of State William Seward. He had

been invited to give a few short remarks at the dedication of a cemetery
for the Union soldiers who had died four months prior. The cemetery
was not finished, and many of the Union soldiers still lay in the temporary graves on the battlefield where they fell. As Lincoln traced the
locations of the most harrowing scenes of the battle, the debris of war
lay all around him. Cartridge boxes, bloody uniforms, rifle pits, earth-
works, haversacks, dead horses, and mounds of shallow graves were all
still there for the president to see. We can imagine Lincoln meditating
silently as he rode over those fields in what historian Martin P. Johnson
has described as "this emerging landscape of memory."[28]

While Lincoln was scheduled to speak at the dedication ceremony,
Edward Everett's duty was to provide the primary oration. In many ways
Everett's life paralleled and even exceeded that of the other great scholar
politician of the era, George Bancroft, who was serving as president of
Harvard University and served as a governor, congressman, senator, secretary of state, and minister to Great Britain. In the previous few years,
he had become the most preeminent lecturer in the nation, traveling
throughout the country to address eager audiences. Originally the dedication was scheduled for October 23, but the organizers postponed it until
November 19, so that Everett would have enough time to conduct the
research he needed.[29] The historian Garry Wills, in his Pulitzer Prize–
winning book *Lincoln at Gettysburg: The Words That Remade America*,
writes, "Everett aspired to more than mere accuracy. Along with Bancroft
and other romantic historians of his time, he meant to create a tradition
that would inspire as well as inform."[30] At the ceremony, Everett vividly recounted the battle, detailing the history of the fighting over the
landscape they could view from Cemetery Ridge. Everett cited numerous historical precedents, especially the ancient Greeks, and he quoted
Pericles's famous funeral oration in his peroration: "'The whole earth,'
said Pericles, as he stood over the remains of his fellow-citizens, who
had fallen in the first year of the Peloponnesian War,—'the whole earth
is the sepulchre of illustrious men.'"[31]

While Lincoln never mentioned Pericles that day, Wills argues that
there are many similarities in both style and substance between Lincoln's Gettysburg Address and Pericles's Funeral Oration (as narrated
by Thucydides in his *History of the Peloponnesian War*). In terms of
style, Wills argues that Lincoln used many of the hallmarks of classical
oratory found in Pericles's address: "compression, grasp of the essential,
balance, ideality, [and] an awareness of the deepest polarities in the situation." There are similarities in substance, as both Pericles and Lincoln
used a series of antitheses, such as life and death, present and the past,

and Athens/America contrasted with other city-states/nations.[32] Wills, however, does not assert a direct Periclean influence on Lincoln or even argue that Lincoln had read this speech. However, Lincoln scholar Anne Wootton observes that Lincoln was likely familiar with Pericles's oration. For one thing, there was a renewed interest and fascination in classical Greek culture during the antebellum years that may have exposed Lincoln to the work. Wootton also points out that Lincoln probably read a reprint of Pericles's speech somewhere, such as in Hugh Blair's *Lectures on Rhetoric and Belles Lettres*. Furthermore, as Wootton notes, there was a copy of Thucydides's *History of the Peloponnesian War*, which contained Pericles's "Funeral Oration," in the White House library, which Lincoln could access at his leisure. Even if he had never read or heard of it before November 1863, he would have read Everett's reference to Pericles, since he had given Lincoln a copy of his address a few days prior to the ceremony.[33] Lincoln is also known to have read many military texts on warfare after the firing on Fort Sumter, and it is not inconceivable that Lincoln would have consulted the most famous work in the Western canon on war and statesmanship, Thucydides's *History of the Peloponnesian War*. Although it is impossible to prove, there is more than a slight possibility that Lincoln was inspired by a famous speech in history when he wrote his most celebrated address.

Lincoln's first line in the Gettysburg Address is a compressed history lesson: "Four score and seven years ago our fathers brought forth on this continent, a new nation, conceived in Liberty, and dedicated to the proposition that all men are created equal."[34] Lincoln grounded his address in the history of the nation, that it was founded on the principles of protecting natural rights and that no man had a right to rule over another because of his birth.

A government founded on these principles was not the natural order of things. As Lincoln had been arguing for the past few years, the current conflict would show if this highly unusual nation could survive: "Now we are engaged in a great civil war, testing whether that nation, or any nation so conceived and so dedicated, can long endure."[35]

Lincoln then proceeded from the distant to the more recent past: "The brave men, living and dead," who fought at Gettysburg would live on in memory because the world "can never forget what they did here." Lincoln then moved from the past to purpose:

> It is rather for us to be here dedicated to the great task remaining before us—that from these honored dead we take increased devotion to that cause for which they gave the last full measure of devotion—that we here

highly resolve that these dead shall not have died in vain—that this nation, under God, shall have a new birth of freedom—and that government of the people, by the people, for the people, shall not perish from the earth.[36]

For Lincoln, the past, both recent and distant, provides meaning and purpose—that they must be "dedicated," take "increased devotion," and highly "resolve" to finish their work. Lincoln's closing parallels the beginning in that he argued the government the Founding Fathers made was worth sacrificing for because it was "of the people, by the people, and for the people."

Although in the coming years appreciation would grow for Lincoln's Gettysburg Address, it was already well regarded immediately after he delivered it, despite a persistent myth to the contrary. Besides the positive reviews in the press, George Bancroft requested that Lincoln write an official copy for him to have it published in a collection of works by the most prominent contemporary American authors.[37]

Conclusion

Lincoln's Gettysburg Address, especially the opening sentence, has come under criticism by some of the most eminent scholars in American history. Although there are some similarities among their critiques, each is distinct and deserves to be addressed separately.

Joseph J. Ellis, a Pulitzer Prize–winning historian and expert on the Revolutionary War, writes in *The Quartet* that "the first clause in the first sentence of Lincoln's famous speech was historically incorrect"—namely, the idea that when the Founding Fathers declared their independence, they were creating a new "nation," was, according to Ellis, not accomplished until the Constitution took effect more than a decade later.[38]

Before proceeding, it is necessary to note that when Lincoln uses the word *nation*, he is not necessarily implying something analogous to a modern conception of a centralized nation-state. Rather, he is using the term *nation* to mean something like a country or even a people.[39] The historian R. B. Bernstein, in his review for the *New York Times*, supports this interpretation when he criticizes Ellis for his conflation of nationhood with a form of government. Bernstein argues that a sense of national identity allowed the American people to fight for independence together, and that the Framers sought a new constitution to preserve rather than to create a nation.[40]

Of course, Lincoln was not the first to refer to the United States as a nation before the Constitution, rather than an alliance or league of states (as Ellis claimed the United States was). One clear example of this was General George Washington, who when resigning his commission in the U.S. Army in 1783, wrote of the United States as a "nation," as a "Republic" that had "assumed its Rank among the Nations." He wrote that the United States had a "national character" and that the "Union" was an "independent Power." He called the United States, "my country." Washington described the United States as a singularity well before the U.S. Constitution was written, while the Articles of Confederation was still in effect.[41] Furthermore, Pauline Maier, author of the definitive history of the Declaration of Independence *American Scripture: Making the Declaration of Independence* and the historian to whom Ellis dedicated his work, writes that the American people had transferred their loyalty from the British empire to "that jerry-built institution, the Second Continental Congress, and the fledgling nation it struggled to lead."[42]

To further critique Lincoln's history lesson, Ellis writes, "In 1776 thirteen American colonies declared themselves independent states that came together temporarily to win the war, then would go their separate ways."[43] Ellis's assertion is also the direct opposite of what Lincoln had been arguing through history since the secession crisis. Whereas Lincoln asserted that the Union was "perpetual," Ellis argues that they had been united "temporarily." In his first inaugural address, Lincoln traces the history of the idea of a perpetual union from the 1774 Articles of Association to the Declaration of Independence in 1776 to the Articles of Confederation and Perpetual Union ratified in 1781 and then to the Constitution itself. When Lincoln uses the word "perpetual," he uses the same word that had been used five times in the Articles of Confederation to describe the Union.[44] It is true that the 1774 Articles of Association said that Americans would "solemnly bind" themselves to each other until Parliament repealed certain acts that they felt violated their rights. However, there is no hint, either explicit or implicit, in the Declaration of Independence or the Articles of Confederation, that the Union was only meant to be *temporary*.[45] Furthermore, the phrase E Pluribus Unum (Latin for "out of many, one" and not "out of many, many") for the de facto national motto did not originate after the Civil War or after the inauguration of the Constitution but rather when the Second Continental Congress appointed a committee, consisting of Benjamin Franklin, John Adams, and Thomas Jefferson, to create a great seal for the new entity they had just created, on July 4, 1776. In 1782 the Continental Congress finally approved a design by Charles Thomson for the great seal with the motto included. Thomson provided a written description to Congress explaining that the design symbolized a "new State taking its place and rank among other sovereign powers."[46] Likewise, when the states of Connecticut, Georgia, Massachusetts, New Hampshire, New York, South Carolina, and Virginia ceded their territorial claims under the Articles of Confederation and Perpetual Union, producing their co-equal states within that perpetual national union, including Vermont, Michigan, Wisconsin, Illinois, Indiana, Ohio, Kentucky, Mississippi, and Alabama, they were not ceding their claims to foreign powers but rather to their own national Union.

Ellis believes that Lincoln, in his context, "had some compelling reasons for bending the arc of American history." Still, he says that Lincoln's opening statement in the Gettysburg Address was a "fundamental distortion of how history happened."[47] Ellis is right to point out that, before the Constitution, the Union was extremely weak and flawed. However, the imperfect nature of the Union does not mean that the Declaration of Independence made the states independent from Great Britain as well as from each other. Even if the Union was fragile, it still was a union, just as an imperfect marriage is still a marriage that, with some work, can be made more perfect. To use Lincoln's words, Ellis does not see the Union as a marriage at all but more of a "free-love arrangement."[48] Of the two historians in this instance, Lincoln is not the one most guilty of bending the arc of American history to suit his needs.

Another related critique is that Lincoln's opening sentence is not based on any historical research performed by Lincoln himself. In critiquing how the Declaration has lived on in memory, Pauline Maier writes that "Lincoln's view of the past," both in his Gettysburg Address and throughout his political career, "was a product of political controversy, not research, and his version of what the founders meant was full of wishful suppositions."[49] To deny that current political controversies informed Lincoln's views would be incorrect in the extreme. However, to deny the extensive research Lincoln performed about the ideas of the Founding Fathers would also be a mistake. Lincoln's views were grounded in diligent research, comprising years of study and carefully testing his ideas in public in front of opponents. As detailed earlier, sometimes his assertions were flawed. Still, the historical arguments that he made based on that research were, in many ways, even more accurate than not only the most eminent scholars of his era but also those of well-regarded historians of later generations. Lincoln's arguments about the past were based on extensive historical research and not wishful suppositions.

Others accuse Lincoln not necessarily of ignorance but rather of a willful manipulation of the past in his Gettysburg Address. For example, Garry Wills, in his *Lincoln at Gettysburg*, argues that by making the historical arguments he made at Gettysburg, Lincoln "performed one of the most daring acts of open-air sleight-of-hand ever witnessed by the unsuspecting. Everyone in that vast throng of thousands was having his or her intellectual pocket picked." How did Lincoln deceive his audience, and how does his deception continue to influence Americans today? Wills argues that Lincoln performed this gigantic "swindle" at Gettysburg when he "revolutionized the Revolution" by earnestly portraying that generation as leading a great liberty movement. Wills argues that the proper reading of the Constitution is as a proslavery document, since it both tolerated the peculiar institution and failed to protect and promote equality within its text.

Conversely, in his excellent *No Property in Man*, the historian Sean Wilentz argues that "constructions of a usable past need not distort past political arguments," and I contend that Lincoln was not guilty of such distortions here. Wilentz argues that, while those who believe in a proslavery Constitution have powerful arguments, those who view it as leaning more toward the side of liberty have just as strong if not stronger reasons to support that view. According to Wilentz, the contentions of Lincoln and like-minded people "were not simply inventions, twisting the words of the framers, their supporters, and their critics to fit new situations and preconceptions. Early versions of these contentions had emerged at the founding itself, during the ratification struggles of 1787 and 1788." Wilentz in his *No Property in Man*, with its title derived from Madison's statement that the Constitution must not be seen to provide moral sanction to slavery, traced the history of the freedom Constitution. Lincoln was working in a long tradition of thinking that went back immediately to the Framers. According to Wilentz in a review in the *New York Times*, "Contrary to Jefferson Davis, Lincoln and the Republicans' triumph did not break the Constitution; it broke the pro-slavery view of the Constitution while vindicating the long beleaguered antislavery view." While there are good reasons to disagree with Lincoln's interpretations of American history, these interpretations were not inventions of Lincoln but had been there right from the beginning.[50]

Like Wills, Pauline Maier also criticizes how historically accurate Lincoln's view of the Declaration of Independence was. She writes that "in many ways, Douglas's history was more faithful to the past and to the views of Thomas Jefferson," because he treated the Declaration as a document of separation from Britain and nothing more.[51] However, it was Douglas, not Lincoln, who in an unsuccessful attempt to maintain the unity of his party, perverted the history of the Revolution to justify a political expedient that he did not really believe in. It was Douglas who mistakenly argued that America, at its founding, was a tabula rasa and that the Founders created a country half-free and half-slave as if that was the optimal condition. In contrast, Lincoln correctly argued that America was born with slavery already established among its colonies and that the revolutionary generation, in their wisdom, abolished it and restricted it in as many places as they could while still holding the Union together.

It was Douglas and not Lincoln who argued that the Founders meant for slavery to be perpetuated forever (including at the time of this writer's present, in 2023, and in your, the reader's, future) rather than wishing that future generations would not get the idea from the Constitution that there had ever been anything as sinister as *property in men* in the United States. It was Douglas, whom Maier even quotes but does not critique, who asserted that only British subjects were included in the phrase "all men are created equal." Just as Lincoln criticized Douglas for arguing that the Declaration of Independence really meant *all British subjects were created equal*, he would equally and vehemently challenge anyone who would argue that the phrase really meant *all men are created equal until we have won our independence from Britain.*[52]

History is the study of continuity and change over time. Lincoln, quite accurately, used the Declaration of Independence as the best expression of the spirit of the revolutionary era to show a continuity in history had been broken and that there had been a great change over time. In his 1854 Springfield and Peoria speeches about the Kansas-Nebraska Act, he argued, "Let no one be deceived. The spirit of seventy-six and the spirit of Nebraska, are utter antagonisms; and the former is being rapidly displaced by the latter."[53] When war broke out, Lincoln analyzed the Southern declarations of independence and argued that, while they claimed to be following the footsteps of the Founders, they were deliberately erasing the principles on which the Founders based their revolution, leading a great anti-liberty movement. When people denied or diminished the principles of the Revolution, they were not only perverting history but they were also, as Lincoln said, quoting Henry Clay, "blowing out the moral lights around us." Lincoln had argued in 1857 that Douglas was turning the Declaration of Independence into nothing more "than an interesting memorial of a dead past." Like Douglas before her, Maier imprisons the values of the Revolution best expressed by the Declaration to only a specific time and place by denying the "vitality" of the past. [54]

In *The Purpose of the Past*, Gordon S. Wood largely accepts Maier's characterization of Lincoln's use of the past, not challenging Maier's assertion that Lincoln did not do research or practice anything remotely close to the work of a historian. Wood calls Lincoln's use of the past a "false heritage," even if he perverted the past for noble reasons.[55] While Lincoln's approach to history was flawed at times, characterizing Lincoln's use of the past as false is misguided. Still, Wood would be correct to characterize Lincoln's opening line of the Gettysburg Address on its own as mere heritage (i.e., collective memory) and not something that resembles the fruits of a historian. However, taking context into account, the Gettysburg Address was not simply a tightly crafted assertion made by a politician making arguments about the past that he had not investigated. That one sentence represents years of research and public debates regarding historical ideas condensed into a single and readily accessible idea. As Edward Everett wrote to Lincoln the day after the ceremony: "I should be glad, if I could flatter myself that I came as near to the central idea of the occasion, in two hours, as you did in two minutes."[56] Lincoln's Gettysburg Address does not have to be considered *either* history *or* heritage, because it was *both*. At Gettysburg Lincoln was able to do what every historian dreams of doing; he distilled years of research and labor into an assertion about the past that has lived on and even become cherished in memory. In other words, Lincoln was able to take history and render it heritage.

Chapter 9

The Almighty Has His Own Purposes (1864–65)

The Will of God Prevails

"There are too many pigs for the tits." This, according to one disappointed visitor to the White House, is how Lincoln explained why he did not have a government job for him.[1] In an era when the Executive Mansion was open to all, anyone patient enough and willing to wait in line, sometimes for days, could get an audience with the president. In an era before polling, these interviews provided the president with a sense of the mood of the people at any given moment. However, they also proved a great trial to the president, as thousands of people from throughout the country traveled to the executive mansion hoping to receive some kind of favor, usually a patronage job for themselves or a friend or relative. Other visitors, especially religious leaders, instructed Lincoln on what God wanted him to do. Lincoln questioned one delegation of Chicago ministers as to why God would reveal his wishes to others, especially those from "that awfully wicked city," rather than directly to himself.[2] Lincoln, perhaps, expected more vexation when he granted access for a small group of Quakers to see him on Sunday, October 26, 1862.

After brief introductions and conversation, a solemn and momentary silence came over the group, save for the sound of the driving rain upon the windows and roof of the White House. Then, a sixty-one-year-old widow, Eliza Gurney, removed her bonnet and began to address the president.[3] She told Lincoln that she knew he was weighed down with burdens and cares and hoped he would take those in prayer to the Lord, who would grant him comfort. The widow said that she knew that thousands on both sides of the Atlantic rejoiced that the Lord had chosen Lincoln "to loose the bands of wickedness, to undo the heavy burthens, to let the oppressed go free," and "that for this magnanimous deed the children yet unborn will rise up and call him blessed in the name of the Lord." Gurney told the president she had seen "how difficult it is to accomplish that which we wish, and how vain is the help of man." She therefore "earnestly desired that the President might repair day by day . . . to this river of God, which is full of water, even to the well-spring of Eternal Life."[4] She then knelt and delivered a solemn prayer "that light and wisdom might be shed down from on high, to guide our President through the troublous times he had to pass."[5]

Gurney's speech and prayer brought tears to the president's eyes. After a moment of silent reflection, Lincoln replied:

> I am glad of this interview, and glad to know that I have your sympathy and prayers. We are indeed going through a great trial—a fiery trial. In the very responsible position in which I happen to be placed, being an humble instrument in the hands of our Heavenly Father, as I am, and as we all are, to work out his great purposes, I have desired that all my work and acts may be according to this will, and that it might be so, I have sought his aid—but if after endeavoring to do my best in the light which he affords me, I find my efforts fail, I must believe that for some purpose unknown to me, He wills it otherwise. If I had had my way, this war would never have been commenced; If I had been allowed my way this war would have been ended before this, but we find it still continues; and we must believe that He permits it for some wise purpose of his own, mysterious and unknown to us; and though with our limited understandings we may not be able to comprehend it, yet we cannot but believe, that He who made the world still governs it.[6]

What is remarkable about this exchange is how frankly Lincoln discussed his religious views with this stranger. Some friends had known him for decades and yet never heard him utter any remark regarding his faith or lack thereof. Clearly, the widow Eliza P. Gurney had touched him, and he expressed himself more openly about his possible faith than he may have ever done before, apparently showing some kind of evolution from his earlier beliefs. Lincoln, likely inspired by Gurney, continued to meditate on this theme for the rest of his life.

At some point during 1862, perhaps after his interview with Eliza P. Gurney, Lincoln expanded on these thoughts in a private note to himself, known today as his Meditation on the Divine Will. Here, Lincoln mused on the meaning of the war:

> The will of God prevails. In great contests each party claims to act in accordance with the will of God. Both *may* be, and one *must* be wrong. God can not be *for*, and *against* the same thing at the same time. In the present civil war it is quite possible that God's purpose is something different from the purpose of either party—and yet the human instrumentalities, working just as they do, are of the best adaptation to effect His purpose. I am almost ready to say this is probably true—that God wills this contest, and wills that it shall not end yet. By his mere quiet power, on the minds of the now contestants, He could have either *saved* or *destroyed* the Union without a human contest. Yet the contest began. And having begun He could give the final victory to either side any day. Yet the contest proceeds.[7]

Even though it is impossible to know what Lincoln sincerely believed in his heart, Lincoln began to ponder, at least privately, that there were greater forces at work in history than human intention.

Lincoln elaborated on this theme in a letter to Albert Hodges of Kentucky on April 4, 1864. Hodges had been part of a delegation who came to the White House to express its concerns about arming Blacks to join the Union forces. After listening to the delegation's complaints, Lincoln delivered a short speech, and the group apparently left satisfied. Before departing, Hodges asked if he could write the speech down for him, which he thought would do much good, and Lincoln obliged.

Lincoln's letter, containing the substance of what he discussed with the delegation, deals primarily with personal history, especially his own long-held beliefs on slavery, and a short history of abolition during the war. He began with his clearest denunciation of slavery: "I am naturally anti-slavery. If slavery is not wrong, nothing is wrong. I can not remember when I did not so think, and feel." He contrasted his private feelings with his public duty: "And yet I have never understood that the Presidency conferred upon me an unrestricted right to act officially upon this judgment and feeling." He had taken an oath to uphold the Constitution. He believed that the Constitution protected slavery in the states in which it already existed, and he would do nothing to disturb the institution under ordinary circumstances. When subordinates attempted to free slaves under their own authority earlier in the war, he revoked their orders because he did not think they were legal, because preservation of the Constitution did not yet necessitate freeing the slaves. However, after many military setbacks, he felt that in order to preserve the Union and the Constitution, he must do what under ordinary circumstances would be inadmissible. He used an analogy to prove his point: "By general law life and limb must be protected; yet often a limb must be amputated to save a life; but a life is never wisely given to save a limb." Thus, "measures, otherwise unconstitutional, might become lawful, by becoming indispensable to the preservation of the constitution, through the preservation of the nation."[8] The experience of the previous year had shown that his Emancipation Proclamation had augmented the strength of the North while at the same time subtracting strength from the South, proving that the best way to maintain the Union was to uphold his emancipation policy.

Lincoln closed his letter with something that he did not address in his short speech in person. Lincoln wrote,

> In telling this tale I attempt no compliment to my own sagacity. I claim not to have controlled events, but confess plainly that events have controlled me. Now, at the end of three years struggle the nation's condition is not what either party, or any man devised, or expected. God alone can claim it. Whither it is tending seems plain. If God now wills the removal of a great wrong, and wills also that we of the North as well as you of the South, shall pay fairly for our complicity in that wrong, impartial history will find therein new cause to attest and revere the justice and goodness of God.[9]

Lincoln acknowledged there were greater forces at work in history than the intentions of any single person or party. Experience had taught him humility but not despair. He would continue to elaborate on these themes in the coming months.

The World Moves

Later that month, on April 18, 1864, Lincoln addressed the Baltimore Sanitary Fair. Sanitary fairs were popular throughout the North to raise funds for sick and wounded soldiers.

Lincoln could not help recalling the past, as it was Baltimore through which he had had to sneak under the cover of darkness on his way to his first inauguration to avoid assassination. It was the people of Baltimore who had rioted and attacked Union soldiers who peaceably passed through the city. It was also in Baltimore where Lincoln first suspended habeas corpus to protect the vital rail link into the city. Now, the people of Baltimore had gathered not to attack Union soldiers but rather to raise funds to support them. Lincoln, who was always sensitive to the contrast between the past and the present, noted in the beginning of his speech,

"We can not fail to note that the world moves. . . . The change from then till now, is both great, and gratifying."[10] What was more, Maryland, which the Emancipation Proclamation did not cover, was then in the process of abolishing slavery on its own initiative.

Baltimore was not an isolated case but was emblematic of a larger process that the country was undergoing. Lincoln argued that neither side expected the war to last this long or believed slavery would be affected so much, but neither side's expectations came true. Lincoln then quoted a famous proverb: "So true is it that man proposes, and God disposes."[11] This sentiment matches not only what he had spoken to Mrs. Gurney but also what he wrote in his Meditation on the Divine Will along with one of his favorite lines from *Hamlet*, which he had been quoting for years: "There's a divinity that shapes our ends, Rough-hew them how we will."[12] Lincoln then argued: "But we can see the past, though we may not claim to have directed it; and seeing it, in this case, we feel more hopeful and confident for the future."[13] While he knew his limitations, he felt more confident in interpreting the past and using it to envision the future.

As he had done so frequently before, he defined a key term, in this case "liberty," and he professed that the war could be considered a conflict over this word's true meaning:

> We all declare for liberty; but in using the same *word* we do not all mean the same *thing*. With some the word liberty may mean for each man to do as he pleases with himself, and the product of his labor; while with others the same word may mean for some men to do as they please with other men, and the product of other men's labor. Here are two, not only different, but incompatable things, called by the same name—liberty. And it follows that each of the things is, by the respective parties, called by two different and incompatable names—liberty and tyranny.

To illustrate his point, he used an analogy of a sheep, who would define liberty as being free from a wolf, while the wolf would define liberty as the right to hunt the sheep. Lincoln remarked with approval that Maryland was then choosing to renounce the wolf's definition of liberty.[14]

Lincoln closed by discussing the news of the Fort Pillow Massacre, where word had arrived that Confederate soldiers had killed three hundred Black soldiers after they had surrendered. While Lincoln acknowledged that the incident still needed investigation and that he did not want to get into a hanging contest with the Rebels by having the North execute its own prisoners, he still promised "retribution" if the rumors were true. It was important for him to see that justice was done because he was the one who issued the Emancipation Proclamation and had authorized recruitment of Black troops; so he felt "responsible for [their deaths] to the American people, to the christian world, to history, and on my final account to God."[15] Increasingly, Lincoln began to feel that he was not just responsible for upholding the Constitution; he began to feel that his responsibilities to history and to God were inseparable.

You Were Right and I Was Wrong: General Grant

To say Lincoln had a strained relationship with his generals in the early years of the war would be an understatement. His generals chafed at his micromanaging, frustrated at taking orders from a man with almost no military experience. For his part, Lincoln felt he needed to micromanage his generals because they had lost so many of the battles in which they outnumbered their enemies (i.e., First Bull Run, the Seven Days Battles, Second Bull Run, Fredericksburg, and Chancellorsville) or failed to take advantage when the enemy was in a precarious position after a victory (i.e., Antietam and Gettysburg).

However, Lincoln treated General Ulysses S. Grant differently. Lincoln wrote a letter to Grant on July 13, 1863, to congratulate him on his capture of Vicksburg nine days prior. He then gave a short history of his thoughts on Grant's Vicksburg campaign. Lincoln wrote that, when he arrived near the city from the north, he hoped that Grant would run his troops past the southern citadel, which is what Grant eventually did. Lincoln then wrote that he thought Grant should move his troops farther south to meet up with another Union army in Louisiana. When Grant instead marched his men east to tear out the vitals of the state of Mississippi, Lincoln thought Grant had made a mistake. However, Grant's brilliant maneuvering allowed him to capture the last Rebel city on the Mississippi, and as a result the South had been finally cut in two. Grant had no notion of Lincoln's feelings, but Lincoln chose to highlight them here: "I now wish to make the personal acknowledgment that you were right, and I was wrong."[16] He did not have to admit his mistake in the past, but after all the failures he had suffered, it must have been gratifying to know he finally had a general who knew better than him. In her *The Scout Mindset*, a book in which she argues that the search for truth is essential to sound judgment, Julia Galef uses Lincoln's confession to Grant as the first example of what the scout mindset looks like. According to Galef, the "willingness to say 'I was wrong' to someone else is a strong sign of a person who prizes the truth over their own ego."[17]

Lincoln possessed the self-confidence and the humility to admit openly when he was wrong and to be able to learn from that mistake.

Before the spring campaign in 1864, Lincoln again wrote to Grant, who would now lead the forces in the East. Unlike the sharp letters he had written to other generals in the past, Lincoln here expressed his entire confidence in Grant:

> The particulars of your plans I neither know, or seek to know. You are vigilant and self-reliant; and, pleased with this, I wish not to obtrude any constraints or restraints upon you. While I am very anxious that any great disaster, or the capture of our men in great numbers, shall be avoided, I know these points are less likely to escape your attention than they would be mine.[18]

Lincoln had learned from the past who he could trust, and he used this experience to guide his present and have hope for the future.

My Most Generous Friend: Owen Lovejoy

Unlike his older brother Elijah, and despite the threats against him, Owen Lovejoy of Princeton, Illinois, died peacefully of natural causes on March 25, 1864. He lived long enough to see the signing of the Emancipation Proclamation, and his life's work was nearly fulfilled. Lovejoy, who was passionate and intemperate, had an entirely different personality than Lincoln, who was cool and calculating. While the murder of Elijah Lovejoy had led Lincoln to maintain that the law must be upheld, Owen Lovejoy learned the opposite lesson, that the law must be *subverted*. However, over the last ten years of his life, Lovejoy developed a personal friendship with Lincoln, and they both had strong feelings of mutual respect. When other abolitionists were indignant at Lincoln's actions at the beginning of the war, especially when Lincoln revoked emancipation orders by his subordinates, Lovejoy never lost his faith in the president.[19] As Lovejoy said, "If the President does not believe all I do, I believe all he does. If he does not drive as fast as I would, he is on the same road, and it is a question of time."[20]

Lincoln wrote a letter to John H. Bryant of Princeton on May 30, 1864, with a few thoughts to celebrate Lovejoy to be read at a meeting to honor their mutual friend. Lincoln wrote in this letter that his acquaintance with Lovejoy for the preceding decade had been "quite intimate" and that "every step in it has been one of increasing respect and esteem." Even though the two men had used very different methods, Lincoln praised Lovejoy for these differences: "It can be truly said of him that while he was personally ambitious, he bravely endured the obscurity which the unpopularity of his principles imposed, and never accepted official honors, until those honors were ready to admit his principles with him." Lincoln, who largely remained silent about his opposition to slavery for the first two decades of his political career, admired the zeal Lovejoy had in spite of all the forces arrayed against him. Earlier in his career, Lincoln had criticized the radicalism of abolitionists, but in this letter, Lincoln tacitly acknowledged that he had been wrong. After celebrating Lovejoy's politics, Lincoln praised him personally, stating that Lovejoy had been his "most generous friend." In closing, Lincoln wrote: "Let him have the marble monument," but more importantly, Lovejoy's memory must live on "in the hearts of those who love liberty, unselfishly, for all men."[21] Although a relatively obscure figure today, the memory of Owen Lovejoy and everything he stood for has never been forgotten in the hearts of the people of Princeton.

An Inestimable Jewel: Messages to the Soldiers

In 1864 Lincoln delivered several speeches to different units of soldiers as they passed through the capital. To the 166th Ohio Regiment, on August 22, Lincoln proclaimed: "It is not merely for to-day, but for all time to come that we should perpetuate for our children's children this great and free government, which we have enjoyed all our lives." According to Lincoln, his personal history was, in some ways, the embodiment of the promise held out by the national history that they were fighting for:

> I happen temporarily to occupy this big White House. I am a living witness that any one of your children may look to come here as my father's child has. It is in order that each of you may have through this free government which we have enjoyed, an open field and a fair chance for your industry, enterprise and intelligence; that you may all have equal privileges in the race of life, with all its desirable human aspirations. It is for this the struggle should be maintained, that we may not lose our birthright—not only for one, but for two or three years. The nation is worth fighting for, to secure such an inestimable jewel.

Likewise, Lincoln told the 148th Ohio Regiment nine days later, "we are striving to maintain the government and institutions of our fathers, to enjoy them ourselves, and transmit them to our children and our children's children forever." Lincoln addressed the 42nd Massachusetts Regiment on October 31, recalling that it was only three short years prior, in the early days of the war, when mobs in Maryland had attacked

Massachusetts men passing through the city. However, at the stroke of
midnight that night, slavery would be abolished forever in Maryland.
As he had expressed earlier that year in Baltimore, Lincoln told the men
that "the world has moved" since those dark early days in the war, and
these soldiers had played no small role in effecting that change. In a letter he wrote that October to a correspondent, Lincoln expressed that not
only did he "wish all men to be free" but that he also hoped for the end
of slavery because it was the "only thing which ever could bring this nation to civil war."[22] By fighting to end slavery, these soldiers were making
sure that their sacrifices would not have been made in vain and that their
sons would not have to fight the same war over again. Lincoln made clear
in these short addresses that the promise held out by the Founders was
no myth or mere abstraction. President Lincoln, born in a log cabin to a
poor, semiliterate father, was a living embodiment of that great promise.
For Lincoln, it was this generation's responsibility to endure tremendous
sacrifice to preserve this sacred heritage for the future forever.

This responsibility was not for the soldiers alone. In those same
weeks that he delivered these speeches to these units returning home,
Lincoln held an interview with two prominent politicians from Wisconsin, Alexander W. Randall and Joseph T. Mills. Lincoln reiterated the importance of the past to illuminate the present, using such expressions as
"my own experience has proven to me" and "let them prove by the history of this war." However, Lincoln's most startling statement was his
comment on his responsibility to the future. Some hoped for the North
to reach some kind of accommodation with the South by returning freed
slaves, including soldiers who had fought bravely for the Union, to their
former owners in the South. Lincoln stated that he must not do that because he "should be damned in time & in eternity for so doing."[23] Lincoln was professing that his responsibility to both history and Heaven
was one and the same thing.

No Mortal Could Make and No Mortal Could Stay: Letter to Eliza P. Gurney

In some ways, just as Eliza P. Gurney had been a minister to others, she
had become one to the president. In 1863 Lincoln sent a message through
a mutual friend inviting Gurney to write to him when she pleased. On
August 8, 1863, she replied that she and many others were praying for
him and that she believed that God had appointed him to his current
position for a special purpose.[24]

We do not know why Lincoln first requested Gurney to write to him, nor do we know why he waited more than a year to reply, but Lincoln wrote her a heartfelt letter on September 4, 1864, shortly after he had learned of Sherman's capture of Atlanta. Lincoln wrote, "I have not forgotten—probably never shall forget—the very impressive occasion when yourself and friends visited me on a Sabbath forenoon two years ago." Nor had he forgotten her letter a year prior. He then expressed his gratitude for all those praying for him and elaborated on themes he began to discuss with her during their first meeting:

> The purposes of the Almighty are perfect, and must prevail, though we erring mortals may fail to accurately perceive them in advance. We hoped for a happy termination of this terrible war long before this; but God knows best, and has ruled otherwise. We shall yet acknowledge His wisdom and our own error therein. Meanwhile we must work earnestly in the best light He gives us, trusting that so working still conduces to the great ends He ordains. Surely He intends some great good to follow this mighty convulsion, which no mortal could make, and no mortal could stay.[25]

Here he continued to argue two primary points. One is that there were limits to man's wisdom and agency. There were forces at work that were greater than human will or understanding. However, while there may be limits, that does not mean that people have not been granted some wisdom and agency, and they must pursue what is right, as God gives them the understanding to do so. Lincoln continued to ponder these thoughts in private, and remarkably, he continued to express his deepest thoughts on God to a woman he had only met once. It is a testament to how deeply Mrs. Gurney had moved him.

Philosophy to Learn Wisdom from: Lincoln's Election Victory Speech

In leading the nation during a time of armed insurrection, it is not easy for us to understand how truly difficult it was to keep the Union united and how the conflict rent apart not only a nation but also innumerable communities within that nation. Lincoln painted his most vivid account of this process to a fractious delegation from the Border State of Missouri in 1863:

> Actual war coming, blood grows hot, and blood is spilled. Thought is forced from old channels into confusion. Deception breeds and thrives. Confidence dies, and universal suspicion reigns. Each man feels an impulse to kill his neighbor, lest he be first killed by him. Revenge and

retaliation follow. And all this, as before said, may be among honest men only. But this is not all. Every foul bird comes abroad, and every dirty reptile rises up. These add crime to confusion. Strong measures, deemed indispensable but harsh at best, such men make worse by mal-administration. Murders for old grudges, and murders for pelf, proceed under any cloak that will best cover for the ocasion.[26]

However, with Sherman's capture of Atlanta and his overwhelming Electoral College victory in 1864, the end of this curse Lincoln spoke of appeared to be near. On the night of November 10 Lincoln delivered a victory speech from the White House window in response to a serenade.

Lincoln opened the speech with a reiteration of his frequent statement that this war was a test for free government: "It has long been a grave question whether any government, not *too* strong for the liberties of its people, can be strong *enough* to maintain its own existence, in great emergencies." Part of that test was whether that government could successfully carry out a presidential election within the midst of that war. Lincoln felt it was necessary because they could not fight for a free government without free elections. The difficulties faced during the election would be instructive for the future. As Lincoln said, "What has occurred in this case, must ever recur in similar cases. Human-nature will not change. In any future great national trial, compared with the men of this, we shall have as weak, and as strong; as silly and as wise; as bad and good." Therefore, what had just happened should be remembered and studied: "Let us, therefore, study the incidents of this, as philosophy to learn wisdom from, and none of them as wrongs to be revenged."[27] In this war that had killed more Americans than any other, many, both North and South, could see the history of this war as a cause to nurse hatred and seek vengeance. For Lincoln, who proclaimed his belief in a useful past throughout his career, history must be seen as the wellspring of wisdom to discern the means to build a better future rather than the root of discord to avenge the wrongs of the past.

King's Cure for All the Evils: The Thirteenth Amendment

Lyman Trumbull, a U.S. Senator from Alton, where Elijah Lovejoy had been martyred, cowrote the Thirteenth Amendment, using much of the same language from the Ordinance of 1787 (which outlawed slavery in the Northwest Territories) that Lincoln had cited so frequently in his pre-presidential speeches. Lincoln worked mainly behind the scenes to get the amendment passed in the Senate in 1864 and then in the House on January 31, 1865. It would be ratified and take effect later in the year. Even though he had no official constitutional role in the amendment process, Lincoln signed the Thirteenth Amendment after the House of Representatives passed it.

In response to another serenade, this time on the day after the House passed the amendment, Lincoln delivered another short speech from the White House. After reminding his audience that they still had work to do to get the states to ratify the amendment, he proudly told the crowd that he had received word that day that his home state was the first to approve it, just a day after its passage in the House. He was hopeful because it would "remove all causes of disturbance in the future." Thus, slavery would be "rooted out." Lincoln was proud to have issued the Emancipation Proclamation. Still, he admitted that it did not free all the slaves and the legality of the proclamation could be challenged in the future, threatening the freedom of those already liberated. Americans must work to get the amendment passed because it "is a King's cure for all the evils. It winds the whole thing up."[28] In Lincoln's view, Americans were fulfilling their great responsibility to history.

The Second Inaugural Address

The six weeks from May 4 to June 15 in 1864 were the deadliest days of the deadliest war in American history. Union and Rebel armies fought and maneuvered across the Old Dominion only to end in a stalemate in the protracted siege of Petersburg outside the Southern capital.

While the Union dead from Grant's Overland Campaign were being buried in their Virginia graves, the Union capital was turning into one vast hospital to care for the thousands of wounded. Steamers brought them almost continuously from the battlefields, and ambulances filled with the wounded crowded the streets from the boats to the tent hospitals that surrounded the city. The president frequently stopped and talked with these men and attempted to provide them comfort. One of Lincoln's lawyer friends from Illinois, Congressman Isaac N. Arnold, recalled meeting the president in his carriage as he rode from the White House to the Soldiers' Home, where he spent most of his evenings during the hot months of the year. Arnold remembered Lincoln's face as being "grave and anxious." Further, he said, "He looked like one who had lost the dearest member of his own family." After greeting him, Lincoln pointed to the lines of ambulances carrying wounded soldiers and said, "Look yonder at those poor fellows. I cannot bear it. This suffering, this loss of life is dreadful."[29]

Friends, family members, and acquaintances who knew him in his early life had all remarked that Lincoln would periodically withdraw within himself and silently meditate for long periods of time. According to those who knew him during his presidency, these grim silences only grew more frequent in the latter years of the war. William Stoddard, who worked in the White House as a secretary, remembered one night when he worked late into the early morning hours hearing the "sentry-like tread" of the president as he silently paced the floor in his room. Stoddard left the White House shortly before three in the morning, and he could still hear Lincoln's footsteps. Stoddard wrote that Lincoln's meditation "was a vigil with God and with the future."[30] Another of Lincoln's secretaries, John Hay, recalled how the war years wore on him:

> Under this frightful ordeal his demeanor and disposition changed—so gradually that it would be impossible to say when the change began; but he was in mind, body, and nerves a very different man at the second in-auguration from the one who had taken the oath in 1861. He continued always the same kindly, genial, and cordial spirit he had been at first; but the boisterous laughter became less frequent year by year; the eye grew veiled by constant meditation on momentous subjects; the air of reserve and detachment from his surroundings increased. He aged with great rapidity.[31]

Not only the president but also the capital had been transformed in the four short years from Lincoln's first to his second inauguration. During the first inauguration, a crane had protruded from the domeless rotunda of the Capitol. Despite the limited money and manpower, Lincoln insisted that construction must continue, and by his second inauguration, workmen had completed the dome and crowned it with the *Statue of Freedom*. While in 1861 Washington had been, to some extent, a Confederate-sympathizing city, by 1865 the Confederate supporters had grown scarce. As the capital's population swelled in the war years, almost all its new residents were pro-Union. Lincoln's first inauguration was a time of uncertainty. Four years later, uncertainty had been replaced with expectation, as the Rebel armies were on the brink of capitulation or disintegration. In 1861 slavery was still very much legal in Washington. By 1865 not only had slavery been abolished in the capital but thousands of the people gathered to see Lincoln's second inauguration were Black, mingling freely with White spectators. While all the soldiers who provided security for the first ceremony had been White, many of those who did the same in 1865 were Black, a direct testament to the president's policies. William Lloyd Garrison, the famous abolitionist and a

virulent critic of Lincoln early in his presidency, summed up the radical
changes the country had undergone during Lincoln's four years in the
White House:

> His Emancipation proclamation of January 1, liberated more than three-
> fourths of the entire slave population; that since that period, emanci-
> pation has followed in Maryland, Western Virginia, Missouri, and the
> District of Columbia, and is being rapidly consummated in Kentucky
> and Tennessee, thus terminating the holding of property in man every-
> where under the American flag; that all the vast Territories have been
> consecrated to freedom and free labor; that all Fugitive Slave laws have
> been repealed, so that slave-hunting is at an end in all the free States;
> that no rebel State can be admitted to the Union, except on the basis of
> complete emancipation; that national justice (refused under every other
> Administration) has been done to the republics of Hayti and Liberia, by
> the full recognition of their independence; that an equitable treaty has
> been made with Great Britain for the effectual suppression of the foreign
> slave trade, through right of search; that a large portion of the army is
> made up of those who, until now, have been prohibited bearing arms,
> and refused enrolment in the militia of every State in the Union; that
> tens of thousands of bond-men have obtained their freedom in Mary-
> land, Kentucky, Missouri and Louisiana, together with their wives and
> children, by their enlistment as soldiers;. that free negro schools are fol-
> lowing wherever the army penetrates, and multitudes of young and old,
> who, under the old slave system, were prohibited learning the alphabet,
> are now rapidly acquiring that knowledge which is power, and which
> makes slavery and serfdom alike impracticable.[32]

However, Lincoln's actions, which had rendered these changes possible,
had come at a dreadful cost, as more than half a million boys and men,
both White and Black, who had been alive at the time of the first ceremony were now dead. While some had been buried in orderly national
cemeteries like those at Gettysburg and Arlington, many others had been
dumped anonymously in mass pits at Shiloh, lay at the bottom of Mobile
Bay, or were consumed by flames in the Virginia wilderness.

The morning of Lincoln's second inauguration, March 4, 1865, was
wet and gloomy, the rain turning the unpaved streets of the capital into
a morass of mud. Reporting for the *New York Times*, the poet Walt Whitman wrote that the morning's weather was "like whirling demons, dark,
with slanting rain, full of rage."[33] By the start of the ceremony, the rain
had stopped, but the skies were still a leaden gray. When the president
emerged from the Capitol and walked to the inauguration platform, he
was greeted with reverberating cheers and applause from the multitude
stretched out below. As Lincoln began to speak, a most curious thing

happened that many in the audience would forever remember. The reporter Noah Brooks wrote, "the sun, which had been obscured all day, burst forth in its unclouded meridian splendor and flooded the spectacle with glory and light. Every heart beat quicker at the unexpected omen, and not a few mentally prayed that so might the darkness which has obscured the past four years be now dissipated by the sun of prosperity."[34]

Lincoln started slowly as he did in so many of his speeches. He used his first paragraph, a full fifth of his address, to tell his audience what he would not say. Lincoln would not detail how the war was going, nor would he discuss any new policies, and Lincoln, who had known failure so many times in the past, would make no predictions for the future. What he would do is give the nation a history lesson. Lincoln devoted the second and third paragraphs, fully 70 percent of the address, to a history of why the war started and its ultimate cause.[35]

At his first inauguration four years prior, both sides hoped to avoid war. Why, then, had this tragedy happened? Lincoln asserted: "Both parties deprecated war; but one of them would *make* war rather than let the nation survive; and the other would *accept* war rather than let it perish." No matter how much they dreaded war, both sides feared another outcome much more. Lincoln used the passive voice to describe what happened next, almost as if the coming of war had been devoid of human volition: "And the war came."[36]

This in and of itself did not satisfactorily explain why the war began, nor could it account for the duration and savagery with which it was fought. Lincoln knew that the historical causes of this war were more than the consternation over the result of one election or a conflict between union and disunion. Lincoln continued: "One eighth of the whole population were colored slaves, not distributed generally over the Union, but localized in the Southern part of it. These slaves constituted a peculiar and powerful interest. All knew that this interest was, somehow, the cause of the war." While admitting with his "somehow" that there is always some uncertainty about historical causality, Lincoln, unlike generations of scholars after him, accurately centered the origin of the Civil War on slavery. As he had done so many times prior, Lincoln argued that *interest* had been a powerful motivating factor in history, blinding those he believed to be otherwise good people from distinguishing right from wrong. This interest was the South's primary reason for rebelling, as they wanted "to strengthen, perpetuate, and extend" slavery, even at the cost of war. Lincoln continued his theme of the limits of human agency, arguing that not only had neither side wanted war but neither side believed it would last so long or that its original cause would be much affected. As Lincoln noted: "Each looked for an easier triumph, and a result less fundamental and astounding."[37]

Both sides were profoundly religious, as faith played a more significant role during this conflict than in any other in American history. Lincoln proclaimed, "Both read the same Bible, and pray to the same God; and each invokes His aid against the other." Just as they had done with their cherished history, Americans would use the cultural touchstone of scripture to develop wildly divergent views on the most contentious issues of the day. Paraphrasing Genesis and echoing an argument made by Elijah Lovejoy three decades prior, Lincoln gave his sharpest critique of the South in his address: "It may seem strange that any men should dare to ask a just God's assistance in wringing their bread from the sweat of other men's faces." However, he followed this critique up by balancing law with Gospel, quoting Matthew 7:1: "But let us judge not that we be not judged." Lincoln then moved to an idea he had been developing since his 1862 meeting with Eliza P. Gurney: "The prayers of both could not be answered; that of neither has been answered fully. The Almighty has His own purposes."[38] No man wanted this war or expected it to last so long. Human agency had failed. Only forces greater than human intention could account for this.

In this address, some of Lincoln's most profound thoughts dwelt on the proper recompense for sin. Quoting Matthew 18:7, Lincoln proclaimed: "Woe unto the world because of offences! for it must needs be that offences come; but woe to that man by whom the offence cometh!" Lest the wisdom of this verse be obscure to his audience, Lincoln clarified:

> If we shall suppose that American Slavery is one of those offences which, in the providence of God, must needs come, but which, having continued through His appointed time, He now wills to remove, and that He gives to both North and South, this terrible war, as the woe due to those by whom the offence came, shall we discern therein any departure from those divine attributes which the believers in a Living God always ascribe to Him?

Lincoln did not say "Southern" slavery but rather "American" slavery, emphasizing that the nation as a whole was guilty of this "offense." Thus, they were all suffering "woe" and "terrible war," just punishment from an active and living God. Lincoln continued with the limits of human intention: "Fondly do we hope—fervently do we pray—that this mighty scourge of war may speedily pass away." However, it was not given to men to determine the length and severity of this "mighty scourge." Lincoln concluded his history lesson: "Yet, if God wills that it continue, until all the wealth piled by the bond-man's two hundred and fifty years of unrequited toil shall be sunk, and until every drop of blood drawn with the lash, shall be paid by another drawn with the sword, as was said three thousand years ago, so still it must be said 'the judgments of the Lord, are true and righteous altogether.'"[39] Many of the men standing guard that day bore the scars on their bodies from the blood "drawn with the lash," and they were the same men who also bore the guns used to end that "offense" through the blood "drawn with the sword."

While Lincoln doubted the extent of human agency, he did not negate its importance. Lincoln concluded:

> With malice toward none; with charity for all; with firmness in the right, as God gives us to see the right, let us strive on to finish the work we are in; to bind up the nation's wounds; to care for him who shall have borne the battle, and for his widow, and his orphan—to do all which may achieve and cherish a just, and a lasting peace, among ourselves, and with all nations.[40]

Lincoln understood that this war would live on in memory, and it is human nature to use the past to create and perpetuate strife. As he had argued in his victory speech a few months earlier, the past must be used to derive wisdom and not inspire vengeance. By laying guilt at the feet of all of America and by arguing that all were paying for that guilt, Lincoln was tearing down the old in order to build up the new. For lasting peace, Americans must not harbor a vengeful memory of the past. They must act with "charity," do "right, bind up the wounds, care" for the suffering, and strive for a "just" and "lasting peace." Lincoln's Second Inaugural Address neatly parallels, and almost was certainly inspired by, the closing verses of the twelfth chapter of the Apostle Paul's Letter to the Romans.

During the ceremony, Lincoln spotted Frederick Douglass in the audience. Even though he had harshly criticized Lincoln at the beginning of his presidency and did not always agree with him now, Douglass had come to respect Lincoln. The two had met in the White House twice before, once upon Douglass's own initiative and a second time at Lincoln's invitation. Douglass later argued that Lincoln was not only a "great President" but also a "GREAT MAN." He wrote, "In his company I was never in any way reminded of my humble origin, or of my unpopular color." When the guards barred Douglass from attending the reception the evening of the inauguration, he sent someone ahead to notify Lincoln, knowing that they were not acting on orders from him. When Lincoln found out, Douglass was quickly admitted in. When Lincoln saw him in the East Room, he announced for all to hear that Douglass was his friend and he was glad to see him. Lincoln, who had spent years developing the themes he explored in his second inaugural address, was eager to hear Douglass's thoughts on the oration, especially given Douglass's reputation as a writer and orator. Douglass replied, "Mr. Lincoln, that was a sacred effort."[41] As Douglass recognized, Lincoln had somehow united the past, the political, and the sacred in this great masterpiece of history.

Now He Belongs to the Ages

Just like Isaac Watts's Indian arrow, events moved swiftly. On April 3 Union troops captured Richmond. Six days later Robert E. Lee and the chief Rebel army surrendered to Grant and his men at Appomattox Courthouse. Soon, the few remaining Rebel forces would lay down their arms, and the war would be over.

Two days after Lee surrendered, Lincoln delivered a victory speech from his window at the White House. While he had been discussing it privately for more than a year, Lincoln announced publicly for the first time that some Blacks should be allowed to vote. (In an 1864 letter to the governor of Louisiana he marked "Private," the president had suggested that some Blacks should be allowed to vote in order to "to keep the jewel of liberty within the family of freedom.") By now, he had largely abandoned the colonization schemes that had been promoted by so many of the leaders who had inspired him in the past. He now was beginning to advocate for Blacks to be not just free from slavery but also full citizens of the Union they had fought for. Near the end of his speech, Lincoln told his audience, "Important principles may, and must, be inflexible."[42] In so many ways, Lincoln had changed course to meet the needs of the present. However, he held fast to the idea that he had learned from history that the American experiment was dedicated to the "elevation of men," a principle from which he would never waver.[43]

At some point during these final days of the war, Lincoln wrote a private note laying out plans for the demobilization of the army. Lincoln looked to the past to guide his present as he had so many times before. He noted that after the War of 1812, the army had been reduced to "about one soldier to 602 souls" and later, in 1820, it had been reduced again to "one soldier to 963 souls." Using these figures from the past as a guide, Lincoln believed that he could safely reduce the army to "one soldier to 1000 souls."[44]

Had he lived, his experience would have shown him that the past, in this case, would not provide an adequate precedent for what would be necessary for the Reconstruction of the South after the war. Lincoln, the one who had done more than anyone else to save the Union of the "almost chosen people," was shot on Good Friday, lingering a few hours into the next morning. He thus passed from a present reality to a memory that would, in the words of Secretary of War Edwin Stanton, "belong to the ages."[45]

Conclusion

Ironically, the man who shaped American history more than anyone else is also the one who most doubted his ability to do so. As the war progressed, Lincoln deepened his conviction that there were greater forces at work than the intentions of any single person or party. Lincoln no longer made the same arguments about historical causality that he had in his early political career, which reduced cause and effect relationships in human affairs as something as simple as a gust of wind extinguishing a candle. However, he never despaired of human volition but instead redoubled his commitment to it. Lincoln frequently appealed to the past in his final years to guide and inspire the nation. By understanding the past, Americans could better understand the present and work towards a better future. By studying the past, we can see the mistakes that are common to all, and so we must not look to avenge the sins of others but rather learn from them and correct them. In order to establish this just and lasting peace, we must look to history not as something to be avenged but rather as something to learn wisdom from.

Chapter 10

The Wisdom of History

Two Eulogies

Less than a year after Lincoln's death, the nation had already begun to celebrate his birthday (February 12). Lincoln's successor, Andrew Johnson, chose the great historian George Bancroft to deliver a eulogy for the martyred president to Congress on what would have been his birthday. Unlike Lincoln, Johnson readily sought Bancroft's advice (as so many influential politicians had done before) to guide him through his first few months in office. Bancroft seemed the perfect choice to celebrate Lincoln's life and put it into context. He spent much of January 1866 crafting his speech, and on February 12 delivered his address to a joint session of Congress.[1]

Before Lincoln's death, Bancroft had privately denigrated the president, writing, "We have a president without brains." He had said that Lincoln was "ignorant, self-willed," and "surrounded by men, some of whom are as ignorant as himself." However, Bancroft gave much praise to the fallen president during his eulogy. He said, "LINCOLN took to heart the eternal truths of liberty, obeyed them as the commands of Providence, and accepted the human race as the judge of his fidelity." Bancroft gave credit to the American people, but it was Lincoln, he said, who "finished a work which all time cannot overthrow," and he would "be remembered through all time by his countrymen, and by all the peoples of the world."[2]

Even though Bancroft praised Lincoln, several who knew the president best harshly criticized Bancroft's eulogy. In the part that would give the most offense, Bancroft professed, "A good President will secure unity to his administration by his own supervision of the various departments." But Lincoln's "supervision of affairs was unsteady and incomplete," and, "he rather confused than advanced the public business."[3] Lincoln's friends might have accepted the criticism as having some merit had Bancroft not implied that the critique meant that Lincoln was not a "good president." Judge David Davis, who Lincoln had known and befriended during his days riding the circuit in Illinois and who Lincoln had elevated to the Supreme Court, harshly criticized Bancroft's eulogy, writing that he "totally misconceived Mr Lincoln's character" because he had never known him personally. What was more, Bancroft himself was "as cold as an *icicle*." One of Lincoln's young secretaries in the White House who would later rise to become secretary of state in the McKinley and Roosevelt administrations, John Hay, used decidedly undiplomatic language to describe Bancroft and his address. The great historian belonged to the "patent leather kid glove set" that could understand the true Lincoln no more "than an owl does of a comet, blazing in his blinking eyes." Hay continued, "Bancrofts address was a disgraceful exhibition of ignorance and prejudice," and said that Lincoln was better understood by the people than by the learned historian.[4]

George Bancroft was an earnest man who did his best with the lights afforded him, which were in no way insignificant as he advanced the study of history perhaps more than any other American to that point. However, despite his invective, Hay touched on something important in his critique of Bancroft. In his commencement address at Harvard in 1817, Bancroft had declared that the learned scholar "feels himself elevated above the common sphere of mankind" as he "lives in an upper world and contemplates with calm indifference the labours of ordinary men, as of inferior beings, like the majestick eagle."[5] Although, as a politician and historian, he professed to support the wisdom and virtue of the common people, his rhetoric never ceased to soar above them, with highly florid abstractions that rarely lowered itself to deal with concrete specificities. In contrast, according to the historian Shelby Foote, Lincoln's rhetoric was "jogtrot prose" that was "compacted of words and phrases still with the bark on" and was more the language of the people.[6] Furthermore, while Lincoln's arguments about the past stressed humility and the fragmentary nature of human understanding, Bancroft, according to his biographer Lilian Handlin, was "self-righteous and absolutely certain of his judgments."[7] In Lincoln's historical narratives, the history of slavery was essential for understanding his era, whereas Bancroft, according to Handlin, made only "occasional innocuous references" to slavery in his narratives that "offended no one," and his books were "as popular in the South as in the North."[8] Finally, for all Bancroft's learning and trans-Atlantic experience, the self-educated Lincoln was the historian who shaped America's memory of the past the most. Adolphe de Chambrun, a French diplomat who came to know Lincoln in his final weeks, wrote, "His incisive speech found its way to the very depths of the soul; his short and clear sentences would captivate the audiences on which they fell. To him was given to see nearly all his definitions pass into daily proverb."[9] Writing nearly a lifetime later in 1908, Horace White, who covered Lincoln's campaigns in Illinois as a young reporter, wrote of him: "Though dead he yet speaketh to men, women, and children who never saw him, and so, I think, he will continue to speak to generations yet unborn."[10] Even though Bancroft performed deeper research and wrote more extensively on the past, Lincoln made a more "just application" of the past and was able to distill his research into burning symbols that would sear themselves into the memory of the American people.

An example of Lincoln's effect on the nation's memory can be seen in another eulogy of the president, this one given by someone whose advice Lincoln had sought: Frederick Douglass. Two months after Lincoln's death, Douglass delivered his tribute at Cooper Union, the same location where Lincoln had delivered the speech that would transform his career five years earlier. While in his most famous eulogy of Lincoln, which Douglass gave in 1876, he described Lincoln as being "preeminently the white man's President," in his 1865 address Douglass declared that Lincoln was "emphatically the black mans President."[11] The difference could be due to context. As he explained earlier, in his 1865 eulogy, Blacks were banned from participating in the procession as Lincoln's funeral train passed through the city. Douglass, in his 1865 speech, was fighting for Blacks to have the right to both participate in and shape the memory of the president. He told his audience at Cooper Union that "no people or class of people in this country, have a better reason for lamenting the death of Abraham Lincoln," than "the colored people." Thus, they desired "to honor and perpetuate his memory."[12] After praising Lincoln, Douglass echoed the same historical argument Lincoln made in his second inaugural address—that the Civil War "was beyond the power of human will or wisdom" to have been prevented. In this eulogy Douglass professes that the epochs of history "are the great teachers of mankind," a sentiment with which Lincoln would have fully concurred. Echoing Lincoln's Gettysburg Address, Douglass described the Declaration of Independence as being signed "four score and nine years ago."[13] In both form and substance Douglass was forming and transmitting the memory of the past that Lincoln had worked so hard to shape. While by the end of his life Lincoln's political views had become almost identical to those of the prophet Frederick Douglass, it was Douglass the prophet who had come to appreciate the morally guided acumen of Lincoln the statesman.

Sense of Historical Meaning: Abraham Lincoln and Reinhold Niebuhr

Perhaps the greatest American theologian of the twentieth century, Reinhold Niebuhr, began his ministry in the small central Illinois town of Lincoln, the only community named for the man during his lifetime. Although known as a theologian, Niebuhr wrote perhaps as much on the philosophy of politics and history as he did on religion. Like an Old Testament prophet, Niebuhr believed these three topics—religion, politics, and history—were inextricably linked. Niebuhr derived his understanding of the past through his analysis of scripture, which, according to him, reveals that people must strive for justice but also that the politician and the interpreter of the past must understand that no person or group is as virtuous or wise as it believes it is. Niebuhr spoke out against, on the one hand, those who recognize no higher good than self-interest (such as Nazis) and on the other hand, those who recognize a higher sort of values but who believe that their wisdom and virtue can perfectly live up to these ideals (such as pacifists, with whom he once identified, and communists, with whom he once sympathized). He understood that there would always be people who cynically promote their own interests by holding up sacred scripture (sometimes literally), who neither read nor heed what is inside. He denounced those who would use religion or history to sanctify their political views, arguing that "the most perennial sin of religion" is the tendency for people or groups of people to use the "transcendent" to "absolutize rather than to criticize the partial achievements of history." Niebuhr accused those who mistake their own ideas for the ultimate truth and their own virtues for the ultimate good with "idolatry." Even though flawed creatures, humans still had a religious duty to work for good. Niebuhr prayed, "Grant us power and grace to resist evil, knowing that even though we ourselves are sinful men you have called us to be instruments of your justice."[14]

Niebuhr brought this religious sensibility not just to his view of politics but also to his view of how the past should be interpreted. According to Niebuhr, the Apostle Paul in 1 Corinthians used a perfect metaphor that can be applied to how we can understand history—namely, "We see through a glass darkly." There are always those who believe that the past can be clearly seen, as clear as a scientist can see and interpret the natural world. According to Niebuhr, however, interpreting the past is "never purely an intellectual enterprise but a moral and spiritual one." Niebuhr elaborates:

> The highest degree of objectivity and impartiality in the assessment of historical values is achieved by a quality of religious humility, which gains awareness of the unconscious dishonesty of judgment and seeks to correct it. The difference between the knowledge of nature and the knowledge and estimate of our fellowmen is this: in the knowledge of nature the mind of man is at the center of the process of knowing; and the self with all its fears, hopes and ambitions is on the circumference. In the knowledge of historical events the self, with all its emotions and desires, is at the center of the enterprise; and the mind is on the circumference, serving merely as an instrument of the anxious self.[15]

Overly confident people do not recognize that "the historical character of man as both agent in, and creature of, history." They lack "the humility to accept the fact that the whole drama of history is enacted in a frame of meaning too large for human comprehension or management. It is a drama in which fragmentary meanings can be discerned within a penumbra of mystery; and in which specific duties and responsibilities can be undertaken within a vast web of relations which are beyond our powers." According to Niebuhr, "The final wisdom of life requires, not the annulment of incongruity but the achievement of serenity within and above it."[16] Some argue that since we cannot see the past clearly, nothing meaningful to guide the present can be discerned. Niebuhr argues that when thinking about the past, we must not be "overwhelmed by mystery" because there are "clues of divine meaning which shine through the perplexities of life." The proper approach to understanding the past is a "combination of humility and trust" that is "precisely defined when we affirm that we see, but admit that we see through a glass darkly." Despite our limitations, wisdom can and should be derived from history. Wisdom, according to Niebuhr, "is not so much an intellectual achievement as the fruit of a humility." While knowledge is important, it is more essential, when pursuing truth, to vanquish "the pride of the heart" than the "ignorance of the mind." True humility, however, is much more difficult to earn than extensive knowledge. Niebuhr posits, "Perhaps that is why the truest interpretations of the Christian faith have come in moments of history when civilizations were crumbling and the processes of history and the judgments of God had humbled human arrogance."[17]

Without question, the American Civil War was one of those moments. It is no surprise that the man who would best embody how a statesman should merge religion, politics, and history would emerge during this trial. While nearly all statesmen in history had fallen short, Niebuhr believed Abraham Lincoln was the exemplar who possessed this highest form of wisdom, especially in his second inaugural address. Niebuhr writes, "Among all the statesmen of ancient and modern periods, Lincoln alone had a sense of historical meaning so high as to cast doubt on the intention of both sides and to place the enemy into the same category of ambiguity as the nation to which his life was committed." Unlike other politicians, Lincoln did not make "more ultimate claims for their cause, whether for the nation or their party, than either a transcendent providence or a neutral posterity would validate." Niebuhr praised Lincoln for believing, just as the prophets of the Old Testament, that there was a meaningful history and that he, like the prophets, excelled at discerning that meaning. "It was Lincoln's achievement," according to Niebuhr, "to embrace a paradox which lies at the center of the spirituality of all western culture; namely, the affirmation of a meaningful history and the religious reservation about the partiality and bias which the human actors and agents betray in the definition of meaning."[18] Lincoln did not feel that religion sanctioned or sanctified his actions but provided judgment and limits regarding how to live with humility and acceptance. According to Niebuhr, people "are never safe against the temptation of claiming God too simply as the sanctifier of whatever we most fervently desire," because, "the true God can be known only where there is some awareness of a contradiction between divine and human purposes, even on the highest level of human aspirations." Niebuhr praises Lincoln as the noble exemplar of the statesman: "This combination of moral resoluteness about the immediate issues with a religious awareness of another dimension of meaning and judgment must be regarded as almost a perfect model of the difficult but not impossible task of remaining loyal and responsible toward the moral treasures of a free civilization on the one hand while yet having some religious vantage point over the struggle."[19] Because of this duality, Lincoln was able to fulfill the ultimate role of a statesman.

There are many, with good reason, who argue that both religion and history should stay out of politics. This is because religion and history are misused in exactly the same ways—to sanctify one's preconceived notions and personal interests. We are guilty of idolatry when we use religion or history to exalt ourselves and attempt to appropriate greater wisdom and virtue than we possess.

Conversely, a religious sensibility born in humility works for both the statesman and the historian. This sensibility recognizes that there are limits to human understanding and virtue, but this does not mean human understanding and virtue do not exist or are unnecessary. Barack Obama, a fan of both Lincoln and Niebuhr, praised the statesman Lincoln as someone who "acts while still admitting doubt."[20] This same sensibility applies to both the historian, who makes assertions about the past while still admitting uncertainty, and any statesman who would attempt to make history useful. For religion and history to be used successfully in politics, they must not be sanctifiers of one's selfish interests but rather motivators and sources of discipline. The same sensibility allowed Abraham Lincoln to see and proclaim that "we are not what we have been" and to use the past to inspire the nation to live up to its highest ideals.

Abraham Lincoln was not free of biases that affected his interpretations or judgments about the past. However, more than any statesman before or since (and more than many historians both past and present), it was the nexus of these three sensibilities—politics, the past, and the sacred—that gave Abraham Lincoln the ability to rise above the narrow interests and interpretations of his own time to discern the wisdom of history and to fulfill his role within it.

Abraham Lincoln and the Wisdom of History

Just as Lincoln believed there was wisdom to be derived from his past, we also can learn much from Lincoln and how he used this history. His approach to and attitude toward the past can continue to inform historians and politicians so long as Lincoln is remembered and studied.

It is evident from Lincoln's earliest writings that he possessed a heightened attachment to the past. From the poetry he read and wrote, the hymns he memorized, and the history he read, it is unmistakable that Lincoln elevated the memory of the past to something sacred. While it is possible to derive meaning from the past through cold logic, the inspiration derived from history more readily propels people to action. Historians put on the cloak of dispassionate reason, but having something approaching a mystical attachment to the past should not be discounted or discouraged. In some ways children see the world more clearly than adults. They are awake to all the sublime beauty and terror, along with everything in between, in the human experience. Slowly this glowing understanding of our world, for most of us, is dulled, and we become deadened to the wonder, including the extent of the beauty and terror of the past. However, if we do not look at the past with at least some sense of wonder, we do not fully see history.

However, this inspiration should also be informed by the reasoned study and craft of history. This process begins not in the knowing of memory but the questioning that is the root of the discipline. Lincoln believed that he could use the study of the past to gain wisdom for his present, and only by accurately and truthfully reconstructing this past could one find this wisdom. This understanding derived from an accurate reconstruction of the past grants power to those who possess it over those who lack such insight. Those who accurately interpret the past can see patterns of continuities and discontinuities, better persuade people open to reason, and make their decisions on the best evidence available rather than on faulty premises. History can cut through the groupthink of commonly held beliefs about the past to arrive at better solutions for the present. Basing decisions on accurate evidence and logical reconstructions of the past does not guarantee success, but it makes success much more likely than if these decisions were based on faulty and untested assumptions. As Lincoln argued, "right makes might," which applies to getting right with history.

While "right" may indeed "make might," this attitude must be tempered with a proper understanding of people's limitations to determine that right. Ultimately, this sensibility is grounded in humility. It means admitting mistakes, as Lincoln did, when one is wrong. This humility understands that while a more accurate account of the past is more valuable than an inaccurate one, it is still restricted by the limitations of human agency and our ability to predict the future. In human affairs, history can show what is *possible*, it can suggest what is *probable*, but it cannot determine what is *inevitable*. As Lincoln demonstrated, there is wisdom in understanding the limits of one's wisdom.

Lincoln well understood the tendency of interest to corrupt one's interpretation of the past. Lincoln accused his opponents of misinterpreting the American Revolution to promote their own financial and political interests. While it is readily apparent how the interest of politicians can skew their historical interpretations, historians, both past and present, are also susceptible to these same forces. Historians as a class have a greater knowledge of the past and possess training in investigating and interpreting it. However, we are not devoid of self-interest and emotions, and as with anyone, those things can cloud our judgment. The interests of the historian are not necessarily concurrent with those of the greater community or aligned with the naked pursuit of truth. Human nature makes it less likely that a historian will reach a conclusion or make an argument that we feel will endanger our ability to sell a book or achieve tenure. As Niebuhr taught, "Even the most rational men are never quite rational when their own interests are at stake."[21] The historian Shelby Foote perhaps best expressed how Lincoln could step back and see outside himself and his own interests: "A very mysterious man, he's got so many sides to him. The curious thing about Lincoln to me is that he could remove himself from himself as if he were looking at himself. It's a very strange, very eerie thing."[22]

Likewise, historians are just as susceptible to groupthink as the rest of society. As Lincoln wrote, fashion plays a powerful force on human actions. Few modern historians are likely to reach the conclusions that are the intellectual equivalent of a nineteenth-century man wearing his wife's bonnet to church. Historians will never be devoid of emotion or self-interest, but we should be mindful of these factors to limit the effects they have on our work. While intelligence, training, and knowledge are essential, they are no substitute for humility and sound judgment. However, historians must not be devoid of emotion. To the greatest extent possible, historians must realize that our emotions must serve our narratives and not the other way around. As Lincoln has shown, passion can be a powerful force in moving the public toward the good, but these emotions must be *informed by* rather than *dictate* history.

Lincoln also understood, as the scholar Alan Jacobs writes in his *Breaking Bread with the Dead*, that "to confront the reality that the very same people who give us rich wisdom can also talk what seems to us absolute nonsense (and vice versa) is an education in the human condition. Including our own condition, which is likewise compounded of wisdom and nonsense."[23] We all have people we look up to in our pasts, and we must recognize that no matter how virtuous or wise, even the greatest of people (including politicians and historians) are still just that—people—with all the limitations, failings, contradictions, and foolishness wrapped up in being human. As Lincoln understood, to blindly follow the great people of the past is to limit human potential, constrict free will, deny progress, and perpetuate past mistakes for eternity. In order to have a usable history, we need to apply a strong filter that retains the wisdom of the past and sifts out its unwisdom. No filter is perfect, but the more it is made of logic and humility, rather than self-interest and self-celebratory materials, the better it will work. For all his love of history, Lincoln understood that the past provides a guide, but not a limit, to human understanding. Throughout his political career, Lincoln informed his understanding of the present by tempering his knowledge of the past with other sources of wisdom such as scripture, literature, humor, and his own personal reasoning. Furthermore, if we have a deep understanding of history, we can better understand if there is an analog from the past that can shed light on the present or if the situation is so unique that all precedent must be abandoned and we must set new precedents. In most of his pre-presidential career, Lincoln was guided by the precedents set by others in the past, but during his presidency, he frequently based his decisions on his understanding that his actions would set precedents for the future. Since he possessed a profound understanding of history, he was able to determine when something could be "fairly judged of by the past" and when it was time to "think anew" and "act anew."

We must also hold fast to historical truth, as we are given the light to understand this truth, and not give in to relativity to pursue power as Lincoln felt Stephen Douglas and his allies had done. We must not be dismayed by the manifold ways that the past is abused by others but rather be inspired by these abuses to pursue the truth more fully and forcefully. This pursuit is vital because there is wisdom in the past that is frequently lost in the forgetfulness of the present. Often the lessons that were necessary in the past will once again become essential in the future. We must understand that for all our technological and social improvements, we have still fallen short of the virtue and wisdom of the Infinite, and the experience of the past still has much to teach us.

Lincoln's memory has lived on in many ways. He is the Great Emancipator, the savior of the Union, Honest Abe, the Rail-Splitter, the self-made man, the comedian, the shrewd politician, and the orator without peer. Abraham Lincoln's political career demonstrates the enduring power of drawing wisdom from the past, a lesson relevant both today and for generations to come. It is essential that Lincoln's adept use of history, unmatched by any statesman before or since, lives on in memory.

ACKNOWLEDGMENTS

This book is an adaptation of my master's thesis, completed in 2021 at Harvard University Extension School. I am grateful for the guidance of Dr. Asher Orkaby, who provided invaluable insight into narrowing my topic. I am thankful that he rejected some of my earlier proposals that were not good and helped me find something that could work. During my first visit he, without prompting, gave me a personal tour of the campus, showing me his favorite spots in the Widener and Pusey libraries. Dr. Donald Ostrowski and Dr. John Stauffer provided valuable feedback and encouragement as I began my work in earnest. Trudi Goldberg Pires and Dr. Ariane Liazos helped with the formatting review and guided me through the final stages of the thesis submission. I must also thank Harvard University for providing people like myself the ability to pursue their studies at the Extension School. This book features significant additions and alterations from my original thesis. All the errors, shortcomings, and imperfections contained within this book are entirely my own.

Despite a global pandemic when I began this project, research centers throughout the country managed to provide me with invaluable aid. Dr. Christian McWhirter, Dr. Daniel Worthington, and everyone at the Abraham Lincoln Presidential Library in Springfield, Illinois, provided assistance and insight for my research. Katie Blizzard of the Washington Papers helped with a question I had about one of Lincoln's references to the first president. Sara Trotta of the Congregational Library & Archives in Boston helped me in my attempt to assess the credibility of a source.

A whole team of librarians at the Hanna Holborn Gray Special Collections Research Center at the University of Chicago Library helped me with the mountain of materials I had requested. Also, the generations of scholars who have made information about Lincoln readily available allowed me to continue my work, even in the height of the pandemic lockdown. These scholars include Anne Wootton, who graciously shared her research with me when I was unable to travel to a library where it was available.

I would also like to thank everyone at the University of Illinois Press. Special thanks goes to Alison Syring Bassford, my editor, who granted me the opportunity to share my work and expertly guided me throughout the process. Leigh Ann Cowan aided me through the final steps of submission. The peer reviewers provided valuable feedback and helped me see certain aspects in a new way. My deepest gratitude goes to Ellen Hurst who copyedited this book with great skill, insight, and patience.

I would like to thank my wife Lyndsey for the years of support. From the beginning when I started my first classes through the entire process of writing the book, she knew that the sacrifices were guaranteed while the rewards were not; still, she provided steadfast support throughout. She always believed in me when I doubted myself and kept me grounded when the risks began to pay off. For this and for everything I am grateful. When I began the research for this book, my son Nathan was two, my twins Eliana and Elijah were still babies, and Sophia had not yet been born. Although writing a book with small children while fully employed proved to be something of a challenge (to say the least), my children brought me incomparable joy throughout the process. I only hope my children someday find some small part of the joy that they have brought me. I would especially like to thank Nathan, who daily built a "nice bed" for his daddy on the floor, made of pillows and blankets. Much of the reading for this project was done with Nathan and his daddy cuddling on the floor. While he was probably too young to remember this, I will never forget.

It would be wrong not to thank the small-town communities that raised me. The longer I have lived, the more I have come to appreciate all those (family members, teachers, coaches, bus drivers, neighbors, Sunday school teachers, friends, parents of friends, etc.) who have done so much for me and treated me with the kindness and grace that I did not deserve. I am especially grateful for my history teacher from Ladd Elementary School, the late Mr. John Kopina. He has been a source of inspiration and set a standard of excellence that I have sought to pursue throughout my career. Growing up, I took this and everything for granted. It is only in recent years that I have realized how truly blessed I have been.

Finally, I would like to thank my parents, Wayne and Melody Derber. For all the sacrifices, known and unknown, and everything you've done for us, I thank you.

NOTES

Introduction

1. Lincoln, *Collected Works*, 8:101.
2. Wood, *Purpose of the Past*, 308.
3. Holzer, *Lincoln at Cooper Union*, 165–66.
4. Maier, *American Scripture*, 206; Wood, *Purpose of the Past*, 308.
5. Ellis, *The Quartet*, 1.
6. Foner, *The Fiery Trial*, 72.
7. Douglass, *Frederick Douglass Papers*, 463.
8. Lincoln, Nott, and Brainerd, *Address of the Hon. Abraham Lincoln*, 3.
9. Holzer, *Lincoln at Cooper Union*, 225.
10. Goodwin, *Team of Rivals*, 166.
11. Foner, *The Fiery Trial*, 333.

Chapter 1. A Living History (1809–39)

1. Holzer, *Lincoln at Cooper Union*, 88–89.
2. Handlin, *George Bancroft*, 112, 115, 245.
3. Howe and Strippel, *Life and Letters*, 2:130–31.
4. Lincoln, *Collected Works*, 4:61.
5. Wilson and Davis, *Herndon's Informants*, 67, 128.
6. Lincoln, *Collected Works*, 3: 511, 4:61.
7. Howe and Strippel, *Life and Letters*, 1. 30.
8. Lincoln, *Collected Works*, 4:62.
9. Wilson and Davis, *Herndon's Informants*, 64, 94, 107, 114–15, 121, 126, 151.
10. Wilson and Davis, *Herndon's Informants*, 90–92, 142.
11. Lincoln, *Collected Works*, 3:405.

12. Arthur Schlesinger, "Education of a Historian," 29.

13. Holzer, *Lincoln at Cooper Union*, cover.

14. *Chicago Daily Tribune*, "The People's Choice," February 12, 1861.

15. Buckingham, *Illinois as Lincoln Knew It*, 32–33.

16. Davis, *Frontier Illinois*, 390–91.

17. Buckingham, *Illinois as Lincoln Knew It*, 30–31, 34.

18. David Davis to Sarah W. Davis, May 3, 1851, in Benner and Davis et al., *Law Practice*, http://www.lawpracticeofabrahamlincoln.org/.

19. David Davis to Sarah W. Davis, May 1, 1851, in Benner and Davis et al., *Law Practice*, http://www.lawpracticeofabrahamlincoln.org/.

20. Wilson and Davis, *Herndon's Informants*, 348, 630.

21. Wilson and Davis, 648, 732.

22. Wilson and Davis, 395–96.

23. Rice, *Reminiscences of Abraham Lincoln*, 218.

24. Buckingham, *Illinois as Lincoln Knew It*, 33–34.

25. Wilson and Davis, *Herndon's Informants*, 540–41.

26. Wilson and Davis, 82, 107–8, 241, 251, 432, 486.

27. Wilson and Davis, 348–49; Herndon, *Herndon on Lincoln*, 142, 158, 183, 205, 240, 254.

28. Wilson, *Intimate Memories of Lincoln*, 584.

29. Speed, *Reminiscences of Abraham Lincoln*, 19.

30. Shakespeare, *Tragedy of Macbeth*, 84.

31. Lincoln, *Collected Works*, 1:1.

32. "Ciphering Book, [1819–1826]," https://papersofabrahamlincoln.org/documents/D200001.

33. Wilson and Davis, *Herndon's Informants*, 107.

34. Lincoln, *Collected Works*, 1:1.

35. Watts, *Hymns*, 181–82.

36. Wilson and Davis, *Herndon's Informants*, 105; "A Leaf from Abraham Lincoln's Earliest," the Abraham Lincoln Collection.

37. Wilson and Davis, *Herndon's Informants*, 107.

38. Lincoln, *Collected Works*, 1:8.

39. Lincoln, 1:6–9.

40. Lincoln, 1:5–8.

41. Simon, *Freedom's Champion*, 45–48.

42. Simon, 52–54.

43. *Alton Observer*, "Rev. Elijah P. Lovejoy," December 28, 1837.

44. Lovejoy, "Anti-Slavery Principles," *Alton Observer*, December 28, 1837.

45. Simon, *Freedom's Champion*, 139.

46. Lincoln, *Collected Works*, 1:108; "History of Westminster," Westminster Presbyterian Church (website), accessed December 10, 2023, http://www.wpcspi.org/history-of-westminster.html.

47. Lincoln, *Collected Works*, 1:108.

48. "Revolutionary War Veterans Reminisce (And Get Their Pictures Taken)," New England Historical Society (website), accessed December 10, 2023, https://www.newenglandhistoricalsociety.com/revolutionary-war-veterans-reminisce-and-get-their-pictures-taken/.

49. Lincoln, *Collected Works*, 1:109–11.

50. Lincoln, 1:112.
51. Lincoln, 1:113–14.
52. Lincoln, 1:115.
53. Gibbon, *History of the Decline*, 1:1.
54. Lincoln, *Collected Works*, 1:108.
55. Bray, *Reading with Lincoln*, 51–55.

Chapter 2. The Emerging Historian (1839)

1. Emerson, *Lincoln the Inventor*, 2.
2. Wilson and Davis, *Herndon's Informants*, 441, 506–7.
3. Whitney, *Life on the Circuit*, 109–10.
4. Speed, *Reminiscences of Abraham Lincoln*, 18.
5. Galef, *Scout Mindset*, ix-14.
6. Roda, prologue to *Abraham Lincoln*.
7. Backstone, *Commentaries*, 1:38, 2:195, 2:202, 2:237.
8. Blackstone, 1:59, 61.
9. Blackstone, 1:61, 68–70, 3:24, 366, 370, 374.
10. Blackstone, 2:94.
11. Greenleaf, *A Treatise*, 1:vii.
12. Greenleaf, 1:3–4, 10–11, 15–16.
13. Greenleaf, 1:58, 93–95.
14. Greenleaf, 1:14, 119–20, 295, 434, 455.
15. Wilson and Davis, *Herndon's Informants*, 58, 238, 347, 499.
16. Herndon, *Herndon on Lincoln*, 5.
17. Lincoln, *Collected Works*, 1:453.
18. Speed, *Reminiscences of Abraham Lincoln*, 23.
19. Wilson and Davis, *Herndon's Informants*, 635–36.
20. Wilson and Davis, 508–9, 519.
21. Whitney, *Life on the Circuit*, 112.
22. Lincoln, *Collected Works*, 1:8, 165–66, 2:60, 148, 158.
23. Henry, "Give Me Liberty."
24. Thucydides, *The Peloponnesian War*, 1.22.4.
25. Callcott, "Historians," 496–500.
26. Breisach, *Historiography*, 1, 227, 255–68.
27. Lincoln, *Collected Works*, 1:184, 209.
28. Lincoln, 1:419.
29. Abraham Lincoln and James H. Thomas to James Buchanan, August 4, 1848, in *Papers of Abraham Lincoln*, https://papersofabrahamlincoln.org/documents/D206860.
30. Buchanan, *Works of James Buchanan*, 8:152.
31. Lincoln, "Transcription of Treaty of Velasco," in *Papers of Abraham Lincoln*, https://papersofabrahamlincoln.org/documents/D210342.
32. Lincoln, *Collected Works*, 1:184.
33. Lincoln, 1:178–79.
34. Churchill, *Never Give in!*, 215.
35. Wilson and Davis, *Herndon's Informants*, 476.

36. Lincoln, "Speech of Mr. Lincoln," https://papersofabrahamlincoln.org/documents/D200193.

37. Lincoln, *Collected Works*, 1:160–70.

38. Lincoln, 1:167.

39. Lincoln, 1:172–73.

40. Ian Webster, "Value of $100," CPI Inflation Calculator, Official Data Foundation (website), accessed December 11, 2023, https://www.officialdata.org/us/inflation/1814?endYear=1838&amount=100.

41. Lincoln, *Collected Works*, 1:173.

42. Lincoln, 1:176, 179.

43. Lander, "Herndon's 'Auction List,'" 17–18, 36.

44. Lincoln, *Collected Works*, 1:174–75.

45. Lincoln, 1:170–71.

46. Lincoln, 1:157–58.

47. 2 Annals of Cong, 2012 (1791).

48. Jackson, "Veto Message."

49. Lincoln, *Collected Works*, 1:170.

50. Hall and Clarke, *Legislative and Documentary History*, 36, 85, 446, 585, 594, 713.

51. Lincoln, *Collected Works*, 1:171–72.

52. Lincoln, 1:172–73.

53. H.R. Doc. No. 25–192, at 2–3 (1839).

54. H.R. Doc. No. 25–192, at 2–3 (1839).

55. Woodbury, "Report on the Finances."

56. Lincoln, *Collected Works*, 1:173.

57. H.R. Doc. No. 25–192, at 2–3 (1839).

58. Lincoln, *Collected Works*, 1:172–73.

59. United States Census Bureau, "Abstract of the Returns of the Fifth Census," 51.

60. Lincoln, *Collected Works*, 1:172–73; and H.R. Doc. No. 25–192, at 2–3 (1839).

61. Lincoln, *Collected Works*, 1:173–77.

Chapter 3. History and Human Nature (1840–53)

1. Miller, *Lincoln's Virtues*, 30–35.

2. Scripps, *Life of Abraham Lincoln*, 31.

3. Wilson and Davis, *Herndon's Informants*, 450.

4. White, *A. Lincoln*, 95.

5. Lincoln, *Collected Works*, 1:272–75.

6. Watts, *Hymns and Spiritual Songs*, 71.

7. Lincoln, *Collected Works*, 1:276–78.

8. Lincoln, 1:272–77.

9. Lincoln, 1:278–79.

10. Wilson and Davis, *Herndon's Informants*, 88.

11. Knox, "Mortality."

12. Watts, *Hymns and Spiritual Songs*, 181–82.

13. Knox, "Mortality."

14. Knox.

15. Knox.

16. Knox.

17. Wilson and Davis, *Herndon's Informants*, 88.

18. Lincoln, *Collected Works*, 1:367.

19. Lincoln, 1:368.

20. Lincoln, 1:368.

21. Lincoln, 1:367.

22. Lincoln, 1:370.

23. Herndon, *Herndon on Lincoln*, 87.

24. Miller, "Lincoln's 'Suicide' Poem."

25. "The Suicide's Soliloquy," *The Sangamo Journal*, August 25, 1838, https://idnc.library.illinois.edu/?a=d&d=SJO18380825&e=en-20-1-txt-txIN.

26. Herndon, "Character of Abraham Lincoln," 431.

27. Lincoln, *Collected Works*, 1:420–22.

28. Lincoln, 1:431–38.

29. Price, *Origins of the War*, 158.

30. Lincoln, *Collected Works*, 1:439–40.

31. Richardson, *Compilation of the Messages*, 4:621.

32. Lincoln, *Collected Works*, 1:482, 485–86.

33. Miller, *Lincoln's Virtues*, 168.

34. Lincoln, *Collected Works*, 1:484–85.

35. Lincoln, 1:509–14.

36. Wordsworth, "I Wandered Lonely as a Cloud," in *Poems, in Two Volumes*, 49.

37. Lincoln, *Collected Works*, 2:10–11.

38. Lincoln, 2:121.

39. Lincoln, 2:121, 124–27.

40. Lincoln, 2:130–31.

41. Lincoln, 2:128–29.

42. Thomas Jefferson to John Holmes, April 22, 1820, the Jefferson Papers, Founders Online (website), National Archives, accessed December 30, 2023, https://founders.archives.gov/documents/Jefferson/03-15-02-0518.

43. Lincoln, *Collected Works*, 2:128–30.

44. Lincoln, 2:132.

45. Herndon and Weik, *Herndon's Lincoln*, 313.

46. Elder, *Calhoun*, 487.

47. Elder, 315.

48. Calhoun, "Speech on the Reception," 224–25.

49. Elder, *Calhoun*, 339.

50. Calhoun, *Speech of Mr. Calhoun*, 8–18.

51. Davis, "Jefferson Davis' Farewell Address."

52. Stephens, "Cornerstone Speech."

Chapter 4. We Are Not What We Have Been (1854–56)

1. Kellogg, "Notes."

2. Lincoln, *Collected Works*, 3:512, 2:282.

3. Foote, *The Civil War*, 1:27.

4. Cong. Globe, Appendix, 32nd Cong., 1st Sess., 68 (1851).

5. Morris, *The Long Pursuit*, 68.

6. Dixon, *True History*, 445.

7. R. White, *A. Lincoln*, 164–65.

8. Linder and Gillespie, *Reminiscences*, 87.

9. Wilson and Davis, *Herndon's Informants*, 519.

10. Lincoln, *Collected Works*, 4:62.

11. Miller, *Lincoln's Virtues*, 233.

12. "Behold, How Brightly Breaks the Morning!" *Illinois State Register*, October 6, 1854.

13. Nicolay and Hay, *Abraham Lincoln*, 1:372, 376.

14. Peck, "New Records," 45.

15. Yungmeyer, "An Excursion," 10; and B. M. Davison, "History."

16. Peck, "New Records," 45.

17. H. White, "Douglas in the Interior."

18. Peck, "New Records," 46.

19. Peck, 61.

20. H. White, "Douglas in the Interior."

21. Peck, "New Records," 59, 74.

22. Peck, 48.

23. H. White, "Abraham Lincoln in 1854," 10.

24. Lincoln, *Collected Works*, 2:248.

25. Lincoln, 2:248–49.

26. Lincoln, 2:250.

27. Lincoln, 2:250–56.

28. H. White, "Abraham Lincoln in 1854," 10.

29. Lincoln, *Collected Works*, 2:255.

30. Lincoln, 2:255–56.

31. Lincoln, 2:256–58.

32. "Seventh Census."

33. Lincoln, *Collected Works*, 2:262–63.

34. Lincoln, 2:264–65.

35. Lincoln, 2:268–70.

36. Lincoln, 2:265–66.

37. Lincoln, 2:266–67.

38. Lincoln, 2:271.

39. H. White, "Abraham Lincoln in 1854," 10.

40. Lincoln, *Collected Works*, 2:271–72.

41. Lincoln, 2:272–73.

42. Lincoln, 2:274.

43. Lincoln, 2:274–75.

44. Lincoln, 2:275.

45. Lincoln, 2:276.

46. "Hon. A. Lincoln's Speech," *Illinois Daily Journal*, October 5, 1854, https://idnc.library.illinois.edu/?a=d&d=SJO18541005&e=en-20-1-txt-txIN.

47. "Lincoln and Douglas," *Illinois Daily Journal*, October 10, 1854, https://idnc.library.illinois.edu/?a=d&d=SJO18541010&e=en-20–1-txt-txIN.

48. Peck, "New Records," 28–32, 62.
49. H. White, "Grand Passage of Arms"; and H. White, "Abraham Lincoln in 1854," 10–11.
50. Nicolay and Hay, *Abraham Lincoln*, 1:373, 379–80.
51. Lincoln, *Collected Works*, 2:249, 4:77, 89.
52. Foner, *The Fiery Trial*, 70–72.
53. 1 Annals of Cong. 352–54 (1789).
54. "Hon. A. Lincoln's Speech," *Illinois Daily Journal*.
55. Lincoln, *Collected Works*, 2:276.
56. Lincoln, *Collected Works*, 2:277.
57. United States Census Bureau, "1850 Census: The Seventh Census."
58. Lincoln, *Collected Works*, 2:277.
59. United States Census Bureau, "1850 Census: The Seventh Census."
60. Lincoln, *Collected Works*, 2:277–79; United States Census Bureau, "1850 Census: The Seventh Census."
61. Lincoln, *Collected Works*, 2:280–82.
62. Lincoln, 2:282–83.
63. Lincoln, 2:319.
64. Lincoln, 2:317–18.
65. Robertson, *Scrap Book*, 25.
66. Lincoln, *Collected Works*, 2:318.
67. Lincoln, 2:318.
68. Simon, *Freedom's Champion*, 134.
69. Lovejoy and Lovejoy, *Memoir*, 292.
70. Simon, *Freedom's Champion*, 148.
71. Bradsby, *History*, 155–69, 326–40, 408–9.
72. Bradsby, *History*, 181.
73. Lovejoy, "Supremacy of Divine Law."
74. Bradsby, *History*, 155–69, 326–40, 408–9.
75. Bradsby, *History*, 334–35.
76. Lincoln, *Collected Works*, 2:346–47.
77. Lincoln, 2:346–47.
78. Lincoln, 2:349.
79. Lincoln, 2:361–66.
80. Lincoln, 2:377–78.

Chapter 5. The Logic of History

1. Lincoln, *Collected Works*, 2:382–83.
2. Lincoln, 2:401, 403.
3. Lincoln, 2:403–4.
4. Lincoln, 2:404.
5. Maier, *American Scripture*, 160.
6. Lincoln, *Collected Works*, 2:405–6.
7. James Lander, "Herndon's 'Auction List,'" 41; Abraham Lincoln, "Scrapbook: Newspaper Clippings, circa 1854–1860," the Herndon-Weik Collection of Lincolniana, https://www.loc.gov/item/mss25791003/, image 47.

8. Jefferson, *Notes*, 269–70.

9. Amar, *Words*, 519–22.

10. Lincoln, *Collected Works*, 2:406–7.

11. Lincoln, 2:405.

12. Lincoln, *Collected Works*, 2:407–8; James D. B. DeBow, *Statistical View*, 83."

13. Lincoln, *Collected Works*, 2:408–9.

14. Foner, *Fiery Trial*, 98.

15. Lincoln, *Collected Works*, 2:409.

16. Lincoln, *Collected Works*, 2:399, 402, 409.

17. Lincoln, *Collected Works*, 2:407.

18. Burlingame, *Abraham Lincoln*, 1:458.

19. R. White, *A. Lincoln*, 248–52.

20. Lincoln, *Collected Works*, 2:461–62.

21. Lincoln, 2:467.

22. Lincoln, 2:461–69.

23. Lincoln, 2:482.

24. Lincoln, 2:485–86, 489–90.

25. Lincoln, 2:486–89.

26. Lincoln, 2:491–93.

27. Lincoln, 2:499–500.

28. Lincoln, 2:500.

29. Lincoln, 2:501.

30. Lincoln, 2:501.

31. Lincoln, 2:490–91, 501.

32. Douglas, "Speech Delivered at Springfield."

33. Lincoln, *Collected Works*, 2:514–18.

34. Lincoln, 2:514–15.

35. Cong. Globe, Appendix, 33rd Cong., 1st Sess., 371–72 (1854).

36. Lincoln, *Collected Works*, 3:276.

37. Guelzo, *Lincoln and Douglas*, 89–95, 204–6.

38. Schurz, Bancroft, and Dunning, *Reminiscences*, 324–26.

39. Lincoln, *Collected Works*, 3:17–18.

40. Lincoln, 3:28; Ford, *A History of Illinois*, 213–22, 304.

41. Lincoln, *Collected Works*, 3:28.

42. Lincoln, 3:29.

43. Lincoln, 3:27.

44. Lincoln, 3:29.

45. Guelzo, *Lincoln and Douglas*, 131–33.

46. Lincoln, *Collected Works*, 3:44.

47. Lincoln, 3:91–92.

48. Lincoln, 3:94–95.

49. Lincoln, 3:95–96.

50. Lincoln, 3:118, 133–35.

51. Lincoln, 3:121.

52. Hume, *Treatise of Human Nature*, 1:467; Bray, *Reading with Lincoln*, 142.

53. Hume, *Treatise of Human Nature*, 467.

54. Lincoln, *Collected Works*, 1:165.

55. Lincoln, 3:121.

56. Lincoln, 3:181, 184.

57. Guelzo, *Lincoln and Douglas*, 217–19.

58. Lincoln, *Collected Works*, 3:228.

59. Lincoln, 3:230–31; Madison, "Power of Congress," The Papers of James Madison.

60. Lincoln, *Collected Works*, 3. 220.

61. Jefferson, *Notes*, 272.

62. Lincoln, *Collected Works*, 3:274.

63. Lincoln, 3:276.

64. Koerner, *Memoirs*, 2:67.

65. Lincoln, *Collected Works*, 3:297–98.

66. Lincoln, 3:303–4.

67. Lincoln, 3:304–5.

68. Lincoln, 3:307–10.

69. Lincoln, 3:310.

70. Lincoln, 3:311, 315.

71. Guelzo, *Lincoln and Douglas*, 285–86.

72. Lincoln, *Collected Works*, 3:340.

Chapter 6. Right Makes Might

1. Charles H. Ray to Abraham Lincoln, July 27, 1858, in Abraham Lincoln Papers, https://www.loc.gov/item/malo108000/; Ray, Medill & Co. to Abraham Lincoln, June 29, 1858, in Abraham Lincoln Papers, https://www.loc.gov/item/malo092900/.

2. Jesse W. Fell, "Jesse W. Fell," 472–77.

3. Lincoln, *Collected Works*, 3:372–73, 510–12, 4:60–68.

4. Robert W. Johannsen, "Stephen A. Douglas," 612–13.

5. Johannsen, "Stephen A. Douglas," 613–16.

6. Stephen A. Douglas, papers, box 46 (folders 9–10, 12), box 47 (folders 5–9), box 48 (folder 5), box 50 (folders 3–4, 8, 12), Hanna Holborn Gray Special Collections Research Center, University of Chicago Library.

7. Johannsen, "Stephen A. Douglas," 613–16.

8. Lincoln, *Collected Works*, 3:397–99.

9. Holzer, *Lincoln at Cooper Union*, 35.

10. Lincoln, *Collected Works*, 3:405, 415.

11. 6 Annals of Cong. 1353 (1803).

12. Jacob Piatt Dunn, *Slavery Petitions*, 5–19, 41–50, 52–73, 79–85.

13. Lincoln, *Collected Works*, 3:416.

14. Lincoln, 3:453–54.

15. Lincoln, 3:502.

16. Herndon and Weik, *Herndon's Lincoln*, 273.

17. Holzer, *Lincoln at Cooper Union*, 10.

18. Herndon and Weik, *Herndon's Lincoln*, 454–55; James Lander, "Herndon's 'Auction List,'" 39.

19. Holzer, *Lincoln at Cooper Union*, 51.

20. Lincoln, *Collected Works*, 4:118–19.

21. Horace Greeley, "History Vindicated."

22. Holzer, *Lincoln at Cooper Union*, 51–53.

23. Holzer, 53.

24. Holzer, 65, 72–73.

25. Holzer, 92.

26. Holzer, 104–14.

27. Lincoln, *Collected Works*, 3:522.

28. Lincoln, 3:522–23.

29. Lincoln, *Collected Works*, 3:530.

30. Lincoln, 3:523–224.

31. Lincoln, 3:524.

32. Lincoln, 3:525–27.

33. Lincoln, 3:528.

34. Lincoln, 3:528.

35. Lincoln, 3:528.

36. Lincoln, 3:529.

37. Lincoln, 3:527.

38. Lincoln, 3:530.

39. Lincoln, 3:531.

40. Blackstone, *Commentaries*, 1:59.

41. Lincoln, *Collected Works*, 3:533–34.

42. Lincoln, 3:534–35.

43. Blackstone, *Commentaries*, 1:68–70.

44. Lincoln, *Collected Works*, 3:535.

45. Lincoln, 3:536–38.

46. Lincoln, 3:538–42.

47. Lincoln, 3:543–44.

48. Lincoln, 3:543–45.

49. Madison, "Power of Congress," The Papers of James Madison, https://founders.archives.gov/documents/Madison/01-10-02-0106.

50. Lincoln, *Collected Works*, 3:546.

51. Lincoln, *Collected Works*, 3:546–47.

52. Lincoln, *Collected Works*, 3:547–49.

53. Lincoln, *Collected Works*, 3:549–50.

54. Lincoln, *Collected Works*, 3:550.

55. Holzer, *Lincoln at Cooper Union*, 144–50.

56. Holzer, 221–24; Charles C. Nott to Abraham Lincoln, August 28, 1860, in Putman, *Abraham Lincoln*, 228.

57. Brookhiser, *Founders' Son*, 152–53.

58. Charles C. Nott to Abraham Lincoln, November 20, 1860, the Abraham Lincoln Papers, https://www.loc.gov/item/malo457200/.

59. "Old Time Sentiments," *Daily Illinois State Journal*, August 31, 1855, https://idnc.library.illinois.edu/?a=d&d=SJO18550831&e=-en-20-1-img-txIN.

60. Abraham Lincoln, "Scrapbook: Newspaper Clippings, circa 1854–1860," the Herndon-Weik Collection of Lincolniana, https://www.loc.gov/item/mss25791003/, image 45.

61. Lincoln, Nott, and Brainerd, *The Address*, 3.

62. Lincoln, *Collected Works*, 3:520–50.

63. Holzer, *Lincoln at Cooper Union*, 221–24.

64. Lincoln, *Collected Works*, 3:550.

Chapter 7. The Mystic Chords of Memory (1861–62)

1. "The Slavery Question: The Congressional Melee about the Lovejoy Debate," *New York Times*, April 14, 1860, https://timesmachine.nytimes.com/times machine/1860/04/14/76651065.html?pageNumber=9.

2. "Slavery Question."

3. John McQueen to Messrs. T. T. Cropper, J. R. Crenshaw, and Others, December 24, 1860, Perseus Digital Library, Tufts University, accessed December 30, 2023, https://www.perseus.tufts.edu/hopper/text?doc=Perseus%3Atext%3A 2006.05.0178%3Aarticle%3Dpos%3D47.

4. "Confederate States of America—Declaration of the Immediate Causes Which Induce and Justify the Secession of South Carolina from the Federal Union," the Avalon Project, https://avalon.law.yale.edu/19th_century/csa_scarsec.asp.

5. "Confederate States of America—Mississippi Secession," the Avalon Project, https://avalon.law.yale.edu/19th_century/csa_missec.asp.

6. "Confederate States of America—Georgia Secession," the Avalon Project, https://avalon.law.yale.edu/19th_century/csa_geosec.asp.

7. "Confederate States of America—A Declaration of the Causes which Impel the State of Texas to Secede from the Federal Union," the Avalon Project, https:// avalon.law.yale.edu/19th_century/csa_texsec.asp.

8. Jefferson Davis, "Jefferson Davis' First Inaugural Address at the Alabama Capitol, Montgomery, February 18, 1861," the Papers of Jefferson Davis, https:// jeffersondavis.rice.edu/archives/documents/jefferson-davis-first-inaugural -address.

9. Lincoln, *Collected Works*, 1:438.

10. Villard, *Lincoln on the Eve*, 71.

11. "Departure of Mr. Lincoln—Parting Address," *Illinois Daily State Journal*, February 12, 1861, https://idnc.library.illinois.edu/?a=d&d=SJO18610212&e=en-20 -1-img-txIN.

12. "Departure of Mr. Lincoln."

13. Lincoln, *Collected Works*, 4: 90.

14. Villard, *Lincoln on the Eve*, 72.

15. "Departure of Mr. Lincoln."

16. Villard, *Lincoln on the Eve*, 74.

17. Lincoln, *Collected Works*, 4:190.

18. R. White, *Eloquent President*, 16.

19. Lincoln, *Collected Works*, 4: 195–96.

20. Lincoln, 4:235–37.

21. Lincoln, 4:240–41.

22. Herndon, *Herndon on Lincoln*, 182.

23. *Register of Books*, 2:95.

24. Williams, *Statesman's Manual*, 1:1–21, 69–78, 2: 808–26.

25. Lincoln, *Collected Works*, 4:265.

26. "Articles of Confederation: March 1, 1781," the Avalon Project, https:// avalon.law.yale.edu/18th_century/artconf.asp.

27. Lincoln, *Collected Works*, 4:265.

28. Wills, *Lincoln at Gettysburg*, 145.

29. Amar, *Words that Made Us*, 262.

30. Lincoln, *Collected Works*, 4: 265–67.

31. "Declaration of Independence, July 4, 1776," the Avalon Project, https:// avalon.law.yale.edu/18th_century/declare.asp.

32. Lincoln, *Collected Works*, 4:268.

33. Morris, *The Long Pursuit*, 210.

34. Lincoln, *Collected Works*, 4: 265–71.

35. Morris, *Long Pursuit*, 213.

36. Lincoln, *Collected Works*, 4:271.

37. "Confederate States of America—Declaration of the Immediate Causes Which Induce and Justify the Secession of South Carolina from the Federal Union," the Avalon Project.

38. Wilson and Davis, *Herndon's Informants*, 286, 296, 313.

39. R. White, *A. Lincoln*, 413–14.

40. "The Revolution," *Daily Exchange*, April 22, 1861, https://chronicling america.loc.gov/lccn/sn83009573/1861-04-22/ed-1/seq-1/.

41. Lincoln, *Collected Works*, 4:341.

42. Lincoln, 4:341.

43. Lincoln, 4:342.

44. Lincoln, 4:342.

45. Lincoln, 4:437.

46. Lincoln, 4:426.

47. Burlingame, *Abraham Lincoln*, 2: 153.

48. Lincoln, *Collected Works*, 4:430–31.

49. Lincoln, 4:433–34.

50. Lincoln, 4:438.

51. Lincoln, 4:439.

52. Lincoln, 5:25–26, 53.

53. Lincoln, 5:371–75.

54. Lincoln, 5:388–89.

Chapter 8. We Cannot Escape History (1862–63)

1. Huyette, *Maryland Campaign*, 28; Dawes, *Service with the Sixth*, 87; Coffin, *Following the Flag*, 187; Monroe, *Battery D*, 13.

2. Monroe, *Battery D*, 13–14; Coffin, *Following the Flag*, 191; Hooker, "Official Report," 57.

3. Coffin, *Following the Flag*, 207, 211.

4. Coffin, *Following the Flag*, 226–27.

5. Graham, *Ninth Regiment*, 293; Buel and Johnson, *Battles and Leaders*, 2:662; National Park Service, "Eyewitness to Battle," https://www.nps.gov/anti/learn/ historyculture/eyewitness-to-battle.htm.; Coffin, "Antietam Scenes," 318.

6. Coffin, *Following the Flag*, 236; Child, *Letters*, 33–34.

7. Douglass, *Narrative*, 119.

8. Douglass, 58–60, 63–64.

9. Douglass, 68–73.

10. Douglass, "Inaugural Address."

11. Douglass, "Spirit."

12. Douglass, "President."

13. Douglass.

14. Lincoln, *Collected Works*, 5:404.

15. Simpson, Sears, and Sheehan-Dean, *Civil War*, 681.

16. Chase, *Inside Lincoln's Cabinet*, 150; Welles, *Civil War Diary*, 54.

17. Lincoln, *Collected Works*, 6:29–30.

18. Wilson and Davis, *Herndon's Informants*, 197, 212, 475.

19. Lincoln, *Collected Works*, 5:518–36.

20. Lincoln, 5:537.

21. Lincoln, 5:537.

22. Lincoln, 6:16–17.

23. Lincoln, 6:17.

24. Lincoln, 6:107–8.

25. Lincoln, 6:261–67.

26. Lincoln, 6:268–69.

27. Lincoln, 6:410.

28. Johnson, *Writing*, 145–52.

29. R. White, *Eloquent President*, 229.

30. Wills, *Lincoln at Gettysburg*, 51.

31. Everett, "Gettysburg Address."

32. Wills, *Lincoln at Gettysburg*, 52, 56–59.

33. Wootton, "Classical Lincoln," 113–14.

34. Lincoln, *Collected Works*, 7: 23.

35. Lincoln, 7:23.

36. Lincoln, 7:23.

37. Lincoln, 7:22.

38. Ellis, *Quartet*, 1.

39. Lincoln, *Collected Works*, 5: 439, 6: 109.

40. Bernstein, "'The Quartet.'"

41. From George Washington to the States, June 8, 1783, the Washington Papers, accessed December 30, 2023, https://founders.archives.gov/documents/Washington/99-01-02-11404.

42. Maier, *American Scripture*, 73–77.

43. Ellis, *Quartet*, 1.

44. "Articles of Confederation: March 1, 1781," the Avalon Project, https://avalon.law.yale.edu/18th_century/artconf.asp.

45. "Journals of the Continental Congress—The Articles of Association; October 20, 1774," the Avalon Project, https://avalon.law.yale.edu/18th_century/contcong_10-20-74.asp.

46. Kass, Kass, and Schaub, *What So Proudly*, 763.

47. Ellis, *Quartet*, 1.

48. Lincoln, *Collected Works*, 4:196.

49. Maier, *American Scripture*, 206.

50. Wills, *Lincoln at Gettysburg*, 38–40; Wilentz, *No Property in Man*, 149–50; Wilentz, "Was the Constitution Pro-Slavery?"

51. Maier, *American Scripture*, 206.

52. Lincoln, *Collected Works*, 2:406–7.

53. Lincoln, 2:275.

54. Lincoln, 2:407.

55. Wood, *Purpose*, 194.

56. Lincoln, *Collected Works*, 7:25.

Chapter 9. The Almighty Has His Own Purposes (1864–65)

1. Sergt. Major [pseud.], "Lincoln and Stanton," *Chicago Tribune*, January 11, 1879.

2. Lincoln, *Collected Works*, 5:420; Rice, *Reminiscences*, 334–35.

3. "Eliza P. Gurney, Interview with Abraham Lincoln," Abraham Lincoln Papers: Series 1, General Correspondence, https://www.loc.gov/item/mal1870500/.

4. Gurney, *Memoir*, 307–11.

5. "Eliza P. Gurney, Interview with Abraham Lincoln."

6. Lincoln, *Collected Works*, 5:478.

7. Lincoln, 5:403–4.

8. Lincoln, 7:281–82.

9. Lincoln, 7:282.

10. Lincoln, 7:301.

11. Lincoln, 7:301.

12. Herndon, *Herndon on Lincoln*, 234.

13. Lincoln, *Collected Works*, 7:301.

14. Lincoln, 7:301–2.

15. Lincoln, 7:302–3.

16. Lincoln, 6:326.

17. Galef, *Scout Mindset*, 51–52.

18. Lincoln, *Collected Works*, 7:324.

19. Foner, *Fiery Trial*, 89.

20. O. Lovejoy, *His Brother's Blood*, 346.

21. Lincoln, *Collected Works*, 7:366.

22. Lincoln, 7:512, 7:528, 8:41, 8:84.

23. Lincoln, 7: 506–7.

24. Gurney, *Memoir*, 313–16.

25. Lincoln, *Collected Works*, 7:535.

26. Lincoln, 6:500.

27. Lincoln, 8:101.

28. Lincoln, 8:254.

29. Arnold, *Life of Abraham Lincoln*, 374–75.

30. R. Wilson, *Intimate Memories*, 236–37.

31. R. Wilson, 586.

32. Garrison, "Professor Newman's Reply."

33. Whitman, "The Last Hours of Congress," *New York Times*, March 12, 1865.

34. Brooks, *Washington*, 239.

35. Lincoln, *Collected Works*, 8:332.

36. Lincoln, 8:332.

37. Lincoln, 8:332–33.

38. Lincoln, 8:333.

39. Lincoln, 8:333.

40. Lincoln, 8:333.

41. Douglass, *Life and Times*, 436.
42. Lincoln, *Collected Works*, 7:242, 8:403, 405.
43. Lincoln, 3: 380.
44. Lincoln, 8:408–9.
45. R. White, *A. Lincoln*, 675.

Chapter 10. The Wisdom of History

1. Handlin, *George Bancroft*, 283–84.
2. Burlingame, *Abraham Lincoln*, 2:204, 436; Bancroft, *Memorial Address*, 49.
3. Bancroft, *Memorial Address*, 46.
4. Wilson and Davis, *Herndon's Informants*, 218, 332.
5. Howe and Strippel, *Life and Letters*, 1:30.
6. Foote, *Civil War*, 1:804.
7. Handlin, *George Bancroft*, 284.
8. Handlin, 172.
9. R. Wilson, *Intimate Memories*, 584.
10. H. White, "Abraham Lincoln," 24.
11. Douglass, *Oration*, 5; Douglass, "Eulogy," 310.
12. Douglass, "Eulogy," 309.
13. Douglass, 314–15.
14. Niebuhr, *Reinhold Niebuhr*, 948, 956, 1063.
15. Niebuhr, 1001–2, 1020.
16. Niebuhr, *Irony*, 63, 81, 88.
17. Niebuhr, *Reinhold Niebuhr*, 985, 1014, 1030.
18. Niebuhr, "Religion, 75, 77.
19. Niebuhr, *Irony*, 63–64, 172–73.
20. Obama, remarks given at the Abraham Lincoln Presidential Museum dedication, April 19, 2005, Abraham Lincoln Presidential Museum, Springfield, IL.
21. Niebuhr, *Reinhold Niebuhr*, 251.
22. Burns, Ken, et al., *Civil War*.
23. Jacobs, *Breaking Bread*, 134.

BIBLIOGRAPHY

Archival Material

Abraham Lincoln Papers at the Library of Congress. Washington, DC. https://
www.loc.gov/collections/abraham-lincoln-papers/.
Annals of the Congress of the United States. 18 vols. Washington, DC, 1789–1825.
The Avalon Project: Documents in Law, History and Diplomacy. Lillian Goldman
Law Library. Yale Law School. New Haven, CT.
Congressional Globe. 46 vols. Washington, DC, 1833–73.
Herndon-Weik Collection of Lincolniana. Library of Congress. Washington, DC.
https://www.loc.gov/collections/herndon-weik-collection-of-lincolniana/.
The Law Practice of Abraham Lincoln Complete Documentary Edition. 2nd ed.
Edited by Martha L. Benner, Cullom Davis, Daniel W. Stowell, John A. Lupton,
Susan Krause, Stacy Pratt McDermott, Christopher A. Schnell, and Dennis
E. Suttles. The Papers of Abraham Lincoln Digital Library. Abraham Lincoln
Presidential Library Foundation. Springfield, IL. http://www.lawpracticeof
abrahamlincoln.org/.
The Papers of Abraham Lincoln Digital Library. Abraham Lincoln Presidential
Library Foundation. Springfield, IL. https://papersofabrahamlincoln.org.
The Papers of Jefferson Davis. Rice University. Houston, TX. https://jefferson
davis.rice.edu/archives/documents.
Stephen A. Douglas Papers. Hanna Holborn Gray Special Collections Research
Center, University of Chicago Library. Chicago, IL.

Newspapers

Alton Observer
Chicago Daily Tribune
Daily Chicago Journal

Daily Exchange
Illinois Daily Journal
Illinois Daily State Journal
Illinois State Register
New-York Daily Tribune
New York Times
Sangamo Journal
Western Citizen

Individual Sources

Allen, Danielle S. *Our Declaration: A Reading of the Declaration of Independence in Defense of Equality*. New York: Liveright, 2014.

Amar, Akhil Reed. *The Words That Made Us: America's Constitutional Conversation, 1760–1840*. New York: Basic Books, 2021.

Arnold, Isaac Newton. *The Life of Abraham Lincoln*. Chicago: A. C. McClurg, 1887.

Bancroft, George. *Memorial Address on the Life and Character of Abraham Lincoln*. Washington, DC: Government Printing Office, 1866.

Barton, William E. *Abraham Lincoln and Walt Whitman*. Indianapolis: Bobbs Merrill, 1928.

Bernstein, Richard B. "'The Quartet,' by Joseph J. Ellis." *New York Times*, May 5, 2015.

Blackstone, William. *Commentaries on the Laws of England in Four Books*. 4 vols. London: Printed by A. Strahan for T. Cadell and W. Davies, 1809.

Blight, David. *Beyond the Battlefield: Race, Memory and the American Civil War*. Amherst: University of Massachusetts Press, 2002.

Bradsby, Henry C. *History of Bureau County, Illinois*. Chicago: World Publishing, 1885.

Bray, Robert C. *Reading with Lincoln*. Carbondale: Southern Illinois University Press, 2010.

———. "What Abraham Lincoln Read—An Evaluative and Annotated List." *Journal of the Abraham Lincoln Association* 28, no. 2 (2007): 28–81.

Breisach, Ernst. *Historiography: Ancient, Medieval and Modern*. Chicago: University of Chicago Press, 2008.

Brookhiser, Richard. *Founders' Son*. New York: Basic Books, 2014.

Brooks, Noah. *Washington in Lincoln's Time*. New York: Century, 1896.

Buchanan, James. *The Works of James Buchanan, Comprising His Speeches, State Papers, and Private Correspondence*. 12 vols. Collected and edited by John Bassett Moore. Philadelphia: J.B. Lippincott, 1908–11.

Buckingham, Joseph H. *Illinois as Lincoln Knew It: A Boston Reporter's Record of a Trip in 1847*. Edited by Harry E. Pratt. Springfield, IL: Members of the Abraham Lincoln Association, 1938.

Buel, Clarence Clough, and Robert Underwood Johnson, eds. *Battles and Leaders of the Civil War: Being for the Most Part Contributions by Union and Confederate Officers; Based Upon "The Century War Series."* 4 vols. New York: Century, 1914.

Burlingame, Michael. *Abraham Lincoln: A Life*. 2 vols. Baltimore, MD: John Hopkins University Press, 2008.

Burns, Ken, Geoffrey C. Ward, Ric Burns, David G. McCullough, George Plimpton, Morgan Freeman, and Jason Robards. *The Civil War*. Hollywood, CA: PBS Home Video, 1990.

Calhoun, John C. *Speech of Mr. Calhoun, of South Carolina, on the Oregon Bill: Delivered in the Senate of the United States, June 27, 1848*. Washington, DC: Towers, 1848.

———. "Speech on the Reception of Abolition Petitions, February, 1837." In *Speeches of John C. Calhoun: Delivered in the Congress of the United States from 1811 to the Present Time*, 222–26. New York: Harper and Brothers, 1843.

Callcott, George H. "Historians in Early Nineteenth-Century America." *New England Quarterly* 32, no. 4 (1959): 496–520.

Chase, Salmon P. *Inside Lincoln's Cabinet: The Civil War Diaries of Salmon P. Chase*. Edited by David Herbert Donald. New York: Longmans, Green, 1954.

Child, William. *Letters From a Civil War Surgeon*. Solon, ME: Polar Bear, 2003.

Churchill, Winston. *Never Give In!: The Best of Winston Churchill's Speeches*. Edited by Winston S. Churchill. New York: Hyperion, 2003.

Coffin, Charles Carleton. "Antietam Scenes." *Century Illustrated Monthly Magazine*, 32 (May–October 1886), 315–19.

———. *Following the Flag: From August 1861 to November 1862 with the Army of the Potomac*. New York: Hurst, 1864.

Davis, James Edward. *Frontier Illinois*. Bloomington: Indiana University Press, 1998.

Davison, B. M. "History of the Illinois State Fair—1853 to 1915." *Prairie Farmer*, September 11, 1915. https://idnc.library.illinois.edu/?a=d&d=PFR19150911.1.5&e.

Dawes, Rufus Robinson. *Service with the Sixth Wisconsin Volunteers*. Marietta, OH: E.R. Alderman and Sons, 1890.

DeBow, James D. B. *Statistical View of the United States, Embracing Its Territory, Population—White, Free Colored, and Slave—Moral and Social Condition, Industry, Property, and Revenue; the Detailed Statistics of Cities, Towns, and Counties; Being a Compendium of the Seventh Census*. Washington, DC: Beverly Tucker, 1854.

Derber, Jesse. "Abraham Lincoln and the Wisdom of History." Master's thesis, Harvard University Extension School, 2021.

Dixon, Susan Bullitt. *The True History of the Missouri Compromise and Its Repeal*. Cincinnati, OH: Robert Clarke, 1899.

Douglas, Stephen. "Speech Delivered at Springfield, Ill, by Senator S. A. Douglas." In Abraham Lincoln Historical Digitization Project (website). Northern Illinois University Digital Library. Northern Illinois University. Dekalb, IL. Accessed December 30, 2023. https://digital.lib.niu.edu/islandora/object/niu-lincoln:35822.

Douglass, Frederick. "Eulogy for Abraham Lincoln." 1865. In *President Lincoln Assassinated!: The Firsthand Story of the Murder, Manhunt, Trial, and Mourning*, edited by Harold Holzer, 308–24. New York: Literary Classics of the United States, 2015.

———. *Frederick Douglass Papers: Series Three: Correspondence*. Vol. 2, *1853–1865*. New Haven, CT: Yale University Press, 2018.

———. "The Inaugural Address." *Douglass' Monthly*. April 1861. https://transcription.si.edu/transcribe/12935/ACM-2007.19.11_01.

———. *Life and Times of Frederick Douglass*. Hartford, CT: Park, 1882.

———. *Narrative of the Life of Frederick Douglass, an American Slave*. Boston: Antislavery Office, 1845.

———. *Oration by Frederick Douglass Delivered on the Occasion of the Unveiling of the Freedmen's Monument in Memory of Abraham Lincoln*. Washington, DC: Gibson Brothers, 1876.

———. "The President and His Speeches." *Douglass' Monthly*. September 1862. https://rbscp.lib.rochester.edu/4387.

———. "The Spirit of Colonization." *Douglass' Monthly*. September 1862. https://transcription.si.edu/view/13220/ACM-2007.19.25_01.

Dunn, Jacob Piatt. *Slavery Petitions and Papers*. Indianapolis, IN: Bowen-Merrill, 1894.

Elder, Robert. *Calhoun: American Heretic*. New York: Basic Books, 2021.

Ellis, Joseph J. *The Quartet: Orchestrating the Second American Revolution, 1783–1789*. New York: Alfred A. Knopf, 2015.

Emerson, Jason. *Lincoln the Inventor*. Carbondale: Southern Illinois University Press, 2009.

Everett, Edward. "Gettysburg Address." Edited by Bjørn F. Stillion Southard. Voices of Democracy: The U.S. Oratory Project (website). University of Maryland. College Park, MD. January 15, 2024. https://voicesofdemocracy.umd.edu/everett-gettysburg-address-speech-text/.

Fell, Jesse W. "Jesse W. Fell." In *The Lincoln Memorial: Album-Immortelles*, edited by Osborn H. Oldroyd, 468–82. New York: G. W. Carleton, 1887.

Foner, Eric. *The Fiery Trial: Abraham Lincoln and American Slavery*. New York: W.W. Norton, 2010.

Foote, Shelby. *The Civil War, a Narrative*. 3 vols. New York: Vintage Books, 1986.

Ford, Thomas. *A History of Illinois: From Its Commencement as a State in 1814 to 1847*. Chicago: S. C. Griggs, 1854.

Galef, Julia. *The Scout Mindset: Why Some People See Things Clearly and Others Don't*. New York: Portfolio, 2021.

Garrison, William Lloyd. "Professor Newman's Reply." *Liberator*. September 30, 1864.

Gibbon, Edward. *The History of the Decline and Fall of the Roman Empire*. Vol. 1. New York: Fred de Fau, 1776.

Goodwin, Doris Kearns. *Team of Rivals*. New York: Simon and Schuster, 2006.

Graham, Matthew J. *The Ninth Regiment, New York Volunteers (Hawkins' Zouaves): Being a History of the Regiment and Veteran Association from 1860 to 1900*. New York: E. P. Coby, 1900.

Greeley, Horace. "History Vindicated: A Letter to the Hon. Stephen A. Douglas on his 'Harper' Essay." *New-York Daily Tribune*. October 15, 1859.

Greenleaf, Simon. *A Treatise on the Law of Evidence*. 3 vols. Boston: Charles C. Little and James Brown, 1842.

Guelzo, Allen C. *Lincoln and Douglas: The Debates That Defined America*. New York: Simon and Schuster, 2008.

Gurney, Eliza Paul. *Memoir and Correspondence of Eliza P. Gurney*. Edited by Richard F. Mott. Philadelphia: J. B. Lippincott, 1884.

Hall, David A., and Matthew St. Clair Clarke. *Legislative and Documentary History of the Bank of the United States*. Washington, DC: Gales and Seaton, 1832.

Hall, James. *Notes on the Western States: Containing Descriptive Sketches of Their Soil, Climate, Resources, and Scenery.* Philadelphia: Harrison Hall, 1838.

Handlin, Lilian. *George Bancroft, the Intellectual as Democrat.* New York: Harper and Row, 1984.

Herndon, William H. "Analysis of the Character of Abraham Lincoln." *Abraham Lincoln Quarterly* 1 (1940): 343–441.

———. *Herndon on Lincoln: Letters.* Edited by Douglas L. Wilson and Rodney O. Davis. Urbana: University of Illinois Press, 2016.

Herndon, William Henry, and Jesse William Weik. *Herndon's Lincoln: The True Story of a Great Life.* Edited by Douglas L. Wilson and Rodney O. Davis. Urbana: University of Illinois Press, 2006.

"History of Westminster." *wpcspi.org.* Westminster Presbyterian Church. Accessed December 10, 2023. http://www.wpcspi.org/history-of-westminster.html.

Holzer, Harold. *Lincoln at Cooper Union: The Speech That Made Abraham Lincoln President.* New York: Simon and Schuster, 2004.

Hooker, Joseph. "Official Report of Major-General Joseph Hooker, Commanding First Army Corps, and Right Wing of the Federal Line of Battle at Antietam, September 17, 1862." In *The Maryland Campaign from Sept. 1st to Sept. 20th, 1862: History and Explanation of the Battles of South Mountain and Antietam, Md.* Edited by George Hess, 54–57. Hagerstown, MD: Globe Job Rooms Print, 1890.

Howe, M. A. De Wolfe, and Henry C. Strippel. *The Life and Letters of George Bancroft.* 2 vols. New York: C. Scribner's Sons, 1908.

Hume, David. *A Treatise of Human Nature: Being an Attempt to Introduce the Experimental Method of Reasoning Into Moral Subjects and Dialogues Concerning Natural Religion.* Vol. 1. London: Longmans, Green, 1890.

Huyette, Miles Clayton. *The Maryland Campaign and the Battle of Antietam.* Buffalo, NY: Hammond Press, 1915.

Jackson, Andrew. "Veto Message [of the Re-authorization of Bank of the United States]." July 10, 1832. In The American Presidency Project (website). University of California Santa Barbara. Accessed December 30, 2023. https://www.presidency.ucsb.edu/documents/veto-message-the-re-authorization-bank-the-united-states.

Jacobs, Alan. *Breaking Bread with the Dead: A Reader's Guide to a More Tranquil Mind.* New York: Penguin Press, 2020.

———. *Notes on the State of Virginia.* London: John Stockdale, 1787.

Johannsen, Robert W. "Stephen A. Douglas, 'Harper's Magazine,' and Popular Sovereignty." *Mississippi Valley Historical Review* 45, no. 4 (1959): 606–31.

Johnson, Martin P. *Writing the Gettysburg Address.* Lawrence: University Press of Kansas, 2013.

Kass, Amy A., Leon R. Kass, and Diana J. Schaub. *What So Proudly We Hail: The American Soul in Story, Speech, and Song.* Wilmington, DE: ISI Books, 2013.

Keller, Timothy. *Counterfeit Gods: The Empty Promises of Money, Sex, and Power, and the Only Hope That Matters.* New York: Dutton, 2009.

Kellogg, William Pitt. "Notes: Interview with the Honorable William Pitt Kellogg of Louisiana." By Ida M. Tarbell. In the Ida M. Tarbell Collection, 1890–1944, Pelletier Library Allegheny College (website). Special Collections. Allegheny College. https://dspace.allegheny.edu/handle/10456/32198.

Knox, William. "Mortality." In *Song of Israel: Consisting of Lyrics, Founded Upon the History and Poetry of the Hebrew Scriptures*. Edinburgh: J. Anderson, 1824.

Koerner, Gustave. *Memoirs of Gustave Koerner: 1809–1896*. Vol. 2. Edited by Thomas J. McCormack. Cedar Rapids, IA: Torch, 1909.

Lander, James. "Herndon's 'Auction List' and Lincoln's Interest in Science." *Journal of the Abraham Lincoln Association* 32, no. 2 (2011): 16–49.

Lincoln, Abraham. *The Collected Works of Abraham Lincoln*. 9 vols. Edited by Roy P. Basler. History Book Club edition. New Brunswick, NJ: Rutgers University Press, 1953.

Lincoln, Abraham, Charles C. Nott, and Cephas Brainerd. *The Address of the Hon. Abraham Lincoln, in Vindication of the Policy of the Framers of the Constitution and the Principles of the Republican Party, Delivered at Cooper Institute, February 27th, 1860*. New York: G. F. Nesbitt, 1860.

Linder, Usher F., and Joseph Gillespie. *Reminiscences of the Early Bench and Bar of Illinois*. Chicago: Chicago Legal News, 1879.

Lovejoy, Elijah P. "Anti-Slavery Principles." *Alton Observer*. December 28, 1837.

Lovejoy, Joseph C., and Owen Lovejoy. *Memoir of the Rev. Elijah P. Lovejoy Who Was Murdered in Defence of the Liberty of the Press at Alton, Illinois Nov. 7, 1837*. New York: John S. Taylor, 1838.

Lovejoy, Owen. *His Brother's Blood: Speeches and Writings, 1838–64*. Edited by William F. Moore and Jane Ann Moore. Urbana: University of Illinois Press, 2004.

———. "Supremacy of Divine Law." *Western Citizen*. September 14, 1843.

Madison, James. "Power of Congress to Prohibit the Slave Trade, [25 August] 1787." In the Paper of James Madison. Founders Online (website). National Archives, accessed December 30, 2023. https://founders.archives.gov/documents/Madison/01-10-02-0106.

Maier, Pauline. *American Scripture: Making the Declaration of Independence*. New York: Alfred A. Knopf, 1997.

Miller, Richard L. "Lincoln's 'Suicide' Poem: Has It Been Found?" *For the People: A Newsletter of the Abraham Lincoln Association* 6, no. 1 (2004): 1, 6. https://abrahamlincolnassociation.org/wp-content/uploads/2021/05/6-1.pdf.

Miller, William Lee. *Lincoln's Virtues: An Ethical Biography*. New York: Alfred A. Knopf, 2002.

Monroe, John Albert. *Battery D, First Rhode Island Light Artillery, at the Battle of Antietam, September 17, 1862*. Providence, RI: Providence Press, 1886.

Morris, Roy. *The Long Pursuit: Abraham Lincoln's Thirty-year Struggle with Stephen Douglas for the Heart and Soul of America*. Washington, DC: Smithsonian Books, 2008.

National Park Service. "Eyewitness to Battle." Antietam National Battlefield Maryland (website). September 15, 2023. https://www.nps.gov/anti/learn/history culture/eyewitness-to-battle.htm.

Newton, Joseph Fort. *River of Years, an Autobiography*. Philadelphia: Lippincott, 1946.

Nicolay, John G., and John Hay. *Abraham Lincoln: A History*. 10 vols. New York: Century, 1914.

Niebuhr, Reinhold. *Reinhold Niebuhr: Major Works on Religion and Politics*. Edited by Elisabeth Sifton. New York: Library of America, 2015.

———. *The Irony of American History*. Chicago: University of Chicago Press, 1952.

———. "The Religion of Abraham Lincoln." In *Lincoln and the Gettysburg Address: Commemorative Papers*, edited by Allan Nevins, 72–87. Urbana: University of Illinois Press, 1964.

Obama, Barack. Remarks given at the Abraham Lincoln Presidential Museum dedication. April 19, 2005. Abraham Lincoln Presidential Museum, Springfield, IL. April 19, 2005. Abraham Lincoln Presidential Museum in Springfield, IL. Video, 1:17:36. https://www.c-span.org/video/?186315-1/abraham-lincoln-presidential-museum-dedication.

Peck, Graham A. "New Records of the Lincoln-Douglas Debate at the 1854 Illinois State Fair: The *Missouri Republican* and the *Missouri Democrat* Report from Springfield." *Journal of The Abraham Lincoln Association* 30, no. 2 (2009): 25–80.

Price, Glenn W. *Origins of the War with Mexico: The Polk-Stockton Intrigue.* Austin: University of Texas Press, 1967.

Putnam, George Haven. *Abraham Lincoln: The People's Leader in the Struggle for National Existence.* New York: G. P. Putnam's Sons, 1910.

Register of Books Loaned to Members of the Legislative Offices and Members of the Illinois State Library: December 16, 1842–April 8, 1876. 2 vols. Springfield, IL: Illinois State Library, 1876.

"Revolutionary War Veterans Reminisce (And Get Their Pictures Taken)." *new englandhistoricalsociety.com.* The New England Historical Society. Accessed December 10, 2023. https://www.newenglandhistoricalsociety.com/revolutionary-war-veteransreminisce-and-get-their-pictures-taken/.

Rice, Allen Thorndike. *Reminiscences of Abraham Lincoln by Distinguished Men of His Time.* New York: North American, 1886.

Richardson, James D., ed. *Compilation of the Messages and Papers of the Presidents.* 10 vols. New York: Bureau of National Literature, 1917.

Rieff, David. *In Praise of Forgetting: Historical Memory and Its Ironies.* New Haven, CT: Yale University Press, 2016.

Robertson, George. *Scrap Book on Law and Politics, Men and Times.* Lexington, KY: A. W. Elder, 1855.

Roda, Joseph F. *Abraham Lincoln and Making a Case: The Story of a Master.* Bloomington, IN: AuthorHouse, 2018.

Schlesinger, Arthur. "The Education of a Historian." *New Republic* 191, no. 11 (1984): 29.

Schurz, Carl, Frederic Bancroft, and William Archibald Dunning. *The Reminiscences of Carl Schurz.* New York: McClure, 1907.

Scripps, J. L. *Life of Abraham Lincoln.* Bloomington: Indiana University Press, 1961.

Sergt. Major [pseud.]. "Lincoln and Stanton." *Chicago Tribune,* January 11, 1879.

Shakespeare, William. *The Tragedy of Macbeth.* New York: Charles Scribner's Sons, 1911.

Simon, Paul. *Freedom's Champion: Elijah Lovejoy.* Carbondale: Southern Illinois University Press, 1994.

Simpson, Brooks D., Stephen W. Sears, and Aaron Sheehan-Dean, eds. *The Civil War: The First Year Told by Those Who Lived It.* New York: Library of America, 2011.

Speed, Joshua Fry. *Reminiscences of Abraham Lincoln and Notes of a Visit to California: Two Lectures.* Louisville, KY: John P. Morton, 1884.

Stephens, Alexander H. "Cornerstone Speech." In *Alexander H. Stephens, in Public and Private: With Letters and Speeches, Before, During, and Since the War*, edited by Henry Cleveland, 717–29. Philadelphia: National Publishing Company, 1866.*The Peloponnesian War*. Translated by Richard Crawley. London: J. M. Dent and Sons, 1910.

United States Census Bureau. "1850 Census: The Seventh Census of the United States." *Census.gov*. United States Census Bureau. 2018. https://www.census.gov/library/publications/1853/dec/1850a.html.

———. "Abstract of the Returns of the Fifth Census, Showing the Number of Free People, the Number of Slaves, the Federal Representative Number, and the Aggregate of Each County of Each State of the United States." *Census.gov*. United States Census Bureau. 2022. https://www2.census.gov/library/publications/decennial/1830/1830b.pdf.

———. "Seventh Census of the United States: 1850-Missouri, The." *Census.gov*. United States Census Bureau. 2015. https://www2.census.gov/library/publications/decennial/1850/1850a/1850a-40.pdf.

Villard, Henry. *Lincoln on the Eve of '61: A Journalist's Story*. New York: A. A. Knopf, 1941.

Washington, George. From George Washington to The States, 8 June 1783. Founders Online. National Archives. Accessed December 30, 2023. https://founders.archives.gov/documents/Washington/99–01–02–11404.

Watts, Isaac. *Divine Songs: Attempted in Easy Language for the Use of Children*. London: Printed for J. Buckland, J. F. and C. Rivington, T. Longman, W. Fenner, T. Field, and C. Dilly, 1780.

———. *Hymns and Spiritual Songs: In Three Books*. London: W. Strahan, J. and F. Rivington, J. Buckland, G. Keith, L. Hawes W. Clarke and B. Collins, T. Longman, T. Field, and E. and C. Dilly, 1773.

Welles, Gideon. *The Civil War Diary of Gideon Welles, Lincoln's Secretary of the Navy: The Original Manuscript Edition*. Edited by William E. Gienapp and Erica L. Gienapp. Urbana: University of Illinois Press, 2014.

White, Horace. "Abraham Lincoln in 1854." New York: Putnam's Sons, 1909.

———. "Douglas in the Interior—Politics-State Fair &c." *Daily Chicago Journal*, October 5, 1854.

———. "Grand Passage of Arms—Douglas and Lincoln." *Daily Chicago Journal*, October 9, 1854.

White, Ronald C., Jr. *A. Lincoln: A Biography*. New York: Random House, 2009.

———. *The Eloquent President*. New York: Random House, 2005.

Whitman, Walt. "The Last Hours of Congress—Washington Crowds, and the President." *New York Times*, March 12, 1865.

Whitney, Henry Clay. *Life on the Circuit with Lincoln: With Sketches of Generals Grant, Sherman and McClellan, Judge Davis, Leonard Swett, and Other Contemporaries*. Boston: Estes and Lauriat, 1892.

Wilentz, Sean. *No Property in Man: Slavery and Antislavery at the Nation's Founding*. Cambridge, MA: Harvard University Press, 2018.

———. "Was the Constitution Pro-Slavery? Jefferson Davis Thought So. Abraham Lincoln Didn't." *New York Times*, November 2, 2021.

Williams, Edwin, ed. *The Statesman's Manual: The Addresses and Messages of the Presidents of the United States, Inaugural, Annual, and Special, from*

1789 to 1851; With a Memoir of Each of the Presidents and a History of Their Administrations; Also the Constitution of the United States and a Selection of Important Documents and Statistical Information. 4 vols. New York: Edward Walker, 1853.

Wills, Garry. *Lincoln at Gettysburg: The Words That Remade America.* New York: Simon and Schuster, 1992.

Wilson, Douglas L., and Rodney O. Davis. *Herndon's Informants: Letters, Interviews, and Statements about Abraham Lincoln.* Urbana: University of Illinois Press, 1998.

Wilson, Rufus Rockwell. *Intimate Memories of Lincoln.* Elmira, NY: Primavera Press, 1945.

Wood, Gordon S. *The Purpose of the Past: Reflections on the Uses of History.* New York: Penguin, 2008.

Woodbury, Levi. "Report on the Finances: December 1838." In Annual Report of the Secretary of the Treasury on the State of the Finances. Washington DC, United States Department of the Treasury, 1838. https://fraser.stlouisfed.org/files/docs/publications/treasar/AR_TREASURY_1838.pdf.

Woods, Michael E. *Arguing Until Doomsday: Stephen Douglas, Jefferson Davis, and the Struggle for American Democracy.* Chapel Hill: University of North Carolina Press, 2020.

Wootton, Anne. "The Classical Lincoln." Honors Thesis. Brown University, 2009.

Wordsworth, William. "I Wandered Lonely as a Cloud." *Poems, in Two Volumes.* 2 vols. London: Longman, Hurst, Rees, and Orme, 1807.

Yungmeyer, D. W. "An Excursion into the Early History of the Chicago and Alton Railroad." *Journal of the Illinois State Historical Society* 38, no. 1 (1945): 7–37.

INDEX

abolitionism: black troops and, 191, 202–3, 212–13; British abolition-ist movement, 116–17, 201; in the Civil War, 177, 178–79, 204, 208; of Elijah Lovejoy, 22, 23; Emancipation Proclamation and, 185-86, 201, 202-3; of Frederick Douglass, 184-85; of Owen Lovejoy, 101–3, 160–61, 206–7; rise of, 71; 13th Amendment and, 210–11
Adams, John, 23, 92, 195
Adams, John Quincy, 44, 50
Alton Lincoln-Douglas Debate, 135–38
Alton Observer, 22
Amar, Akhil Reed, 111, 169
Annals of Congress, 45, 146
Arnold, Isaac N., 211
Atchison, David Rice, 73

Baltimore: assassination plot against Lincoln, 171–72, 203; 1864 sanitary fair speech by Lincoln, 203–5, 208; habeas corpus, Lincoln's suspension of, 173, 174–75, 203; Lincoln, response to petitions from, 173–74, 203; mob violence in, 171, 172–73, 203, 208; petitions to Lincoln, 172–73

Bancroft, George: career, 7–8, 9, 10, 11, 39, 192; consultation by Nott and Brainard, 155; correspondence with Lincoln, 177; 1860 meeting with Lincoln, 11, 147; eulogy of Lincoln, 219–21; and Lincoln's Gettysburg Address, 194; work with Stephen Douglas, 8, 11, 142
Bank of the United States, First, 42–44, 46–48
Bank of the United States, Second, 47–48
Barksdale, William, 160, 161
Barton, Clara, 182
Bates, Edward, 185
Bernstein, R. B., 194
Black Hawk War, 64, 125
Blackstone, William: *Commentaries*, 31–33, 151; Lincoln's use of, 33, 80, 82, 118, 142, 148, 150, 151, 153
Boston Courier, 12
Brady, Matthew, 7, 8, 11, 147
Brainard, Cephas, 5, 155–57
Bray, Robert, 26
Brayman, Mason, 155
Brookhiser, Richard, 6, 156
Brooks, Noah, 214
Brooks, Preston, 122–23
Brown, John, 145, 152, 161

JESSE DERBER is an independent scholar.

The University of Illinois Press
is a founding member of the
Association of University Presses.

———————————————————

University of Illinois Press
1325 South Oak Street
Champaign, IL 61820–6903
www.press.uillinois.edu